THE POLITICS OF THE YUKON TERRITORY, 1898–1909

CANADIAN STUDIES IN HISTORY AND GOVERNMENT

A series of studies edited by Goldwin French, sponsored by the Social Science Research Council of Canada, and published with financial assistance from the Canada Council.

Edinburgh University
Library

THE POLITICS OF
THE YUKON TERRITORY,
1898-1909

DAVID R. MORRISON

UNIVERSITY OF TORONTO PRESS

© University of Toronto Press 1968
Printed in Great Britain

SBN 8020 3203 6

PREFACE

THIS BOOK presents a narrative of political development in the Canadian Yukon Territory during and after the Klondike gold rush. Although not cast in a theoretical mould, it offers a case study of political behaviour in an environment of economic decline; thus, it concentrates more upon the responses of territorial inhabitants to socio-economic changes and external political forces than upon the place of the Yukon among the national political issues of the early twentieth century. However, it does attempt to shed some light on Canada's experience as an imperial power, a role that the government of the country accepted in opening up the west and north—even before the attainment of full independence from Britain. It is hoped as well that the study will make some contribution to the continuing debate over what form Canadian territorial governments should take in the future.

In preparing this volume for publication, I received assistance from several people, some of whom must be singled out for special acknowledgments. I am particularly indebted to Professor Norman Ward, under whose supervision the research was undertaken, and the late Professor Vernon Fowke, whose teaching and counselling were greatly appreciated by all who had the good fortune to come under his influence. I should also like to thank the following people for their help during the period I conducted research on the Yukon: the late Professor J. B. Mawdsley, formerly Director of the Institute for Northern Studies, University of Saskatchewan, Saskatoon; Mr. J. R. Lotz, formerly Northern Research Officer, Northern Co-ordination and Research Centre, Ottawa; Mr. G. R. Cameron, formerly Commissioner of the Yukon Territory; Mr. F. B. Fingland, formerly Administrative Assistant to the Commissioner of the Yukon; and Mr. J. Jamieson, formerly editor of the *Whitehorse Star*. I am grateful for the help given me by many residents of Whitehorse and Dawson City, by several officials of the Department of Northern Affairs and National Resources and of the government of the Yukon Territory, and by the staffs of: the Murray Memorial Library, University of Saskatchewan, Saskatoon; the Saskatoon Public Library, Saskatoon; the Public Archives of Canada, Ottawa; the National Library of Canada, Ottawa; the Northern Affairs Library, Ottawa; the University of Washington Library, Seattle; the Public Archives of British Columbia, Victoria; the Public Archives of Saskatchewan, Regina; and the University of Sussex Library, Brighton, England.

Of the authors relied upon in the text that follows, I should like to acknowledge the contributions of Mr. Pierre Berton and the late Professor H. A. Innis; Berton's masterful portrayal of the men and women who dominated the gold rush (in *The Klondike Fever*) made my subject seem living and exciting, and Innis's thorough study of the Yukon economy (in *Settlement and the Mining Frontier*) simplified my task of analysing the influence of economic factors on political behaviour.

Among those who read the manuscript at one stage or another, the following made particularly useful comments and criticisms: Professors R. Graham, R. Kautz, K. Rea, and D. Spafford, all of the University of Saskatchewan; Mr. A. Mohiddin, lecturer in political science, Makerere University College, Kampala, Uganda; and Professor Kenneth McNaught of the University of Toronto. In addition, I am grateful to Professor Goldwin French of McMaster University, editor of the Canadian History and Government Series, for his assistance and his recommendation that this volume be included in the series. Mrs. Sally Wismer was the happy choice of the University of Toronto Press for copy-editor. I alone, of course, am responsible for any errors or omissions.

I wish to thank as well Mrs. J. B. Cyr of Saskatoon and Mrs. Arlene Davis and Mrs. Gloria Holmes, both of Peterborough, for their typing and secretarial assistance.

The Canada Council, the Institute for Northern Studies, and the Northern Co-ordination and Research Centre provided generous financial aid at various stages of my research. The book has been published with the help of a grant from the Social Science Research Council of Canada, using funds provided by the Canada Council.

To my wife, who typed the revised manuscript and assisted me in innumerable other ways, I owe a deep debt of gratitude.

D. R. M.

October 1967
Peterborough

CONTENTS

THE POLITICS OF THE YUKON TERRITORY, 1898–1909

A*

CHAPTER ONE

INTRODUCTION

ON JULY 15, 1897, the *San Francisco Call*, for lack of competing news, reported that men with fortunes in gold reaped from the creek beds of the distant north had arrived in San Francisco aboard the steamer *Excelsior*. William Randolph Hearst, dismayed that his *San Francisco Examiner* had been scooped, authorized that paper and the *New York Journal* to enliven the already exaggerated story of the glittering gold of the Klondike region. Then, the *Post-Intelligencer* reported that a "solid ton of gold" had been shipped to Seattle on the *Portland*. The highly spiced accounts were circulated by Associated Press, which, with its effective communications organization, made the name "Klondike" famous throughout North America within a matter of days. The excitement generated in a people who had suffered from a prolonged economic depression, and who had seen their hopes of a return to bimetallism defeated with Bryan in 1896, was electrifying. The yellow press of America had set in motion one of the most sudden and dramatic population movements in the history of man—the Klondike gold rush.[1]

As a result of diplomatic agreements among the great powers many years earlier, the Klondike happened to be in the Yukon, a provisional district of the Canadian North-West Territories.[2] Thus, when the epidemic of "Klondike fever" spread across North America in the summer of 1897, the government of Canada found itself accountable for the administration of a distant land to which thousands would soon emigrate in search of wealth, glamour, or a means of escape from civilization. Clifford Sifton, as Minister of the Interior, was the man primarily responsible for devising policies for the Yukon and overseeing their execution.

The experience of half a century, covering a dozen countries, all went to show that a gold camp, even in areas comparatively accessible to the influence of government, tended to become one of the most lawless places on earth, where primitive conceptions of commercial morality and equally primitive methods of adjusting differences prevailed. What would happen in the Klondike which was removed from Ottawa four thousand miles by distance, over a month by time, and to which a policeman could not be sent except through the territory [Alaska], and with the consent, of another power [the United States]? These were some of the things which the Minister of the Interior had to think about while angry patronage-hunters buzzed about his head, and a thousand other questions . . . pressed for [his] attention.[3]

While Sifton and other ministers of the Crown worked out solutions to the problems of the Yukon, many people within the region struggled to gain some measure of control over the administration of their public affairs and over the course of their economic development. The purpose of this study is to render an account of the relationship between government and governed in the Yukon during the period from 1898 to 1909.

Before this relationship is examined, it is useful to consider the economic and social setting within which it developed. The story must begin with gold.

Placer gold is formed as a result of erosion in which gold is carried down and distributed by water, coming to rest by virtue of its specific gravity on the bottoms of creeks and rivers. Fine gold or flour gold may be washed down long distances and deposited on river bars. Methods of discovery and extraction rely primarily on the specific gravity of gold and on its affinity for quicksilver. Pans are used for testing gravels for evidence of gold. The discovery of flour gold leads to a search for the tributaries which have been the original source and in turn for coarse gold found in areas nearer the lode originally broken down.[4]

The gold in the Klondike was placer gold, and, not being bound in quartz, could be easily extracted on a small-scale basis with relatively simple capital equipment. Consequently, when news of the discovery of rich placer deposits was spread throughout North America in the summer of 1897, it was not surprising that thousands joined a pilgrimage to the Canadian north where they expected great material rewards to come their way quickly and with little effort. But several factors, which they could not foresee, militated against their success.

Although transportation facilities between the south and the ports of Skagway and Dyea on the Alaska panhandle were excellent, the remainder of the journey to the gold-fields, some 500 miles, was extremely difficult.[5] Furthermore, most of the stampeders arrived at the ports of entry after the inland navigation season had closed in the autumn of 1897, and were forced to spend the winter there or in northern British Columbia until the ice broke up in May 1898, by which time many of them could not proceed owing to insufficient funds and supplies. Of the 100,000 or more people who set out for the Klondike, only about 40,000 reached their destination,[6] and, of the latter, few found gold-bearing land left for them to stake, for most of it had been claimed either by men already in the district or by the Canadian government. Those who did discover, purchase, or win claims soon realized that the permafrost and the harsh northern winters rendered Yukon placer mining far more difficult than they had imagined it would be.[7]

The Klondike did not fulfil the dreams of many who participated in the rush, but those who reached Dawson (the main settlement) and the surrounding creeks made a tremendous impact upon the social and economic life of the region. They transformed a small placer camp into a semblance of the American frontier west, for, like the mining centres of bygone days in California, Nevada, Montana, and Dakota, the Yukon was opened wide to hard drinking, bawdy entertainment, gambling, and prostitution.[8] Citizens of the United States, comprising perhaps more than 75 per cent of an extremely cosmopolitan population,[9] dominated all phases of activity during the rush era. Among the few traits which gave the Yukon a character different from Alaska were the prominence of Canadian officials and the presence of French Canadians. For the most part, it was an American district on Canadian soil.

To the economy, in which transportation and trading enterprises had grown to meet the demands of the placer gold industry, the rush added a new economic base—sheer numbers of people demanding the amenities they had enjoyed in the south. Many of those who came in with the stampede served to meet these demands, augmenting the existing small supply organization by opening professional offices, businesses, banks, newspapers, hotels, saloons, and gaming and prostitution houses. But the economic superstructure they built upon the foundation of gold and people expanded too rapidly and too speculatively to remain stable. The weakness lay in the inability of the economy to absorb those who came to win their fortunes directly from the gold-fields. Although few stampeders were able to acquire mining rights to placer ground, many secured high wages for working on existing claims or obtained "lays" from men who controlled several rich properties.[10] Others, having inflated the economy by spending the funds in their possession,[11] left the Yukon to seek their fortunes elsewhere or to return home disappointed. Yet others, through illness, remained to become indigent wards of the state.

Despite the instability inherent in the regional economy, sufficient gold was produced and enough jobs were created to prevent the sudden and complete collapse that had frequently beset other communities based on placer gold. Many men, excited by the prospects of Cape Nome, Alaska, rushed there in 1899 and 1900,[12] but their departure from the Yukon, although curbing business expansion, served to stabilize the economy—albeit at a lower level—by removing some of the stresses of excessive speculation caused by the temporarily bloated population. Between 1898 and 1901 the population of the Yukon decreased from 40,000 (or more) to 27,219, and then remained stable until 1903. In that year depleted sources of rich gravels, technological innovations, and a failure to diversify the resource base brought about the beginning of a gradual economic decline, from which the Yukon did not recover for years. By 1911 the population had shrunk to 8,512; by 1921 to a mere 4,157.[13]

At first, the exhaustion of the best placer beds did not lead to a contraction of the economic system because advances in transportation, brought about by the rush, "revolutionized mining technique" by reducing costs attendant upon the importation of equipment for more efficient gold production. The most important improvement was the White Pass and Yukon Route, a railroad between Skagway and Whitehorse constructed by a syndicate confident of continued immigration. Completed in 1900, it provided, in conjunction with a steamship service between Whitehorse and Dawson, an immensely cheaper and shorter transportation system than had been available before. Roads, constructed from Dawson to the creeks to augment the rail and water route, further lowered transportation costs.[14] The chief government officer in the region noted the changes with satisfaction in his annual report for 1901–2: "Every reduction in freight rates, every reduction in the cost of living in the Yukon . . . makes possible the introduction and operation of a higher class of machinery and cheaper production of gold. It may be said with perfect confidence that the progress of the Yukon . . . during the last year has been of a very satisfactory character. The evolution from an uncertain, unstable and excited mining camp to a steady, permanent, and prosperous community has proceeded in a rapid and striking manner."[15] Although this "higher class of machinery" did increase the ratio of capital to labour, it did not significantly reduce the absolute demand for labour until the more pronounced exhaustion of good ground made necessary the introduction of large-scale hydraulic and dredging equipment. Between 1903 and 1909, therefore, there was a sharp decline in the number of producers and in the need for labour. Furthermore, because the transformation to higher-order techniques of extraction occurred slowly, the production of gold fell rapidly.[16]

The impact of the conversion upon the economy was disastrous. During the rush and the subsequent boom, several "industries based on local raw materials which could be utilized in various products for the carrying on of the mining industry [had] received a strong impetus," but lumbering, coal mining, and other dependent industries had no potential for sustained growth once gold output fell.[17] Owing to the inaccessibility of the Yukon to the outside world and to the existence of plentiful sources farther south, silver and copper deposits discovered near Mayo and Whitehorse respectively could not be exploited fully enough to stimulate secondary development or to absorb the labour force no longer employed in gold production. When rich gold-fields were discovered in the Tanana Valley in 1903, thousands of men, disenchanted with the Klondike and out of work, moved there in the years that followed.[18] Others left the northland altogether. Their departure weakened "the position of the distributing organization which had grown in relation to the demands of large numbers" and curtailed production in a young agricultural industry, which, despite the severe climate and the poor soil, had developed to supply local needs.[19] Thus, placer gold and the influx of people to exploit it had created a great mining frontier in the Yukon, but, unlike mining frontiers elsewhere, it did not give way to lumbering, ranching, and farming. Gold acted as the catalyst for, and the mainspring of, economic activity, but when sources were relatively depleted, and new forms of production were introduced, it could not sustain an economy that failed to diversify owing to the geographical location and the geological limitations of the region.

While the Yukon was experiencing this economic transformation, it underwent several marked social changes, which brought it closer to becoming a psychological as well as a physical part of Canada. The population remained cosmopolitan, but the proportion of Americans in the region fell to 53 per cent in 1900, 32 per cent in 1901, and 21 per cent in 1911.[20] The relative decline in American influence that resulted, together with pressure from eastern Canada and a drop in the transient segment of the population, led to tighter control over vestiges of the frontier such as gambling and prostitution, and eventually to the partial adoption of the stricter social mores that prevailed elsewhere in Canada. Despite these changes, the Yukon remained a separate community. The gold rush brought many of the amenities of civilization to the Klondike, but these comforts did not lead to the establishment of normal life or end the privations of the long, dark, dreary, and cold winters.[21] Moreover, the isolation of Yukoners from the rest of the world, called the "outside" (as it is still in 1968, despite modern transportation and communications facilities), gave rise to the development of a distinct set of attitudes to all phases of life.

Political conflict is prevalent in every society, but where the environment is fluid, as it was in the Klondike, this conflict becomes more intense. Because of the sweeping economic and social changes that beset the Yukon from 1898 to 1908, the region was a fertile breeding ground for discontent. The agitation that resulted was directed towards public authorities, who, many Yukoners believed, were capable of solving all problems once shown the proper means of approaching them. The changing demands made of government are illustrated in later chapters, but first attention is directed towards official efforts to cope with the problems of governing a remote and inaccessible land.

CHAPTER TWO

THE COLONIZATION OF THE KLONDIKE

IN 1870 the young Dominion of Canada, yet a colonial appendage of the United Kingdom, acquired a vast continental colonial empire of its own through the annexation of Rupert's Land and the "North-Western Territory."[1] Over a period of forty years and by policies of "trial and error,"[2] the southern portion of this wilderness was tamed, settled, and developed, but little attention was paid to the territory from the fifty-fourth parallel of latitude to the North Pole, all of which belonged to Canada after 1880. Until well into the twentieth century, this northern area, with one exception, was the domain of the fur trader, the Indian, and the Eskimo, who were free to behave as they wished, untrammelled by Western civilization or government. The single exception, the most remote region of all, was the mountainous terrain through which the mighty Yukon River flows from its source into the American territory of Alaska.

The land of the Yukon, inhabited by few Indians and no Eskimos, was penetrated by white men in the late 1830s and during the 1840s, when Robert Campbell and a party of men in the employ of the Hudson's Bay Company established posts to conduct their trade with the Indians. In 1847 they built Fort Selkirk and Fort Yukon, but were forced to retreat from the former when it was destroyed by Indians in 1852, and from the latter when, in 1869, it was found to be in American territory. Prior to the Company's departure from the region in 1869, some of its men were reported to have found deposits of coarse gold, but they left the exploitation of the precious metal to men who, discouraged with prospects on creek beds farther south, began to filter into the Yukon district in 1873. By 1885 a thousand men, provisioned by the Alaska Commercial and the Northern Trading and Transportation companies, were combing the tributaries of the Yukon and finding paying quantities of gold on several of them, notably on Fortymile Creek near the international boundary.[3]

The federal government first displayed interest in this portion of Canada's northern possessions in 1887 when it commissioned Dr. George Dawson and William Ogilvie to survey the area drained by the Yukon River.[4] However, nothing was done to provide for the administration of the region following submission of their report, partly because the government was preoccupied with the development of more southerly areas and partly because Ogilvie felt that the miners, preponderantly of American nationality, would resent Canadian anthority. In 1893 he changed his mind, recommending action "in the matter of establishing authority over the Yukon in the goldfields, or we might, if the work were delayed, have to face annoyances, if not complications, through possession, without protest from us, by American citizens."[5] The same year, the government received a formal submission from W. C. Bompas, Anglican Bishop of Selkirk, who requested that a force of men be sent to the Upper Yukon River region to quell drunkenness among Indians supplied with liquor by Americans crossing the international boundary from Circle City, Alaska.[6] The

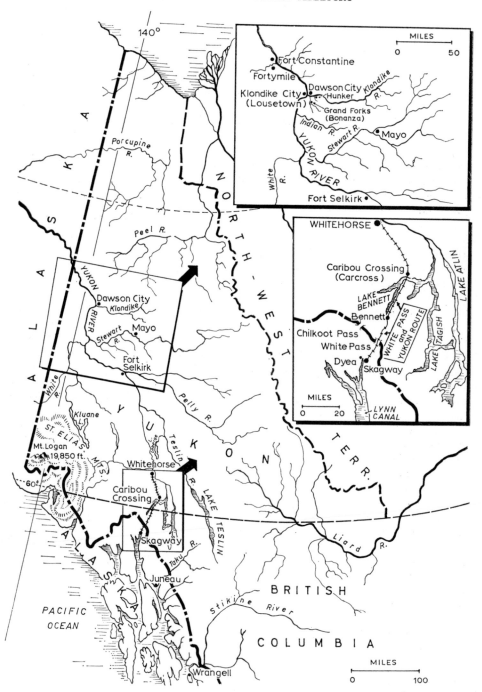

The Yukon Territory, 1900

federal cabinet, uncertain of the location of the border and afraid of a small force being outnumbered by miners "who respected no law apart from that of their own making," refused to take action.[7]

Later in 1893 Bompas wrote once more, noting that matters had grown much worse and requesting that a magistrate and a detachment of North-West Mounted Police (N.W.M.P.) be dispatched with full powers to enforce prohibition.[8] In 1894 C. H. Hamilton, an official of the Northern Trading and Transportation Company, visited Ottawa and, in a letter to the government, stated that the country "is settling up fast now, with miners and others, and the outlook for gold there is very encouraging," and that police protection and a collector of customs were badly needed. Feeling that prohibition would be impossible to enforce, Hamilton recommended a licensing system. What was probably the most significant portion of his representation dealt with potential public revenue, which, he confidently asserted, would be more than sufficient to pay the expenses of sending a party of officials to the area. "I cannot urge too strongly the necessity of immediate action in this matter. The United States Government are sending Customs officers in there this year, and unless your Government does the same we will be compelled to buy all our merchandise in the United States."[9]

T. M. Daly, the Minister of the Interior, considered sending a force of six men to establish order in the region, but, on the advice of the Comptroller of the N.W.M.P., he decided instead, "in the interests of the peace and good government of that portion of Canada . . . and of the Public revenue," to dispatch an Inspector of the N.W.M.P. to the Yukon to act as "Agent of the Dominion Government."[10] The Agent, to be assisted only by a non-commissioned officer, was empowered to take possession of the area, to protect the Indians, and to exercise the functions of all government departments, particularly those associated with customs duties, the liquor traffic, and land administration. However, despite the assignment of such an impressive role to two men, their real task was to investigate conditions and to recommend measures for the proper administration of the territory.[11]

After spending five months of 1894 in the gold-bearing district, the Agent, Inspector Charles Constantine, recommended that a force of forty officers and men be sent to the Yukon to fulfil the functions assigned him by the government.[12] The cabinet, however, was of the opinion that the job could be done by fewer men, and in June 1895 Constantine returned, accompanied by a customs collector and a force of eighteen men.[13] The exact area under his jurisdiction was clarified by an order in council demarcating the Yukon as a separate district of the North-West Territories.[14]

The major task facing the Inspector was the necessity of purging the only previous form of law and order—the miners' meeting—of its authority.

The American miners' meeting, which operated in the Canadian town of Fortymile, had the power of life and death over the members of the community. It could hang a man, give him a divorce, imprison, banish, or lash him . . . . Any prospector could call a meeting simply by posting a notice. An elected chairman performed the functions of judge, while the entire meeting acted as a jury. Both sides could produce witnesses and state their cases, and anybody who wished could ask a question or make a speech. The verdict was decided by a show of hands.[15]

With some difficulty, Constantine managed to abolish this institution, and to establish his authority. He commissioned the building of Fort Constantine near Fortymile, and dispersed his men to the various creeks and ports of entry to settle disputes and prevent smuggling.[16] In his report for the year 1895 the Inspector noted that the force had been successful in carrying out most of its duties, but that civil courts were urgently required to settle disputes arising from refusals to pay small debts, and that it "is necessary in the interests of traders and capitalists, that an office for the registration of transfers, mortgages, deeds, and other papers of title be established."[17] Despite these recommendations, the government's only notable provisions for the Yukon in 1896 were the rejection of a thinly veiled offer of annexation from the Legislative Assembly of British Columbia and the appointment of William Ogilvie as surveyor to lay out building lots and mining claims.[18] Shortly thereafter, political leaders in Ottawa were preoccupied with a general election and a subsequent transfer of power from the Conservatives of Sir Charles Tupper to the Liberals of Wilfrid Laurier.

Meanwhile, Ogilvie found himself far busier than anyone had imagined, following the discovery (on August 17, 1896) of rich placer beds on Bonanza Creek, a tributary of the Klondike River.[19] In reporting the event on September 6, he requested both the appointment of an official to act as mining recorder and land agent, and the establishment of legal machinery, without which, he predicted, civil justice would become once more the preserve of miners' meetings. In the months that followed, when it became increasingly apparent that the discovery was far richer than any of the placer beds exploited earlier, his submissions became stronger. He indicated that creeks other than those in the "Klondak" had been abandoned, while confusion reigned on Bonanza and Eldorado creeks, where, as the only competent official in the area, he was expected to settle disputes over claims. Somewhat reluctantly, he surveyed the creeks and a townsite at the confluence of the Klondike and Yukon rivers, calling it Dawson in honour of the man under whom he had worked in the survey of 1887.[20]

In one of his final reports before resigning his Yukon post, Ogilvie claimed that "within a year or two" the Klondike would be inhabited by 10,000 people. Despite the forecast, the government remained sceptical, although it did appoint Thomas Fawcett as Gold Commissioner and Land Agent after Constantine asked to be relieved of his supervision over mining.[21] When Fawcett—formerly a surveyor in the Saskatchewan District—arrived in Dawson on June 15, 1897, he replaced Constantine as Dominion Agent and assumed the duties of chief mining recorder, arbiter of miners' disputes, and administrator of the Dominion Lands Act regulations.[22] In a résumé of his first two months in office he noted that conflicts among the miners were frequent and difficult to resolve, and complained that he had to sleep in his office to protect it from thieves.[23] Not a man to take bold decisions, he constantly worried about his performance; honest and painstakingly careful, he could not handle a job that entailed using great discretionary powers because of the poor communications facilities between Ottawa and Dawson.[24] Fawcett's isolation from the national capital was well illustrated by his report of September 16: "If the latest reports contained in American [news] papers can be relied upon, we will soon have both a judge and an administrator. If these appointments have been made, I shall feel my responsibility very much lessened, more especially if a judge is sent who will undertake to decide all those civil disputes and fraudulent dealings which day to day become more numerous."[25] The reports were correct: on August 17 the government had appointed Major James Morrow Walsh as Chief Executive Officer of the Government of the Yukon Territory and T. H. McGuire as Judge of the Court of the Yukon Provisional District.[26]

Clifford Sifton, the Liberal Minister of the Interior, may well have regretted his inattention to the submissions of Ogilvie and Constantine regarding the future of and the requirements for the Yukon because, following the press reports of a new Eldorado in July 1897, he suddenly found himself responsible for the administration of a distant land to which thousands of people were being lured by the glitter of gold and the glamour of the frontier. Speed was essential, for, in the absence of continued Canadian authority, the district could have fallen prey to anarchy or American annexation. In addition to the appointments of Walsh, McGuire, and other civilian officials, the government changed the placer mining regulations in the interests of revenue— by decreasing the size of placer claims, reserving alternate ten claims for the Crown, and imposing a royalty of 10 to 20 per cent on the gross output of gold—and, in the course of the last half of 1897, increased fivefold the strength of the N.W.M.P. detachment.[27]

The major concerns of the cabinet during the frenzied period of the gold rush were to secure adequate revenue to defray increasing administrative costs in the Yukon, to assist the influx of gold-seekers to reach their destination with a minimum of disorder, and to keep the Klondike under Canadian control. The police played the most important role in attaining these objectives by collecting $150,000 in customs duties, by overseeing 40,000 people along the Canadian sections of routes to the gold-fields, and by securing possession of the summits of the White and Chilkoot passes just a few miles inland from the American ports of Skagway and Dyea.[28]

While, in actual fact, the N.W.M.P. had little difficulty in maintaining law and order, the Laurier ministry, during the winter of 1897–98, began to worry that the size of the police force in the district was insufficient to control the large number of aliens who were expected to rush to Dawson in the spring. On March 10, 1898, F. W. Borden, the Minister of Militia and Defence, announced that the government intended to send 200 men, one-quarter of the Canadian militia, to the Yukon to assist the police.[29] Some two months later, the details of the scheme were announced to the House of Commons. The Minister stated that the Yukon Field Force, as the detachment came to be known, "would have a decided moral effect upon the scattered population through the district, and, if necessity demanded, would be ready to assist in enforcing law and maintaining order." He justified the proposed expenditure by noting that the American government had stationed four companies in Alaska,[30] implying thereby that the Americans, in an imperialistic mood at the time, might try to annex the gold-fields. Unfortunately for the government, which had to defend an expenditure of $45,000, but fortunately for the people of the Yukon, the force was never used for military purposes, although some of the men participated in a different sort of action as firemen in Dawson.[31] Furthermore, the militia did not reach the gold-fields until September 11, 1898, over two months after it set out and long after the danger of disorder reached its peak in June.[32]

More embarrassing to the government than the dispatch of the Field Force was the abortive policy to open up an all-Canadian route to the gold-fields, which would provide water and rail transportation from Vancouver to Dawson. The cabinet decided to build at first a wagon road, and then a railroad, from the Stikine River in northern British Columbia to Lake Teslin, head of navigable waters flowing to the Klondike. The Stikine passed through territory claimed by the United States, but the British had secured navigation rights upon it through their treaty with the Russians in 1824. Late in 1897 a syndicate offered to build a wagon road for compensation of $1,000 per mile or a railway for $6,000 per mile, but, a month later, withdrew its offer to construct the railroad.[33] The government, now determined that only a rail link would do, negotiated an agreement with Messrs. William Mackenzie and Donald Mann (who later constructed the Canadian Northern), promising the contractors 25,000 acres per mile in return for the 110-mile line.[34] Despite Sir Charles Tupper's personal support for the idea, the Leader of the Opposition acceded to the wishes of his caucus and conducted a strenuous campaign against the plan. Not only was the government offering to give the builders some of the world's richest gold-bearing lands, opposition critics exclaimed, it was doing so without even opening public tenders for the project.[35] The contract was subsequently defeated by the Conservative majority in the Senate, and the government was ordered by the courts to pay damages of $327,000 to Mackenzie and Mann.[36]

The embarrassment suffered by the government over opposition criticisms of the Field Force and the railway policy was trifling in contrast to that which it endured as the result of a bitter attack upon the conduct of civilian officials in the Yukon. Dissatisfied with the performance of regular civil servants, Sifton had chosen, in Walsh, a man he thought fully equipped to make bold decisions because of his proven record as a superintendent of the North-West Mounted Police during the force's westward expansion in the 1870s.[37] But Walsh's Yukon career, with the exception of the manner in which the policemen conducted themselves under his supervision during the rush, blackened the image of the government. Even Walsh's appointment had been irregular. The order in council appointing him described his position as "Chief Executive of the Yukon Territory"[38] at a time when the "Yukon Territory" did not yet exist. Sir Charles Hibbert Tupper, in a scathing denunciation of the government's Yukon policy and administration, declared the appointment extra-legal and lacking in statutory authorization, an opinion later supported by David Mills, the Minister of Justice, in a confidential communication to the Prime Minister.[39]

Walsh was given complete authority over all officials in the district, full command of the N.W.M.P., and sweeping powers to vary, alter, or amend the regulations issued by the Governor in Council under the provisions of the Dominion Lands Act.[40] However, he was virtually unable to exercise these powers because he did not arrive in Dawson until May 21, 1898, fully nine months after his appointment and at a time when he had already decided to submit his resignation. Originally, the Major, in agreeing to accept the post for a year, had stipulated that he could not depart for the Yukon until September 1897.[41] In that month, he left for the Klondike in company with a party of officials, including Sifton for part of the trip, but had barely managed to get through the White Pass when the navigation season closed. He spent the winter at Tagish, some 400 miles south of the gold-fields.[42] F. C. Wade, the newly appointed Registrar of Lands, who went on to Dawson by dog-sled, wrote his old friend Sifton to complain about Walsh's decision not to proceed to the territorial capital. "There is no reason," he said, "why Major Walsh could not have been here months ago. . . . The general opinion amongst us all is that Major Walsh . . . [stayed at Tagish] from sheer fear of his ability to cope with the situation."[43]

As a consequence of Walsh's decision not to go to Dawson in the winter of 1897–98, Fawcett remained in immediate command in the Klondike region, and had to bear the brunt of mounting dissatisfaction resulting from the new placer mining regulations, particularly the one imposing a royaly on gold output. The discontent took the form of accusations of dishonest behaviour on the part of officials in the Gold Commissioner's office. Tappan Adney, a correspondent for *Harper's Illustrated*, offered complaints typical of those expressed in the district prior to the rush in the spring of 1898:

The registry books, or copies thereof, which elsewhere in Canada are considered public property, were not accessible to the public, and the clerks were quick to take advantage of this state of affairs to begin a "side-door" business, selling to individuals, for cash or interest in claims, information on unrecorded claims. Afterwards, emboldened by the impotency of the Gold Commissioner to correct these abuses, favored ones began to be admitted during office hours, upon passes, and recorded claims ahead of men who had been waiting often for days in line outside. It became recognized by everyone who was obliged to deal with the office that the only way of getting what belonged to him was to bribe an official. Appeal to the Gold Commissioner was as likely as not met with dismissal in an arbitrary, unjust, or illegal manner.[44]

Although many charges were groundless, it is certain that some officials were bribed, and others had special interests in mining properties.[45] Fawcett remained honest, but he was guilty of negligence, for far more serious than the petty corruption was the chaotic and inefficient way in which his office, staffed by patronage appointees, operated. Records were lost; claims were recorded in the names of two different miners; and on one occasion the Gold Commissioner actually registered two discovery claims on one creek.[46]

Wade found administrative effectiveness and morale in a deplorable state when he arrived in Dawson. He noted that Fawcett's office was understaffed and overcrowded; that, owing to the absence of a safe, the records, of which there were no duplicates, could go up in flames at any time; and that the work was months behind. Fawcett, he said, "must give up his clerical work, and look after the larger interests here. . . . He must shake loose from civil service traditions and get his mind out of the small official groove." It may be added that Wade himself did not do his utmost to maintain administrative harmony: before Walsh arrived, Wade had a bitter argument with Judge McGuire and Inspector Constantine over whether hotels should be licensed by federal authorities to sell liquor. "I issued notices . . . to the hotels over which we should have no end of power; over this Constantine became impudent and I had to call him down. . . . He is now particularly ugly. [Furthermore, McGuire] . . . has the unhappy faculty of sticking his nose into everything that does not concern him."[47]

When Walsh finally did arrive in Dawson, the newly established *Klondike Nugget* expressed the hopes of many Yukoners, proclaiming that "the people now turn to Major Walsh, the supreme authority in this district, to show them that they have one friend left."[48] But the editors, and many others as well, were soon disappointed in the Major who refused to make important decisions for fear of interfering with the work of his successor. Although he and the police kept disorder to a minimum, Walsh performed less creditably when confronted by problems with which he was less familiar, such as how to care for the indigent sick, how to go about building and repairing roads, and how to settle legal conflicts among quarrelling miners. Furthermore, despite his full authority over officials and the mining regulations, Walsh did not take action to curb administrative excesses in the Gold Commissioner's office and did little to amend the mining laws to lessen the hardships they imposed.[49] According to one of his dog-drivers, the Chief Executive frequently said: "This is a placer camp. It won't last long. Make money as quick as you can and get out."[50] A better summary of his attitude towards his task in the Yukon would be hard to find.

Charges of petty corruption in, and mismanagement of, the Gold Commissioner's office, and of administrative ineptitude on the part of Walsh gave the Conservative opposition in Ottawa an excellent opportunity to criticize the Laurier administration for its handling of Yukon affairs, but had it not been for one specific incident—later called the Dominion Creek scandal—the opposition would have been able to talk only in vague generalities. The story[51] of the incident began in November 1897, when Fawcett decided to close Dominion Creek to further staking after discovering that claim-jumping and errors in recording had taken place. Then, in April 1898, when it was discovered that deposits of gold were to be found on the hills and benches as well as the creek beds below, prospectors began to stake hill and bench claims along the creek. J. D. McGregor, the Inspector of Mines—another of Sifton's appointees who had proceeded to Dawson in the winter—decided to close these new claims as well, a decision supported by Walsh and a majority of officials apparently against Fawcett's protests. Rumours spread quickly that the deposits were extremely rich, and it became evident to "the Commissioner[52] and everybody else . . . that as soon as any announcement was made declaring the creek open there was bound to be a great stampede." To overcome the possibility of violence and confusion, Walsh resolved to open all of Dominion Creek only to those who obtained special permits, but, at Fawcett's insistence, decided to reserve certain areas for those who had attempted to file claims before McGregor issued his order in April and to allow anyone else to stake on the remaining hills and benches. Then came the difficulty. The original order requiring permits had been posted to take effect July 11, but the order rescinding it and declaring all but reserved claims open was posted undated on July 9. Stories began to spread that some men, informed of the change the night of July 8, had rushed the sixty miles from Dawson to Dominion Creek and staked claims before the general public became aware of the new ruling the next morning. Later, Major Walsh was implicated when it was discovered that a cook in his employ, Louis Carbeno, had been one of those who staked on Dominion Creek on July 8.[53] The story became even more damning when it was disclosed that Carbeno had agreed to give Lewis Walsh, the Major's brother, three-quarters interest in any claims he secured in return for the capital required to begin production.[54]

The *Klondike Nugget*, as a result of the Dominion Creek muddle, began a campaign against the administration, choosing Fawcett as the villain rather than Walsh, apparently because the Gold Commissioner had once ordered the editor of the paper out of his office.[55] On July 12 it called upon Fawcett to "retire," and, a few days later, when Fawcett claimed he had acted on orders from Walsh, the *Nugget* concluded that he was weak and a liar.[56] From that time forward, the newspaper refused to leave Fawcett alone, even though he was demoted to a minor position in October.[57] William Ogilvie, who replaced Walsh as Commissioner in August, told Laurier that "a black-guard sheet here called the *Klondike Nugget* whose principal object seems to be to vilify everyone who in any way runs counter to its wishes or thoughts . . . [abused Fawcett] until it nearly broke the poor man's heart."[58]

Meanwhile, the government in Ottawa began to hear complaints about the Dominion Creek episode, which, in addition to earlier charges, worried the Prime Minister. He wrote Sifton:

We made a good stroke last year when we appointed a Commission to investigate . . . the Crows Nest Pass matter. If we had not done that, we would have found ourselves in a rather unfortunate position during the last session. I deem it absolutely important that we should investigate the complaints now made. . . . We must preserve the good name of the Government in that distant land, and see that the miners have their claims whenever they have staked them, and that no pretense should be given them, such as that the books were closed . . . , to deprive them of their rights.[59]

After wiring the substance of the communication to Sifton in cipher,[60] Laurier received the following reply: "*There are no complaints to investigate.* To appoint a commission

. . . would place the Government in an indefensible position."[61] Then, on August 25, the ministry received a petition from a committee of Klondike miners requesting a commission of inquiry with full powers "to subpoena and protect witnesses."[62] That same day, Sifton wrote Laurier saying that Walsh and Fawcett had done their best to solve the Dominion Creek problem, and concluding that "it is perhaps open to question if they acted wisely, but I do not think there is any ground for believing there was anything wrong."[63]

However, agitation in the Yukon could not be ignored. Early in September a Yukoner, claiming to be a government supporter, wrote the Prime Minister, urging him to appoint a commission of inquiry to vindicate the administration and to stop the growing scandal.[64] In reply, Laurier stated that, although a commission could be appointed if specific charges were laid against officials, he had heard only complaints of a general nature, but added that he would sincerely appreciate the correspondent's efforts if some of these grievances were forwarded in a confidential letter.[65] There is no record of the man writing again, but when Laurier's old friend, J. E. Girouard, the newly appointed Registrar of Lands, beseeched the Prime Minister to undertake an investigation of "charges of malfeasance" arising from the Dominion Creek affair,[66] Laurier decided to act. On October 7 William Ogilvie was appointed a commissioner under the provisions of the "Act Respecting Enquiries concerning Public Matters" with power to investigate the complaints registered in the miners' petition of August 25.[67]

Owing to the fact that W. H. P. Clement, the Legal Adviser, did not arrive in Dawson until January 1899, the Commission did not sit until February,[68] some five months after the petition making complaints against the administration had been drawn up. Ogilvie, following his terms of reference, decided to disallow any charges brought before him that referred to incidents that had occurred after August 25, 1898.[69] This decision served to increase agitation, the *Klondike Nugget* carrying on a strenuous campaign of denunciation and the major plaintiffs walking out of the hearings. In his report, Ogilvie exonerated Walsh and Fawcett of dishonesty or of seeking personal gain in the Dominion Creek affair, and found groundless several minor charges. Only one official, a clerk, was found guilty of accepting bribes and for admitting people to the Gold Commissioner's office out of turn; the only other indefensible act, committed by several employees, was the acceptance of money for work done before and after working hours.[70]

In the opinion of Sir Charles Hibbert Tupper, opposition spokesman on the Yukon, the report was a biased and partisan document, and the evidence accompanying it seemed a powerful denunciation of the government's handling of Yukon affairs. For two sessions of Parliament—1899 and 1900—he devoted great zeal and energy to a campaign to blacken the image of the Laurier administration by attacking its performance in the Klondike basin. His major speeches of 1899, one before and one after the evidence was printed, were among the longest orations ever delivered in the Canadian House of Commons.[71] The first one, during the Address in Reply to the Speech from the Throne, contained several general criticisms of government policy and administration, and was well answered by Sifton.[72] The Minister frankly admitted that he had waited too long before making provision for the administration of the region, but had thought Ogilvie's early reports on the prospects of the gold-fields too optimistic. He went on to defend the original appointees to the Yukon service, each of whom had been condemned by the younger Tupper.

Tupper's second speech was somewhat stronger than the first, and contained specific charges of maladministration and corruption, either inferred from the evidence of the Commission or obtained from private sources in the Yukon.[73] After citing the details, the Conservative spokesman accused Sifton of favouritism and partiality in the administration of the laws and regulations of the North-West Territories; Walsh of misbehaviour in office; F. C. Wade of using his official position for personal gain; the Minister of Customs of gross and scandalous abuses in his oversight of the collection of customs in the Yukon; the Minister of Marine and Fisheries of appointing an official who had previously been dismissed for misconduct; the Postmaster General of gross neglect in the administration of his department's affairs in the Klondike; and William Ogilvie of conducting partial hearings. He then proposed a resolution requesting the appointment of a royal commission of two or more judges of the Supreme Court of Canada to investigate fully all of the charges he had laid before the House.

Sifton replied at length, devoting most of his time to a defence of himself, Walsh, and the manner in which Ogilvie handled proceedings of the Commission of Inquiry.[74] With respect to the Dominion Creek scandal, the Minister pointed out that, although Walsh's cook, Carbeno, had indeed staked a claim upon learning of the reopening of the creek, the servant had later declared under oath that he learned of Walsh's decision, not from the Commissioner himself, but from a dog-driver who overheard a conversation in which the plans had been discussed. Said Sifton, ridiculing Tupper, "an Indian servant lets out some information, and a cook, by a mistake of the Gold Commissioner, gets a claim which, perhaps, he should not have got, and this is brought before us as a corrupt act, as an indictment of Major Walsh and of his administration of the Yukon." Sifton neglected to mention that Carbeno had also declared that he had received Walsh's permission to go to Dominion Creek and was certain that the Major would not have thought "I was just going for a walk."[75]

Political tempers exploded as the debate continued, particularly when the other ministers accused of irresponsibility spoke in defence of themselves.[76] Party lines were broken by Liberals Frank Oliver and R. L. Richardson, both of whom declared themselves in favour of Tupper's resolution. Oliver's deviation is particularly noteworthy, for, just six years later, he succeeded Sifton as Minister of the Interior and, as such, minister in charge of Yukon affairs. Some of the fervour with which he delivered his speech carried over to his later administration. He said:

I will vote for the motion of the hon. member for Pictou, not because I support all that his motion contains or the position he takes in every particular, but because I wish to place before the House and the country, in the most emphatic manner possible, my desire that the offences which have been committed against the pioneers of the Yukon by certain officials of the Government should be punished and punished as severely as possible, as the result of any investigation that may be held. I consider that it is necessary to hold an investigation for the credit of the officials as well as for their punishment. All were not guilty and all were not equally guilty, but that certain officials were guilty has been proven by the investigation . . . held by Mr. Ogilvie.[77]

The Liberal majority defeated Tupper's amendment, but a third Liberal—W. W. B. McInnes, later to become Commissioner of the Yukon Territory—joined Richardson and Oliver in support of Tupper and the opposition.[78]

The same charges came up again in the session of 1900, prior to the federal election of that year. The administration of the Yukon under Walsh and Fawcett was discussed four times on motions to go into Committee of Supply and twice on motions to adjourn to discuss urgent business.[79] Again Sir Charles Hibbert Tupper spearheaded the attack, which continued, after dissolution, into the election campaign. Tupper and Sifton even clashed personally in a debate in Brandon,[80] but, when the smoke of the battle had cleared, it appeared that the Yukon scandals had not moved an electorate, satisfied with Laurier's first term of office and enjoying the fruits of Canada's unprecedented economic expansion.

The opposition's criticism of the government's handling of the Yukon during the Klondike gold rush brought to a close the story of the colonization of the Klondike. The Laurier ministry, although it could have acted sooner, had suddenly found itself faced with the problems of controlling one of the most rapid migrations in the history of man,[81] and had had to act quickly without previous similar experience to solve these problems. Every action was uncertain; overly optimistic policies were framed; mistakes were made; and unexpected difficulties were encountered. Tappan Adney wrote:

The ... difficulties [such as poor communications facilities between Ottawa and Dawson] that stood in the way of putting into immediate operation an effective government were so great that one should not judge ... [the administration] too harshly. On the other hand, if there were not serious disorders, it was due less to the quality of government than to the orderly character of the population, and to the fact that men were there enduring the privations of the Arctic climate to make their fortunes and get away, not to help set in order the political households of their Canadian friends.[82]

It would take the government a long time to undo the damage of the Walsh–Fawcett regime because discontent among Yukoners, set in motion during the rush, did not die down quickly. Nevertheless, the excitement was over, and some permanent measures could be taken to prevent a recurrence of earlier difficulties.

CHAPTER THREE

THE YUKON BECOMES A TERRITORY

ALTHOUGH government arrangements for the administration of the Yukon were provisional during 1897–98 and remained so in the years that followed, about the time the Yukon scandals began to make headlines in the Canadian press, developments of significance to the future government of the region occurred almost unnoticed. When, in the wake of these developments, the Yukon was created a separate territory and given its own government, officials in Ottawa began to realize that the Klondike would not die the quick death of many placer mining camps, but would become a permanent settlement, requiring government services similar to those provided in other parts of Canada.

In the winter of 1897–98, the governments of Canada and the North-West Territories became embroiled in a jurisdictional dispute over the Yukon liquor traffic. At first, because the Yukon was a district of the North-West Territories, those who sought to ship liquor to the Klondike had had to obtain permits from the Lieutenant Governor of the Territories acting on the advice of the Minister of the Interior. However, late in 1897, Frederick Haultain, whose Executive Council had just won responsible government for the territories, claimed that the Lieutenant Governor was now obliged to accept the advice of his territorial ministers with respect to the Yukon liquor trade and all other purely territorial matters.[1] The federal government, which had dispatched a Chief Executive Officer to the Klondike to oversee all government responsibilities, was of a different mind. In somewhat equivocal terms, Clifford Sifton explained the situation to the House of Commons on March 11, 1898: "The Government of the North-West Territories claims that permits should be issued by the Lieutenant Governor, with the advice of the Executive Council. That is not the interpretation placed on the statute [presumably the North-West Territories Act] by the Government here; but there is no real dispute between the two Governments." No permits, he said, would be issued by either the federal or territorial government until the affair had been straightened out.[2]

Despite the Minister's decision not to allow the issuance of liquor permits, Haultain dispatched G. H. V. Bulyea, a member of the territorial Executive Council, to Dawson to collect licence fees from hotel and saloon operators,[3] previously licensed by Constantine without fee. Major Walsh met Bulyea in Tagish, and wrote ahead to Inspector Constantine advising him of the councillor's mission. The Chief Executive noted that, although Premier Haultain had sent a letter authorizing Bulyea to issue permits for importation of liquor and licences for hotels and saloons, "I informed him that we could not recognize his authority in either instance. . . . Do what you can to make his visit pleasant, but you will in no way recognize his authority in this District."[4] Bulyea proceeded to Dawson where, apparently without serious opposition from Constantine (who previously had opposed Wade's plans to impose similar taxes in the name of the federal government), he collected $2,000 in licence fees from sixteen hotel and saloon owners.[5] A confrontation between the rival authorities occurred in May when Walsh arrived in the capital, and, claiming that his jurisdiction was complete, ordered drinking outlets to operate as they had before Bulyea's arrival. Not a man to acquiesce easily, the territorial councillor brought before the courts a test case against a saloon proprietor who had sold liquor without the permission of the Lieutenant Governor in Council of the Territories.[6] However, before a decision could be rendered, the Canadian Parliament, at the behest of the Laurier ministry, took action to remove Yukon affairs from the authority of the government of the North-West Territories.

The federal cabinet may have considered taking such a step as early as August 1897 when it appointed Major Walsh Chief Executive Officer of the "Yukon Territory," but nothing was done until June 1898 after the liquor dispute had proven the existing constitutional arrangement unworkable: the Yukon, so isolated that even telegrams took six to eight weeks to reach it from other parts of Canada, simply could not be administered by separate governments 2,000 miles distant from one another in Ottawa and Regina. The problem was solved, although not without a protest from the Legislative Assembly of the North-West Territories,[7] by "An Act to Provide for the Government of the Yukon Territory," which created the Yukon a separate territory and provided it with a full complement of executive, legislative, and judicial institutions.[8] By no means a definitive constitution, the Yukon Bill was introduced to the House of Commons by Sifton as a tentative measure "to clothe the Government with power to maintain order and administer the country for a year or two until we shall have a better opportunity of knowing what kind of community we shall have to provide for."[9]

Executive powers were conferred upon a Commissioner, responsible for administering the government of the territory under instructions given him by the Governor in Council or by the Minister of the Interior; and upon a Council of six officials, charged with assisting the Commissioner in his supervision over the government.[10] In essence, the executive was two-tiered, consisting of the federal cabinet in Ottawa and the Commissioner and Council, which, with the exception of two councillors, was within the hierarchy of the Department of the Interior in Dawson City. Orders in council, promulgated by authority of the Yukon Act, created certain administrative offices and gave the Commissioner in Council the power to set up others. Those filling the former were to be appointed and recompensed by the federal government, while those occupying the latter were to be selected by the Commissioner, subject to the Minister's approval, and paid from territorial revenues.[11] The orders established machinery for the administration of territorial and other responsibilities of the Department of the Interior, but, owing to the great distance and poor communications facilities between Ottawa and Dawson, the Commissioner was given authority over all officers of the federal government in the territory,[12] including employees of the Post Office, Public Works, Justice, and Customs departments, and officers and men in the ranks of the North-West Mounted Police and Yukon Field Force.

Most law-making powers were delegated by the Canadian Parliament to two executive institutions—the Governor in Council and the Commissioner in Council. The former was granted authority to legislate for the peace, order, and good government of the Yukon, while the latter was assigned "the same powers to make ordinances for the government of the territory as are at the date of this Act possessed by the Lieutenant Governor of the North-West Territories, acting by and with the advice and consent of the Legislative Assembly thereof to make ordinances for the government of the North-West Territories," with the exception of any powers denied by the Governor in Council.[13] Assuming that none was withheld and omitting those relating to elections, the powers granted by implication to the Commissioner in Council were: direct taxation for territorial and local expenditure; the establishment of a territorial civil service to be financed by the territory; the establishment, maintenance, and management of prisons; the incorporation of municipal institutions; the imposition of shop, saloon, tavern, auctioneer, and other licences; the incorporation of certain companies; the solemnization of marriage; the protection of property and civil rights; the administration of justice; the imposition of punishments—by fine, penalty, or imprisonment—for infractions of any territorial ordinances; the expenditure of funds and money appropriated by Parliament for territorial purposes; superintendence over all matters of a merely local or private nature; and the provision of educational facilities.[14] Thus, unless the cabinet decreed otherwise, the Commissioner in Council had authority to legislate on all topics that were normally provincial matters with the exception of the territorial constitution (the Yukon Act), the borrowing of money, the management and sale of public lands, and the construction of major public works such as railways and canals.[15]

Despite this delegation of legislative subjects, Parliament's abdication was not complete. Neither executive body could, without the authority of Parliament, impose any tax, customs duty, or penalty exceeding $100; alter or repeal punishments provided in acts of Parliament; or appropriate public moneys, land, or property of Canada. Furthermore, all ordinances passed by the Commissioner in Council, subject to disallowance within two years by the Governor in Council, were to be laid before the Senate and the House of Commons.[16]

The Yukon Act changed the judicial structure by replacing the Court of the Yukon District with a superior court of record, styled the Territorial Court and consisting of one or more judges. It provided further that judicial procedure and administration were to conform as closely as possible to the practices found in the North-West Territories, that the Commissioner, councillors, judges, and commissioned officers of the North-West Mounted Police were to possess the powers of one or two justices of the peace, and that all jurors were to be British subjects.[17]

In framing a constitution for the Yukon, Sifton and his associates were fortunate in being able to consult precedents which earlier federal regimes had followed in governing other parts of the north and west. Given the inaccessibility and rapid development of the region, it was certainly not deemed desirable to provide the new territory with an administration that functioned wholly outside its boundaries. Even in circumstances not as demanding as those in the Yukon, experiments with an external seat of government had proven unsatisfactory in the North-West Territories from 1870 to 1876 and in the old Keewatin Territory from 1876 to 1881.[18] The model chosen instead was that of the North-West Territories Act of 1875 by which the territories were governed from 1876 to 1888, partly from Ottawa and partly from capitals located inside the territorial borders.[19] Only one major provision distinguished it from the Yukon Act: in the latter no allowance was made for the future development of representative institutions. Feared by federal authorities because of the frontier and cosmopolitan nature of the mining community, this aspect of political evolution had to await a response to organized pressure from within the Klondike basin.

One of the slight differences between the acts of 1875 and 1898 seemed to imply a status for the Yukon inferior to that of the North-West Territories: the new chief executive was to be designated as Commissioner rather than as Lieutenant Governor. However, this departure from convention was one of semantics rather than of substance. Major Walsh, who could not have been accorded the title of Lieutenant Governor during his tenure of office because the Yukon was still a district of the territories, was commonly called "Commissioner." To avoid confusion among the populace, the act of 1898 merely legalized the previous usage.[20]

Another provision of the Yukon Act, the establishment of the Council, also had historical roots, for in the last few months of his regime Major Walsh had consulted what he termed his "council." Consisting of the Crown Prosecutor, the Gold Commissioner, the Mining Inspector, and some minor officials,[21] this group—judging from Thomas Fawcett's testimony before the Ogilvie Commission of Inquiry—was no more than an advisory committee on administrative matters. Fawcett claimed that its activities were limited to ratifying Walsh's executive orders,[22] an observation that prompted Sir Charles Hibbert Tupper, in one of his verbal attacks upon the Yukon administration, to accuse the Major of constituting the "council" to shield himself from having to accept full responsibility for his own actions.[23]

When the provisions of the Yukon Act were brought into force, the government appointed, as Commissioner, William Ogilvie, a man well acquainted with at least the physical characteristics of the territory.[24] Four men were selected for the Council: F. C. Wade, Legal Adviser; J. E. Girouard, Registrar of Lands; T. H. McGuire, Judge of the Territorial Court; and S. B. Steele, commanding officer of the N.W.M.P.[25] However, by the time sittings of the Council were held in October, Wade and McGuire had been replaced on Council and in their respective offices by W. H. P. Clement and C. A. Dugas, respectively.[26]

When Ogilvie arrived in the Klondike in September 1898 he found it far different from the small placer camp he had left less than two years before. Perhaps as many as 40,000 people "from all over the world and from every background and creed"[27] swarmed the streets of Dawson and the nearby hillsides. He and his fellow officials and councillors were confronted by many problems that were unique in the history of Canadian administration. Services were required by an isolated area suddenly ten times its former population, and by Dawson, a booming settlement of 17,000, which had no municipal institutions to serve its people. Ogilvie found his position involved not only the responsibilities of Commissioner, but also those of Dawson mayor, city engineer, and fire chief.[28] His job was a demanding one, even more so because he was constantly sought out by people who thought he, as Commissioner, could work miracles. He reported:

Immediately after my arrival I was beset by a great multitude, each individual of whom expected that he or she was going to secure everything that was just and right, and, of course, their own views were just and right, as compared with the views of those opposed to them. For weeks after my arrival I was beset by this multitude daily; not one moment of the long day—generally from eight in the morning until well towards midnight—was I at peace. . . . It appears it was thought I was armed with exceptional powers, such only as the most absolute autocrat on the face of the earth could have; it was expected I would reverse decisions without hearing anything but a simple statement made by one party . . . and because I couldn't do this, great disappointment was expressed.[29]

In addition, it should be remembered that Major Walsh, for fear of complicating his successor's work, had left Ogilvie with almost every problem of government unsolved. Although the surveyor-turned-administrator battled bravely to overcome his personal limitations for a position with discretionary powers[30] and the tremendous obstacles confronting the goal of establishing good government, a man who knew him well claimed Ogilvie suffered through "one long nightmare" during his tenure in office.[31]

The needs of Dawson were foremost in the minds of the administration, for disease and fire were constant dangers in a community of overcrowded and hastily constructed shacks and buildings. Ogilvie set up a fire department and a board of health and appointed medical health and sanitation officers. With the authorization of Council, he oversaw the construction of "paved" streets, sidewalks, schools, and a drainage system for the town site.[32] He convened Council several times a week[33] to deliberate on policy and to frame ordinances to replace the often inapplicable laws of the agrarian North-West Territories. Ordinances were passed during the last three months of 1898 on such diverse matters as the requirement for a College of Physicians and Surgeons to license doctors, the necessity of muzzling dogs within the limits of Dawson, and the need for detailed regulations to govern the liquor trade.[34]

Because by no means all the people who rushed to the Klondike were physically and financially equipped to withstand the rigours of the frontier, the government's greatest responsibility during and just after the rush was caring for the indigent sick. Living in an era before the rise of the welfare state, Ogilvie seemed shocked that such a service should have to be provided, but he took great pains to defend an expenditure of $100,000—48 per cent of total territorial expenditures in 1898–99—on indigents. "We, as a civilized Government, could not allow these men to die like beasts, consequently we had to take care of them. The hospitals made vain appeals to the people for support, but all to no effect; the universal cry seemed to be, 'Let the Government look after the sick; they get all the taxes and . . . should attend to these matters.' "[35]

As difficulties in Dawson were surmounted, others appeared in new communities, three of which grew rapidly: Klondike City (Lousetown), across the Klondike River from Dawson; Grand Forks (Bonanza), at the confluence of Bonanza and Eldorado creeks; and Whitehorse, 300 miles south of the gold-fields on the route between Skagway and Dawson. Then, too, there were the problems of securing adequate transportation facilities from Dawson to the creeks, and of housing the rapidly expanding territorial and federal offices. Late in 1898 a franchise was granted to "Pioneer Tramway Co." to build a tramway from Dawson to Grand Forks, but it was revoked the following winter when the owners, T. W. O'Brien and Hill Henning, began charging tolls for a sled trail they built over the proposed route.[36] Although Council set aside $10,000 to construct roads to the major centres of gold production,[37] that small sum was insufficient, and it took several years before adequate transportation was provided. The Gold Commissioner's quarters and the Post Office were badly cramped for space, particularly the Post Office, which, Ogilvie noted, "entails as much work as that of a city of 150,000 inhabitants . . . because there is no city delivery as in other cities, and every resident of the territory has either in person, or by proxy, to resort to Dawson for mail."[38] Gradually, buildings were constructed by the Department of Public Works,[39] but, by the time they were completed, the need was not as great as that existing when the plans were drawn up.

The territorial government was also faced by the need to find sources of revenue to pay for the rapidly expanding services for which it became responsible after the passage of the Yukon Act. The federal government continued to obtain revenue from royalties on gold output, mining licences, land sales, timber fees, and customs duties,[40] but the territorial administration had to look elsewhere. Although the Governor in Council maintained control over the manufacturing and importation of liquor, receipts from permits were given to the territory,[41] which augmented these with retail liquor licences, and other minor fees and taxes, such as those for practising law, auctioneering, operating ferries, and running music halls.[42]

One difficulty that did become less acute was communication between Ottawa and Dawson. On September 20, 1899, telegraph lines constructed by the federal government and the White Pass and Yukon Route were opened to link the territorial capital and Skagway. Whereas messages had previously taken about two months to transmit, they now took only five days, the time necessary for steamers to make the trip from the Alaska panhandle to Vancouver or Seattle. Two years later, three alternative telegraph systems made possible instantaneous contact between the territory and the "outside."[43]

Communications within the Yukon civil service were another matter. Low administrative morale, a problem throughout the Walsh–Fawcett regime, continued to plague the administration during Ogilvie's tenure as Commissioner. The Prime Minister and the Minister of the Interior were kept busy trying to ease tensions among senior civil servants. Early in 1899 Ogilvie complained that F. C. Wade, now Crown Prosecutor, was occupying "incompatible positions," for, in addition to his primary duties, he acted as Clerk of Court and as private counsel for several firms. Ogilvie noted that, on one occasion, Wade had actually represented two opposing interests in a case before the Territorial Court.[44] The Crown Prosecutor was quite bitter about Ogilvie's interference and told Sifton that the Commissioner "as an administrator . . . is simply useless."[45] The government in Ottawa also heard strong criticisms of J. E. Girouard and W. H. P. Clement, both of whom were conducting private legal practices after hours.[46] Although the two officials protested Ogilvie's attempts to restrict them, claiming that they had accepted positions in the territory on the understanding that they could augment their salaries by practising,[47] the government responded with an order in council forbidding such activity.[48] Girouard and Judge Dugas became embroiled in a similar conflict with the Commissioner over their propensity to "spend too much time to the acquirement of claims."[49] However, before Ogilvie's complaint reached Ottawa, the cabinet, because of opposition charges that F. C. Wade had grown rich on mining properties, had passed an order restricting all officials from staking, purchasing, or sharing profits from mining claims.[50]

In Council itself, a more serious conflict arose between English-speaking and French-speaking members. Clement wrote Sifton to explain his side of the story:

I dislike very much to take a position as critic of my brother members of Council, but the attitude which Judge Dugas [and] Girouard are taking is so . . . hostile to you that I feel bound to give you a word of warning. They both are outspoken in their criticism of *your* anti-French, anti-Catholic policy in reference to the Territory, the latest move being a motion in Council for a return of all employees of the Government here. It's a great pity the Judge was not . . . removed from the Council; he will make trouble, if he can. At present he is out on the war-path against the Good Samaritan Hospital (under Presbyterian control) because, he says, it is unduly favoured by the Commissioner and the Comptroller at the expense of St. Mary's, a R.C. concern. In the matter of schools, too, he will do what he can to embarrass you. In fact, he is prepared to raise the race and religion issue if he can do so; and Girouard will support him, because you would not allow him his travelling expenses out last summer.[51]

While Clement confided in Sifton, Girouard and Dugas wrote their compatriot, Laurier, urging the appointment of more French Canadian civil servants and higher salaries for themselves—the lowest paid members of Council.[52] Although the Prime Minister later increased Girouard's pay,[53] the hostility between the two groups within the service did not subside, and from time to time the "race and religion question" spread from those in the employ of the government to the society at large, where, as in other parts of Canada, it became a burning issue.

The bickering among these men of disparate backgrounds was but one of the problems of establishing a government in a region characterized by economic and social flux. Unrest existed among the people as well. Those who had been in the Yukon prior to the summer of 1897 resented changes in government policy that accompanied the gold rush, and they, as well as those who came in 1897–98, became dissatisfied with the way in which the affairs of the territory were being administered. They began to organize in order to gain some measure of control over and participation in government. As a result, in addition to the numerous other difficulties besetting it on the Yukon frontier, government—both federal and territorial—had to contend with active political agitation.

CHAPTER FOUR

THE POLITICS OF PROTEST

THOSE WHO participated in the Klondike gold rush and those who had come to the Yukon prior to its occurrence had abandoned their normal ways of life in the hope of finding a rainbow's end in the wilderness of the north. Thus, when government appeared to interfere with their economic success, they began to protest; protest led to organization, and organization to the selection of positive goals. Interrelated and rooted in the initial feeling of protest, two aims came to dominate the behaviour of pressure groups and the press: first, to change the mining laws and to initiate projects that would stimulate economic development; and, second, to secure some measure of direct popular influence over the actions of government.

The initial vehicle of protest was the mass meeting, an institution owing its origin to the miners' meeting that had earlier dominated political organization. One or more people would announce a meeting and advertise it as widely as possible, and when a crowd assembled—sometimes in the open, other times in closed quarters if available— men would come to the platform, one by one, to harangue the government and to propose reforms. Motions would be made and put to a vote, and resolutions sent to those with either the power or authority to bring about desired changes. Often, but not always, a hat would be passed to collect funds to defray the costs of renting a hall (if one were used) or of drawing up a petition.[1]

Late in 1897 a mass meeting of miners chose two delegates—one representing Americans and the other French Canadians—to travel to Ottawa to seek changes in the placer mining regulations. They were commissioned to object to the reduction in the size of claims, to the royalty, to the reservation of gold-bearing lands for the Crown, and to other rules issued by the Laurier administration following the epidemic of "Klondike fever" that spread across North America in the summer of 1897. The two men, when reporting to a mass meeting in July 1898, claimed that they had found Laurier most co-operative but unaware of conditions in the Klondike, that they had been instrumental in bringing about the defeat in the Senate of the proposed Stikine railway scheme, and that they were certain that beneficial results would soon come from their mission.[2]

The meeting was one of several convened that summer—just at the peak of the gold rush when the passions of the people could be pushed to fever pitch. The demonstrations began shortly after a small committee had been organized by miners who had been in the country for several years. The committee advertised, through the press and by word of mouth, that it would hold an open air mass meeting on July 9, at which time a series of resolutions would be presented to the public for its approval. J. F. (Barney) Sugrue called the reported 3,000 in attendance to order, and, after announcing that the intention of the gathering was not to attack the government, he proceeded to condemn the administration for paralysing the country through its

B

"iniquitous" mining laws. He concluded with a resolution, passed "unanimously," asking for abolition of the royalty, enlargement of placer claims, and a host of other changes.[3]

Frank Dunleavy, a former South African miner, charging that Sugrue's meeting had been too mild and that free discussion had been prevented, organized another meeting a few days later, at which he systematically censured every government regulation, and called upon the crowd to appoint committees to wait upon Fawcett and Walsh with their grievances. Just as the committees were chosen, a fight broke out and the N.W.M.P. dispersed the crowd—again numbering 3,000 according to press reports.[4]

The original group persuaded Dunleavy to join its ranks, and held several more mass meetings in July and August. At one, E. J. Livernash and Maxime Landreville, the two delegates to Ottawa, spoke to a crowd of 7,000; at another, Fawcett's handling of the Dominion Creek muddle was discussed, and a committee of eleven was chosen to prevent further official misdemeanours.[5] The committee of eleven drew up the petition containing the charges that later formed the basis of the Ogilvie Commission of Inquiry,[6] and, finally at the insistence of Dunleavy, it decided to form a permanent organization to keep the needs of the people before the government. At a mass meeting of August 12, those assembled voted to found the Miners' Association.[7] In September the committee of eleven and other instigators of the agitation met in the Presbyterian Church, where they drew up a constitution and elected a slate of officers for the association.[8] George Armstrong and Colonel Donald McGregor, both of whom remained prominent in further political activity, were chosen president and vice-president respectively. It was decided that only men holding miners' certificates could join. By October a membership drive had enlisted 137 persons, 22 of whom gave their occupations as miners;[9] the rest, presumably, had obtained mining licences so that they could join.

Meanwhile, the second goal of political pressure had begun to emerge, for, as early as July, Dunleavy called upon the government to appoint an advisory committee of miners and tradesmen to assist the Commissioner in the performance of his duties.[10] Also in July, in a letter to the Klondike Nugget, C. M. Woodworth, an attorney, suggested that the first step should be incorporation of Dawson, reasoning that Ottawa could not ignore the wishes of a municipal council as easily as it did those of mass meetings. Under the provisions of the Yukon Act, he continued, the newly created Commissioner in Council, once in office, could satisfy the demand for incorporation.[11] Woodworth, who was also a member of the Miners' Association, called a mass meeting early in September to discuss his proposal. He presented a resolution, passed, as always, "unanimously," petitioning Commissioner Ogilvie to confer municipal institutions upon Dawson, "a city of eighteen thousand serving a population of thirty-five thousand," and requesting that all property holders, whether British subjects or not, be given the franchise.[12] Other meetings were held, and more resolutions calling for incorporation were ratified by those in attendance.[13]

Towards the end of September, Armstrong, McGregor, and others—calling themselves the "Citizens' Committee"—announced their intention to meet the public to discuss the advisability of establishing a "Political Association for the Yukon Territory" to seek federal representation.[14] At the meeting, however, most speakers declared it their preference to leave this objective to the Miners' Association, although one thought that it should not be sought at all until incorporation was secured.

Woodworth agreed that one organization was sufficient for all purposes, and strongly urged the Miners' Association to add representation not only in Parliament but also on the Yukon Council to its goals which previously had been solely associated with mining regulations.[15] At the October meeting of the Miners' Association, resolutions were passed calling on the Laurier ministry to provide the Yukon with representation in the House of Commons and requesting the Commissioner in Council (which, incidentally, had no jurisdiction over the matter) to add two elected members to the Yukon Council.[16]

Pressure group activity became somewhat less pronounced during the winter of 1898–99, when the Miners' Association began to act more as a social than as a political organization. The executive did appear before the Ogilvie Commission of Inquiry, but most of the officers boycotted the hearing after learning that the terms of reference permitted the Commission to consider only those grievances tendered before August 25, the date the committee of eleven had forwarded its petition to Ottawa.[17] By spring the association had disbanded.

The agitation did not cease, however, for the press of the Klondike filled the void left by the inactivity of pressure groups. Two newspapers began operations in June 1898—the *Klondike Nugget* (to which reference has already been made) and the *Yukon Midnight Sun*—and a third, the *Klondike Miner*, commenced publication later that year. All three were American-owned, but, shortly after its establishment, the *Sun* was purchased by Canadian interests and, thereafter, was given the patronage of the territorial administration.[18] The other two bitterly opposed the government—the *Nugget* in more sensational fashion—and pledged themselves to protect what they considered to be the rights of Yukoners. Both entered the campaign for representation and endeavoured to keep the issue before the public. On one occasion, the editor of the *Nugget*, in a rare gesture, complimented Council for rescinding certain objectionable features of the ordinance to muzzle dogs, but then went on to write: "had the Yukon Council been dependent upon the citizens of Dawson for their tenure in office, such an act would never have been passed. In a word, being independent of the public, no obligation rests upon them to consult public opinion when laws are to be passed. As a natural sequence, . . . unpopular legislation must be expected."[19]

Council's passing of revenue ordinances caused the *Klondike Miner* to expound that:

A great deal has been said and written about the apparent lack of wisdom shown in the governing of this territory and in the laws and regulations under which we operate. After all is said and done does not the greater part of the trouble arise from the government of Canada attempting to keep this distant country directly under its own eye and control through local officers who of very necessity, do not feel their responsibility to the people of the locality as they do to their own immediate superiors, the Dominion officials—the source of their authority here. It is not the first time in the history of the world when an ignominious failure has followed the attempt to pass laws for the government of a country at an enormous distance from the place of execution, and it reflects no particular discredit by reason of its failure. . . . The two principles that are being violated in the government of this country . . . [are] that of the necessity . . . to have the opportunities to easily present grievances for speedy redress . . . and [that] the citizens . . . if they are to continue to be taxed . . . shall be permitted to have a voice in the spending of their money and that it shall be used for their good and for the development of this land and not to make good . . . deficits in the general running expenses of the Dominion.[20]

The animosity which this editorial expressed towards the government was mild in contrast to that in the following excerpt from the *Klondike Nugget:*

In view of the probable permanence of the territory, we believe it not only our privilege but our duty to object to a "nigger" government—or more properly speaking, a government elsewhere only forced upon underdeveloped races which have given unmistakeable evidence of the lack of those qualities of self-government which have made our own race famous.

Britishers and Canadians should take action, the editor declared, as should Americans, who properly deserve the vote by virtue of their prominence in opening up the country.[21]

The two newspapers had other interests as well—attacking Council's newspaper ordinance, the O'Brien Tramway, and the Ogilvie Commission of Inquiry.[22] With respect to the latter, the *Nugget* again was the more sensational of the two papers, claiming that Ogilvie had written Sifton to say nothing was wrong "long before the royal investigation farce commenced."[23] The *Nugget*'s greatest project was announced in January 1899, when the editor melodramatically proclaimed that the paper would save the Yukon by sending its own representatives, George Allen and William Semple, to Ottawa to secure concessions on the basis of a ten-point programme of desired action. Many times following the return of the two men in May,[24] the *Nugget* took credit for governmental changes which it felt were beneficial.

Shortly after he returned from Ottawa, William Semple left the *Nugget* to establish the *Dawson Sunday Gleaner*. Pierre Berton quotes Bert Parker, "who sold it on the streets," and who "described it as 'one of the hottest sheets ever published in Canada and I don't except the *Calgary Eye-Opener*.' The paper was published twice a week, and more in the interests of circulation than public spirit, roasted the government unmercifully. 'They blamed the government for everything, not excepting the weather,' Parker recalled."[25] Few issues of the *Gleaner* survive, but those that do indicate that Parker's statements were not exaggerated. After Council imposed a two-dollar fishing licence fee, Semple proclaimed in glaring headlines, "THE NEXT THING WILL BE A TAX ON YOUR MOUTH."[26] When Council adjourned in September 1899 the paper asked, "How can the . . . exclusive franchise seekers get along now?"[27] In December Semple was sued for, and convicted of, criminal libel; he disbanded the *Gleaner* and left Dawson shortly thereafter.[28] However, the Klondike could still afford four newspapers (selling at twenty-five cents an issue), and, about the time of Semple's trial, the *Dawson Daily News* began publication.[29]

In 1899 the federal government acted on some of the grievances and requests presented to it by the Miners' Association the previous fall. Although the royalty was not reduced, an exemption of $5,000 on gross output was allowed,[30] thus making the tax less burdensome upon those who had to expend large sums on capital equipment before beginning to work their claims. Also important was the "Bill to Amend the Yukon Act" which eliminated the restriction in the original statute that neither the Governor in Council nor the Commissioner in Council could impose a shop, tavern, or similar tax exceeding $100 without the authority of Parliament; prohibited the manufacturing or importation of liquor without the permission of the Governor in Council; and constituted the Supreme Court of British Columbia as the Court of Appeal for the territory.[31] More significant, however, was a change included in this same bill after second reading in the Senate. During the debate Senator Power of Nova Scotia suggested that an additional clause be inserted to empower the Governor in Council to appoint "at least one local man to the Council. . . . This principle of governing without the consent of the governed is not a good one at this period of the nineteenth century, and there are sufficient number of intelligent and respectable Canadians in the Yukon country now to enable the government to select some reputable and capable man to assist the gentlemen who are sent by the government from outside into the country."[32] David Mills, the Minister of Justice, replied that the government had thought of allowing the people to elect two representatives to Council, but, because it could give this right only to British subjects (who were a minority), it was afraid of raising difficulties in Canada similar to those existing in South Africa. Power responded that the Americans could become naturalized—they were "hardly oppressed like the Uitlanders"—and that representation would prevent a recurrence of the embarrassment suffered by the government as a result of statements in the *Klondike Nugget* and other Yukon newspapers. Mills agreed to frame an amendment providing for the election of two councillors for a two-year term at a time chosen by the Governor in Council.[33] The bill passed both Houses of Parliament with little comment.

When the government had not acted to implement the new electoral provisions by late 1899, the *Nugget* printed the following editorial:

The government appears to have been only handing a "sop" to Yukoners during the late session of Parliament when it passed a law giving us representation on the Yukon-Ogilvie-Star-Chamber. . . . With two members on this Ogilvie Star Chamber dependent for their position—not upon the estimation of Sifton—but of the miners of the Yukon, one vast stride towards purity of administration will have been made. . . . The self-governing traditions of the race, developed through centuries of empire, are all trampled upon to perpetuate a wealth-creating ring rule in this corner of the earth. The greed of those in control is so vast that it is hopeless to look for a time when they shall voluntarily say, "We have enough; let further spoliation cease".[34]

Having received a new impetus from the depressed economic conditions which began to develop when the gold rush boom ended, pressure group activity was further stimulated by the lack of government action. C. M. Woodworth, the attorney who had first suggested that the old Miners' Association seek representation on the Yukon Council, called a mass meeting of British subjects in February 1900 to discuss ways and means of forcing the election of two Yukon councillors.[35] Woodworth spoke to the audience of 150, decrying taxation without representation, and noting that Prince Edward Island, Nova Scotia, New Brunswick, and Manitoba all had had smaller populations than the Yukon when given not only representation but also provincial status. After several others spoke, the meeting passed a resolution requesting that representation be granted, and chose a committee of seven to urge the Commissioner and Council to "negotiate" with Ottawa.[36] Composed of miners Colonel Donald McGregor, A. D. Williams, and James Sturgeon, lawyer C. M. Woodworth, banker T. McMullen, stenographer Joseph Clarke, and mine owner "Big Alex" McDonald (known as the "King of the Klondike"), the group of seven was shortly thereafter dubbed the "Citizens' Committee."[37]

The committee drafted a letter to Council urging it to petition the Laurier ministry to implement the provisions conferring representation. Thus seen as a useful institution through which to work for federal reforms, Council decided to meet the committee to discuss the necessity of the matter.[38] When the conference took place, Commissioner Ogilvie asked the Citizens' Committee to draft, and present to Council, a memorial setting out its reasons for requesting representation.[39] The *Nugget* expressed great confidence following Ogilvie's recommendation, noting that all councillors favoured the movement for more popular control, and that the two members, once elected, would be able to exert strong influence on the federal government to alter the mining regulations.[40]

The resulting memorial stated that strong public feeling favoured a partially elective council; that, of the more than 20,000 people in the territory, at least 3,000 would be able to vote as resident British subjects; and that the implementation of the electoral provision would forestall "large migration to Alaska."[41] When Council subsequently passed a resolution "that an immediate census of the Territory be taken, that in the meantime the Commissioner communicate by telegraph to the Minister of the Interior the purport of the petition received from the citizens' committee and forward the original by mail,"[42] the committee met and denounced the councillors, first, for not endorsing its demand, and, secondly, for ordering a census as a delaying tactic to prevent a spring election. The committee also decided to broaden its scope by seeking two federal representatives for the territory and by opposing, until incorporation was granted, Council's intention to pass an ordinance providing for property and income taxation in Dawson.[43]

On March 17 the *Nugget* alleged that discord over the petition of the Citizens' Committee had arisen in Council between Commissioner Ogilvie and Judge Dugas, the former opposing immediate representation and the latter supporting it. The newspaper condemned the councillors for sitting behind closed doors, claiming that the public ought to know who was for, and who was against, the people. "Representatives of the press are not permitted to be present at [the Council's] deliberation, and the clerk of that body is not permitted to give out for publication one jot or tittle of what takes place until the minutes are . . . submitted to the rigid inspection of . . . Governor Ogilvie. That official reads the minutes with care and deliberation, blue pencilling any and all items which to him may appear best suppressed from publication." The *Nugget* proceeded to poll the members of the Council on the question of secrecy and reported that Messrs. Dugas and Girouard favoured open meetings, Mr. Clement opposed them, and Superintendent Perry refused to comment. Commissioner Ogilvie also rejected the idea, not on the grounds that Council was an executive institution but rather because the chamber was too small to accommodate the press, let alone the general public.[44]

When the Citizens' Committee called a second mass meeting for March 23, 600 British subjects crammed the lower floor of the Palace Grand Theatre. They heard the committee's report, which denounced the census as "mere subterfuge" and secret sessions as "a menace to good government and an outrage to loyal subjects," and made "an indignant protest . . . against [the abuse of] that inalienable right of a free people, which renders illegal taxation without representation." Barney Sugrue, one of the founders of the defunct Miners' Association, exhorted the people to appeal over the heads of the Canadian cabinet ministers by submitting "the whole problem of maladministration" to British Colonial Secretary Joseph Chamberlain, but his motion to do so was tabled for a month. The government was defended by F. C. Wade, the Crown Prosecutor, who attacked the Citizens' Committee as an organ of the Conservative party designed, by its members, to embarrass the Laurier administration. Despite Wade's protests, the resolutions of the committee condemning the census and Mr. Clement, praising Judge Dugas, the *Nugget*, and the *News*, calling for open council sessions and no taxation without local and territorial representation, and expressing loyalty to the Queen and the empire were passed "unanimously." Auguste

Noel, an attorney, and Alex Prudhomme, a contractor, were added to the Citizens' Committee.[45]

After the mass meeting, Council refused to pledge itself to securing representation, causing the *Dawson Daily News* to conclude that:

It is to be regretted that every stumbling block appears to have been placed in the way of securing this representation now, and the only inference to be drawn from these protracted delays is the fear of the party in power to submit to an election in the Yukon Territory at the present time. In other words, the election of two Conservatives to seats in the Yukon Council might prove detrimental to the political prestige of the present government at Ottawa and lessen to that extent its possible success at the coming [federal] election.[46]

However, the Citizens' Committee must certainly have been pleased with some of Council's decisions in the weeks that followed: liquor licences were lowered to suit altered economic conditions in the territory, the Dawson assessment bill was deferred, and the councillors expressed their intentions to permit incorporation as soon as the citizens of the city demanded it.[47] Just when it seemed that agitation might die down, the government-supported newspaper—the *Yukon Sun*—echoed Wade's charges that the Citizens' Committee was an organization inspired by Conservatives,[48] and thus, in effect, not a pressure group seeking to influence public policy, but a political party attempting to bring about the defeat of the government. To these allegations, Woodworth, Clarke, McDonald, and McGregor replied that they had voted Liberal in 1896, while Noel claimed no affiliation and Prudhomme admitted he was a Conservative.[49] As this controversy was reaching its climax, Council provoked more criticism from the Citizens' Committee by deciding to pass the assessment ordinance after all.[50]

On May 2, after the census returns were made public,[51] Ogilvie telegraphed Sifton, saying, "Council sees no objection to granting local representation,"[52] but, of course, he could not divulge the contents of the communication to the press until he had received a reply. Consequently, conflict over the matter persisted, and the Citizens' Committee held its largest mass meeting of the year to discuss what action to take now that the census had shown that there would be approximately 4,000 British subjects eligible to vote. Those in attendance reaffirmed all previous resolutions and passed three more—requesting the abolition of the royalty, immediate federal representation, and the recall of Commissioner Ogilvie. When the last one was proposed, a Dawson physician, William Catto, moved an amendment to remove the Minister of the Interior instead because "Ogilvie is merely the creature of Sifton." The amendment was defeated and the original motion was carried, although by no means unanimously.[53] Ogilvie, interviewed about the resolution, said he had no comment to make apart from being personally in favour of a *completely elective council*.[54] Colonel McGregor later announced that the resolution would not be forwarded to Ottawa because it was poorly supported and might jeopardize the chances of securing territorial and federal representation. Woodworth went further, saying "our committee is organized to secure representation, not to eject government,"[55] thereby affirming, albeit implicitly, his belief that the Citizens' Committee was a pressure group, not a political party. Joe Clarke, secretary of the committee, did not agree, and, apparently without the permission of his fellow committeemen, forwarded the controversial resolution to Lord Minto, Governor General of Canada.[56]

Pressure on government was also exerted by the merchants of Dawson who established the Board of Trade at about the same time the Citizens' Committee was formed.

At first, the board restricted its demands to sweeping changes in placer gold regulations, but, later in the year, it advocated federal representation and authorized a board of trustees to collect $50,000 to bring the state of affairs in the Yukon before the people of Canada.[57]

Meanwhile, in Ottawa, the official opposition, still debating charges of maladministration and misbehaviour in the period 1897–98, saw the denial of representation as a promising issue on which to attack the ministry for its Yukon policy. On March 20, in reply to a Conservative query asking why the provisions of the 1899 amendment had not been brought into effect, Senator David Mills, the Minister of Justice, stated that the people had not yet acted to secure representation. But, said Sir Mackenzie Bowell, the Conservative Senate leader, "just last night" he had read an account of a public meeting in Dawson "protesting in the strongest possible manner against the authorities" for not calling a territorial election.[58] Some three months later, Sir Charles Hibbert Tupper, after reading the petition of the March 23 mass meeting to the House of Commons, condemned the government for not giving the people of the Yukon their political rights. His fellow Conservative George Foster asked why the cabinet had not put the electoral provisions into effect the previous year. "Not by lack of protestation by the people themselves, for the people have been protesting and protesting, and I have before me . . . papers which have been brought down, and I find that after all their protest they have been unable to stir . . . the government." The present constitutional arrangements in the Yukon, he said, have created "a government by officials—an autocracy; because everybody knows that the Minister of the Interior . . . will have his will carried out, though he . . . has no apparent supervision, and assumes no responsibility." Foster concluded with a demand for immediate federal representation so that the House, at last, would be able to obtain first-hand information concerning conditions in the territory. Laurier replied that, although he intended to implement the provisions of the 1899 amendment soon, federal representation would have to await the 1901 census. After all, he exclaimed, the Yukon was only four years old and several constitutional advances had already been made.[59]

Gradually, however, the rewards of political protest in the Klondike became apparent. One of the goals of the Citizens' Committee was achieved on May 31 when Council decided to open its meetings to the public and to adopt a modified form of parliamentary procedure.[60] As a result of this change, Council was transformed from an executive to a legislative institution, although its legal role was not altered. Thus, beginning in June 1900, the Commissioner in Council acted (in the traditional language of British institutions) as a legislature when sitting in open session and as a cabinet when meeting *in camera*. Yet more important was the decision of the Governor in Council on July 13 to permit the Yukon Council to make preparations for a territorial election any time after August 13.[61]

The Citizens' Committee had won its first battle, and, for a time during the summer of 1900, it became dormant. In fact, after all the agitation for open meetings of Council, only Joe Clarke and representatives of the press attended the first public session.[62] But other goals remained—federal representation, incorporation of Dawson, and changes in the mining regulations—and it was not long before renewed pressure was exerted upon the federal and territorial governments. Soon, too, new structures appeared in the political process, for organization was required to wage the first electoral campaign in the short history of the territory.

CHAPTER FIVE

SIGNS OF VICTORY

THE LULL in political activity lasted only until the fourth week of July 1900, when the federal government made two announcements that greatly concerned those involved in territorial politics—the Earl of Minto, Governor General of Canada, would visit the Klondike in August, and an election for two Yukon councillors would be held as soon after August 13 as Council could arrange it.[1] Excitement mounted as preparations were made for both events.

F. C. Wade, on hearing of Minto's proposed visit, began to worry that the Laurier administration would be embarrassed by the import of the petitions that would undoubtedly be presented to the Governor General. He wired Sifton (in code), imploring him to come as well, but the Minister replied that it would be impossible for him to do so. Instead, Sifton asked Wade to persuade the "representative" bodies to agree on an address that "is not objectionable."[2] The Crown Prosecutor then joined the Board of Trade

which is the only representative body in the City and became Chairman of the Committee on Reception. . . . I urged the Board not to deliver political addresses, but it . . . consists largely of American citizens—a good many of whom could not understand the idea, so to satisfy all parties we sent a telegram to the Governor's secretary asking if he would receive any addresses, and got a reply that he would receive any addresses which did not deal with politics. This was satisfactory and settled matters on the Board of Trade for the time being although I had to combat Woodworth and a lot of other Tory members who insisted on the right to present petitions to Her Majesty's representative under any circumstances.[3]

However, the "Tory members" of the Board of Trade also could work through the Citizens' Committee, and there was little Wade could do to stop the latter body's presenting a petition. He attempted to induce Commissioner Ogilvie and Major Wood to prevent the committee from seeing the Governor General, only to be obstructed, he claimed, by Ogilvie who "took the Citizens' Committee to his arms."[4]

Lord Minto arrived in Dawson on August 14, and, that same day, standing on a platform constructed on one of the city's streets, he heard the Citizens' Committee deliver its petition before "thousands." The document recited the grievances of the people dating back to Fawcett's administration of the Gold Commissioner's office, and concluded with a list of eleven requests including those for a wholly elective Yukon council, two members in the House of Commons, a reduction of the royalty, better transportation facilities, improved liquor regulations, and more effective administration of justice.[5] In reporting the event to his political superior, Wade labelled the address "seditious" because it claimed that maladministration and crippling regulations had prevented the territory from growing to a population in excess of 100,000.[6] The petition of the Board of Trade was more subdued, although it, too, contained essentially the same requests, with the significant addition that the federal cabinet delegate its authority over mining regulations to the territorial Council.[7]

B*

Much to Wade's dismay, the Governor General stated publicly that he agreed to a certain extent with many of the demands.[8] In a report to Laurier, Lord Minto noted that "I found myself in the somewhat dangerous predicament of being hailed as the possessor of a magician's wand before whom all grievances were to vanish." However, he felt he had dispelled that notion by convincing the people that he was there only to gain information and not to express opinions. He sent copies of both petitions to Sir Wilfrid, stating that they embodied public opinion, although that of the Citizens' Committee tended to exaggerate conditions to a slight degree.[9]

In his private account of his stay in Dawson, the Governor General made some rather interesting observations.[10] He confided that he had sought the opinions of "everyone of influence" on the contents of the petitions, and found that, with one exception, they agreed with the demands set forth. "The only exception I met with was from a creature, Wade by name, a Government official, who after having accompanied the Board of Trade representatives in their interview with me, returned to tell me he did not agree with a word that had been said." Personally, Minto doubted the advisability of an entirely elected council "in a society of such recent formation as that of Dawson—it is far more easy . . . to advocate representation in the Dominion Parliament" but he felt that the other recommendations were "fair and reasonable." Part of the agitation in the territory, he continued, resulted from the character of Ogilvie who "in the opinion of everyone is a perfectly honest man—but he is weak and vacillating, and does not even possess any social weight." But, far more important, was the way in which the Minister of the Interior provided for the Yukon's administration. Apart from the charges against Sifton which the Governor General heard from many citizens of the area, Ogilvie, although reputed to be on good terms with Sifton, "told me things which in the opinion of ordinary people would *utterly condemn* the Minister."[11] Some of the complaints were that Sifton had insisted on the appointment of J. D. McGregor as "issuer of liquor licences," but Council had refused because of Superintendent Steele's assertion that the former Inspector of Mines had been tried for horse stealing; that the Minister had then arranged to send Steele to the Boer War to rid himself of the officer's opposition;[12] that Ogilvie had received back his annual report with several changes and had been requested to sign it; and that the liquor permit system was controlled by Sifton for his own political profit. "In any country but this, public opinion of the Minister as expressed in ordinary conversation would be enough to ruin any man. My verdict is criminal administration by the Minister of the Interior." He concluded that recent reforms such as the addition of two elected members to Council and the royalty exemption had been granted only because the government feared that new scandals in the Yukon would hurt its image in the forthcoming federal election.

Meanwhile, as soon as it was announced that preparations could be made for a territorial election, the Citizens' Committee called upon Ogilvie to appoint a returning officer to conduct the election under the conditions prescribed in the North-West Territories election ordinance. However, Mr. Clement, the Legal Adviser, claimed that a new law was needed, and that, for Council to pass one, a quorum was required.[13] This requirement was met when the cabinet appointed Major Z. T. Wood to Council to replace Superintendent Perry who had been dispatched elsewhere;[14] the councillors then proceeded to frame an election ordinance.[15] Election day was fixed for October 17.[16] The *Klondike Nugget* set the stage for the ensuing campaign when it noted, on August 22, that there would probably be twenty candidates in the running.

In this number are several good men who, if chosen, will prove of value to the [Council] and who will reflect the honor and credit both to themselves and their constituency. And there are others who are working equally hard, but whose election to the position would be disastrous to the district and her interests. But as the people can usually be trusted to do the right thing at the right time, there is little room for apprehension that the best men will not be selected.[17]

The idea implied by the editorial—that both supporters and opponents of the government would tender their nominations—was given more weight shortly thereafter when it was rumoured that a convention would be held to nominate anti-administration candidates.[18] The Citizens' Committee convened a mass meeting on August 28 to discuss whether or not it would enter the campaign—thereby converting itself, if it did so, from a pressure group to a political party. Violent disagreement occurred between Auguste Noel and other members of the committee, most speakers favouring a convention to select two candidates and Noel supporting an unlimited number of contestants. Having ejected Noel, the meeting decided to hold a convention on September 8 after preliminary meetings to select delegates had been conducted in Dawson, in the surrounding communities, and on the creeks. The men nominated by the convention were to have the full support of the "Citizens' Yukon Party."[19]

The convention, numbering ninety-one delegates, placed the names of sixteen men in nomination, but only five allowed their names to stand. After three ballots had been taken, Arthur Wilson and Alexander Prudhomme were declared the winners, and the defeated aspirants moved that the vote be unanimous. The *Nugget* proudly displayed the biographies of the victors the next day. Wilson, a Liberal "on the outside," had joined in the rush to the Klondike in 1897, leaving Nanaimo where he had been a coal miner and municipal councillor; now he owned three placer claims and was "well known" throughout the creeks. Prudhomme, a Conservative and member of the Citizens' Committee, had come to the Yukon from Quebec early in 1897, and, after trying his hand at mining, turned to his old trade—contracting and building. Both men were in their early thirties.[20]

The Citizens' Yukon Party had hoped that its nominees would run unopposed, but, even before the convention took place, Thomas O'Brien and Auguste Noel declared their intentions to contest the election as independents.[21] O'Brien, a Liberal, had been involved in trading and transportation in the Yukon district since 1886.[22] Unfortunately for his chances of electoral success, his name had been blackened just two years before when he and his partner had charged tolls on the sled trail between Dawson and Grand Forks over their proposed tramway route. Noel, also a Liberal, though he attempted to disguise the fact, had come to the Yukon to practise law during the rush. Although both men declared themselves independent of party and faction,[23] they were served by a common campaign committee, and there was little doubt that they had official support.[24] It is significant to note the importance attached to the French-Canadian minority by those who contested the election—each ticket consisted of one English-speaking and one French-speaking candidate.

After nominations closed on September 19 with only the four candidates in the race,[25] a heated campaign ensued. On September 20 the Citizens' Yukon Party announced that its men would run on a platform of sixteen demands similar to those presented to Lord Minto.[26] All but three (proper schools, free and good roads and bridges, and a miners' lien ordinance) dealt with objectives that could be met only by acts of Parliament or orders in council. Once again, Council was seen as a vehicle through which pressure could be exerted upon the authorities in Ottawa to effect changes, while the electoral campaign itself was viewed by the Citizens' Committee as part of its general assault upon the government. If the Citizens' Yukon Party candidates hoped that the sixteen planks would become issues, they were disappointed because O'Brien and Noel, presumably realizing they would not be in positions of authority anyway, contested the election on an identical programme.[27]

The basic issue, as it turned out, was whether or not Noel and O'Brien were supporting the government. They did their best to conceal any such allegiance,[28] but Wilson and Prudhomme sought to identify their opponents as closely as possible with the Laurier ministry and the territorial administration. Supporters of the "independents" felt that this attempt to foster identification succeeded and therefore that certain government actions prior to and during the election campaign influenced the outcome of the voting. Two decisions were particularly significant: first, Council passed an ordinance, on instructions from Ottawa, restraining the lodging of civil suits or petitions for damages against any officers of the Crown for acts resulting from government rules, regulations, orders, or instructions before July 1900;[29] and, second, Ogilvie announced that, although he had received a letter from Sifton requesting the suppression of gambling and "lewd women," he would leave any action to Major Wood because he, himself, did not favour the idea.[30] Antagonism towards Sifton, although not particularly towards Ogilvie and local officials, mounted as a result of these measures, and such concessions by the federal government as the rescinding of the orders reserving alternate placer claims for the Crown and the promise that the royalty would be reduced did little to offset the hostility.[31]

Most of the campaigning was done on a person-to-person basis and at small gatherings held by each of the candidates, but, on one occasion, all four of them addressed a public meeting in Dawson. Because there were no issues apart from the political affiliation of the candidates and past government activities, personal attacks dominated the proceedings. The *Nugget* reported that not many of the speakers' points could be heard because supporters of the two factions attempted to "howl each other down." Mr. Noel, the attorney, was jeered the most when he claimed to know as much, if not more, about mining than Mr. Wilson, the miner.[32] In the last few days before the election, most controversy centred around a feud between the *Daily News* and the *Nugget*, when the former accused the latter of deserting Prudhomme and Wilson as a result of being bribed by O'Brien and Noel.[33] The *Nugget*, which had written only one editorial in favour of the Citizens' Yukon Party candidates and had remained silent during the rest of the campaign, denied the charges, claiming its silence was due solely to an attempt by supporters of Wilson and Prudhomme to buy its front and editorial pages for the two weeks preceding the election. It proceeded to attack the editors of the *News* for seeking the highest bid before backing one side or the other.[34]

Apart from the sensationalism of the two newspapers, election day was quiet with "no shrewd . . . methods so frequently employed elsewhere being used" and no arrests being made during the "wild celebration" that occurred when the polls closed and the saloons opened.[35] The victory of Wilson and Prudhomme was announced late that night, and the *Nugget* declared the next day that the result was a "condemnation of the past methods of administration which have prevailed in this territory." However, the editor wrote, the losers did much better than they would have done six months earlier because government "has generally improved." The final results were Wilson 1,417, Prudhomme 1,209, O'Brien 875, Noel 642. The Citizens' Yukon Party and the independent faction won ten and three polls respectively, and the tickets were split in ten others. The fact that ticket-splitting occurred in almost half the polls would seem to indicate that the affiliation of the candidates was not an important issue, but all ten of these polls were outside the Klondike region, where, owing to poor communications, many of the voters would have been unaware of the two factions. In these, it would seem that the national origin of the contestants was the dominant factor because Wilson and O'Brien won all but one of the polls.

Local Liberals were somewhat dismayed by the results. Wade reported to Sifton that many aliens voted because the "bad election ordinance" did not provide for an enumeration, but noted that the defeat went beyond the law to the Commissioner, who "should be our political head, but is if anything against us politically." Most of the officials actively supported Noel and O'Brien, but their help was not enough. "The new members are . . . hostile. We see how necessary political reorganization is. The Liberals are meeting . . . and will do something desperate unless matters are improved."[36] Several leading Liberals, including Wade and O'Brien, telegraphed Sir Wilfrid himself.

Friends here wish you all the success in the present [federal election] campaign. Defeat here was unfortunate, but has served to organize the Yukon. We feel time has arrived when friends here must be taken into your confidence. Notorious incompetence of Commissioner of the Yukon is a reproach to the Government and every Liberal supporter. Another similar appointment would be a calamity. We press upon you and your Government the advisability and even necessity of consulting friends here before another Commissioner is chosen. The future success of this Territory depends on the next Commissioner.[37]

The Prime Minister replied that he would confer with Sifton about replacing Ogilvie.[38] In February, the Commissioner announced his resignation. Although Sifton denied Conservative charges that Ogilvie had been dismissed,[39] there can be little doubt that the Commissioner's job was made as unpleasant as possible following the territorial election. In giving the standard reason of poor health for his decision, Ogilvie added that he had other reasons, "some of which are personal dislike of many things in connection with my position."[40]

By the time Ogilvie resigned, the Liberals of the territory had established an association through which future electoral campaigns could be waged effectively.[41] But because, like any political party, the Yukon Liberal Association also existed to play some part in influencing policy and selecting leaders, the first task it undertook was to guide the cabinet in its choice of a successor to Ogilvie. Unhappy with the political acumen of the first Yukon Commissioner, the territorial Liberals desired not only a capable administrator, but also a strong Liberal and a party leader. The party executive therefore telegraphed a unanimous request to the Prime Minister supporting F. C. Wade; the latter was also favoured in separate representations from several individuals, including Auguste Noel.[42] However, after being informed by Israel Tarte, the Minister of Public Works, that Wade would be unacceptable to "*nos compatriates* [*sic*]," Sir Wilfrid appointed instead James Hamilton Ross, a man admirably qualified for the position, at least in so far as the characteristics sought by the Yukon Liberal Association were concerned.[43]

Ross was the most distinguished individual appointed to the Commissioner's chair during the period under discussion, and the only occupant who had been an active participant in a political environment somewhat similar to that in the Yukon. Born in London, Ontario, in 1856, he moved to Manitoba with his father and brother in the 1870s. In 1882, after acquiring some capital in the lumbering business, the young Ross brothers trekked westward again, this time to the Assiniboia District of the North-West Territories where they established a ranch near Moose Jaw. Only a year later James embarked upon a political career and won election to the territorial Council. Thereafter, while a representative in first the Council and then the Legislative Assembly, he ardently sought responsible government for the territories. Successively private member, Speaker, and member of the Assembly's Executive Committee, Ross played a key role in the campaign that led to the realization of that goal in 1897. From then until his Yukon appointment, his offices of Commissioner of Public Works and Territorial Treasurer placed him in a position second only to that of Premier Haultain. Besides his political experience in a developing frontier community, he had the desired qualification of long and loyal support of the Liberal cause. It is true that the territorial group which fought for responsible government was non-partisan, but Ross played an important part in creating a federal Liberal organization and had campaigned actively for the party in national elections. If he could succeed in overcoming the grievances of Yukon politicians, the post of Commissioner promised to open the door to a potentially significant career in Ottawa.[44]

While Yukoners expectantly awaited the arrival of their new chief executive, Ogilvie continued to call frequent sessions of Council, which was now wholly transformed from an executive to a legislative body because of the addition to it of Wilson and Prudhomme, the elected councillors. They were sworn in on December 6, 1900, and, under the headline "Nothing Happened," the Klondike Nugget reported: "If there were those present who expected Patrick Henry speeches or a display of fire works they went home disappointed, as there was nothing more vivid than the necktie of Mr. Prudhomme to attract attention or to keep in mind the fact that great things were expected."[45] Nevertheless, Wilson and Prudhomme were persistent in pressing for the reforms promised in their election platform. Their major success was the passage, late in 1901, of an ordinance to protect miners' wages. On March 28 Wilson introduced a miners' lien bill requiring mine owners to pay the wages of labourers prior to meeting the claims of creditors except those who provided credit before mining operations were undertaken.[46] F. T. Congdon, Clement's successor as Legal Adviser,[47] arguing that the provisions were too favourable to the labourer and too harsh on the capitalist, succeeded in persuading Wilson to withdraw the bill in favour of a miners' protective wage ordinance, which, when passed, gave the Court the powers to appoint a receiver for the output of mines and to decide the priority of claims against them.[48] Wilson and Prudhomme had made an advance, but the problem of miners' liens, far from being finally solved, became a heated issue again.

The new councillors were active in other spheres as well. When Council forwarded a memorial to the Governor in Council seeking a reduction in the royalty, larger placer claims, and other changes in the mining regulations, the Citizens' Yukon Party representatives sent a minority petition requesting representation in Parliament and a wholly elective council.[49] Later, when no action had ensued on the royalty (a reduction had been promised in the election campaign) or on the size of claims, they presented a motion to telegraph Ottawa, but were defeated by the appointed members who proposed an amendment to defer action until an answer to the original submission had been received.[50] Shortly thereafter, the reply came—the royalty would be reduced to 5 per cent and larger claims would be permitted.[51] Although another victory had been won, the stronger opposition elements in the Citizens' Committee seemed disappointed that they could no longer complain about the "paralyzing" effect of the tax. When, at the April meeting, one member proposed a vote of thanks to the government for the concessions, Barney Sugrue retorted, "Thank God and not the government." The resolution was not passed.[52]

For the most part, good will prevailed as authority was transferred from Ogilvie to Ross after the new Commissioner arrived in Dawson on April 12.[53] Council passed a resolution naming a new bridge over the Klondike River for Ogilvie and presented an address of welcome to Ross, who was promised that he would be aided in every way possible. A lavish banquet was held to honour both men. However, two incidents marred the proceedings. At the Citizens' Committee meeting mentioned above, one member moved a vote of thanks to the federal government for removing Ogilvie pursuant to the resolution passed at the mass meeting the previous year. The motion was withdrawn when C. M. Woodworth said it would bring discredit to the committee, but not before Joe Clarke accused his fellow committeemen of "lacking backbone." F. C. Wade, when asked by the *Nugget* whether Ogilvie would be honoured at the banquet, was quoted as saying: "He will take no part. The Ottawa government kicked him out without even giving him notice. We will have nothing to do with him." The Crown Prosecutor denied making the statement, but then inadvertently admitted his guilt by claiming that his remarks had been confidential.

A major task confronting Ross upon his assumption of office was to quell discontent arising from an order Ogilvie, against his better judgment, had issued to the police to suppress gambling, prostitution, and dancehalls. The initiative for the order had come from Ottawa. Early in 1900 Clifford Sifton and other cabinet ministers began to receive complaints from church and temperance organizations against these Klondike institutions. A representative of the Women's Christian Temperance Union, the most vocal pressure group, wrote the Minister of the Interior on June 27: "In the interests of our 'Social Purity Department' we implore you . . . that you would do all in your power, both by personal influence and vote, to suppress so grave and shameful evils, that are a disgrace to our Christian civilization. . . . For the sake of our Motherhood, . . . our Wifehood, . . . our Boyhood, we pray you to act speedily in this matter."[54] Following receipt of this letter, Sifton asked Ogilvie to provide information on vice in the Yukon.[55] The Commissioner supplied these statistics: gaming houses 8, gamblers 110, dancehalls 2, dancehall girls 42, prostitutes 49.[56] In the letter that Ogilvie made public just prior to the territorial election campaign, Sifton demanded immediate suppression, but, as noted above, the Commissioner refused to act.[57] He told his Minister that abolishing gambling would merely force it underground, wherein the "square game" played currently would be replaced by dishonest practices. In so far as music halls were concerned, Ogilvie deemed them "necessary evils" because, once out of work, many of the dancehall girls "would not resort to ordinary prostitution but would become leeches on the general mining public."[58] Sifton and his Deputy Minister, James Smart, continued to write the Commissioner demanding action, until finally, on February 27, 1901, Ogilvie acquiesced and ordered dancehalls and gambling palaces to close their doors at midnight, March 15.[59]

When the order was made public, a great uproar ensued, particularly among leading businessmen who claimed that suppression would have serious short-run and long-run repercussions on the territorial economy. The managers of the Alaska Commercial and the Northern Trading and Transportation companies appealed to the Commissioner to rescind the order, and the Board of Trade circulated a petition around Dawson and the creeks to forward to the national capital. Major Wood wrote Sifton, requesting a postponement of the order until the navigation season opened, but the letter did not reach the Minister who was in the West on a political mission.[60] The order was carried out, and, for a day, Dawson was a quiet town. Then, on March 18, all establishments reopened after Sifton, back in Ottawa, wired an authorization to grant a postponement until June 1.[61]

Dr. A. S. Grant of the Dawson Presbyterian Church was incensed by the temporary revocation, writing Sifton: "It is nothing more or less than a standing disgrace to our country and an insult to the people of Dawson."[62] When Ross arrived, he was met by loud protests from the clergy over postponement and from businessmen over the proposed June 1 closure. Although Sifton directed the new Commissioner to enforce the order, Ross compromised—forbidding faro, roulette, and craps, but permitting blackjack and poker until November—thus enabling Dawson to make the transition.[63] Prostitutes were ordered to leave Dawson, whereupon they moved to Klondike City, although not without a strong protest from the residents of this town across the river from the capital.[64] Music halls were permitted to stay open until 1902, when Council passed ordinances prohibiting dancing on licensed premises, open passageways between music halls and bars, and women from selling drinks on percentage.[65] By the end of that year, although "temperance dancehalls" continued to operate,[66] Dawson's entertainment facilities were not much different from those in many Canadian cities of comparable size.

Ross used diplomacy in another matter as well, when he became determined that some provision had to be made for the government of Dawson. The city, smaller than it had been during the rush, was still the responsibility of the Commissioner and Council and required a great deal of attention. A good example of the ludicrous demands made upon the territorial government is furnished by a *Klondike Nugget* editorial calling upon Council to solve the problem of municipal garbage disposal.[67]

Incorporation had been an issue in the autumn of 1898 and the winter of 1900, and it appeared again after the Council election when the *Nugget* proclaimed that "now incorporation must follow."[68] Although the newspaper reversed its stand shortly afterwards when it learned that the large companies opposed the measure because it would increase taxation, C. M. Woodworth and other members of the Citizens' Committee called a mass meeting in January 1901 to discuss the advisability of seeking municipal institutions.[69] A committee was chosen to urge Council to pass an incorporation ordinance, but Commissioner Ogilvie refused to meet with it because he had already received a petition from businessmen taking the opposite viewpoint. Following a second mass meeting, the Commissioner did agree to suspend parliamentary procedure to allow members of the committee to state their case before Council, but he answered their plea by remarking that it seemed inconceivable to him that an incorporated city could manage its own affairs in view of the fact that Council was already spending one-half of its revenue on Dawson.[70] At one point, when Ogilvie announced that he would suppress dancehalls and gambling, it appeared that those favouring and those opposing incorporation would reconcile their differences: some of the leading businessmen, along with the Board of Trade, suddenly reversed their stands in the hope of electing a liberal city council to rescind the order—until they were informed that a city council would be powerless to take action because gambling houses and dancehalls contravened sections of the Canadian Criminal Code.[71]

Consequently, when Ross took office, he was confronted by two groups irreconcilably opposed to one another.

In July, shortly after the new Commissioner announced that he favoured some form of local government for Dawson and the nearby townsites, Council passed an "Ordinance respecting Unincorporated Towns," empowering the Commissioner to incorporate towns and to make provisions for the election of overseers once the municipalities had been established.[72] Later that month, the Citizens' Committee convened a mass meeting, which declared itself in favour of a mayor-council system of government and ratepayer franchise (enabling alien property-holders to vote) for Dawson.[73] The special Dawson incorporation bill which Ross subsequently placed before Council compromised between the factions opposing and supporting municipal institutions by providing for a plebiscite to give the voters the option of adopting an appointive commission of three or an elective council and mayor.[74] However, because both the Board of Trade and the Citizens' Committee objected to a clause permitting only British subjects to vote on the plebiscite and, if the elected council were chosen, in municipal elections, a deputation composed of men from the two factions appealed to Ross to broaden the franchise to include all ratepayers. When the Commissioner refused, the Board of Trade convened a mass meeting at which several speeches were delivered in favour of wide suffrage, including two from councillors Wilson and Prudhomme, who somewhat equivocally promised to secure the vote "for all who are entitled to it." Another meeting somewhat reluctantly accepted the Commissioner's decision, and proposed several minor amendments to the bill.[75] The ordinance was given assent on December 16, and the plebiscite was set for January 9.[76]

The campaign leading up to the date of the plebiscite was fervent.[77] Some of the more radical members of the Citizens' Committee—calling themselves the "Kid Committee"—as well as the *News* and the *Miner* crusaded for the elective plan, while a "Taxpayers Committee," the *Nugget*, and the *Sun* solicited votes for the appointive commission. In the end, after bitter name-calling and charges of tampering with the voters' list, the mayor-council system was chosen by a slim margin of 383 to 308.[78] The "Taxpayers" and the "Kids" each nominated a slate of candidates for the ensuing municipal election, and, this time, the former group was successful, electing the mayor and four of the six aldermen.[79]

In his report for the year ending June 30, 1902, Commissioner Ross noted with pride the advances made in local government: "The people of this territory are gradually acquiring self-government. Since my last report Dawson has become an incorporated city, . . . and the Yukon Council has been relieved from the government of what is perhaps one of the most progressive cities in Canada. . . . Grand Forks has also been incorporated under the name Bonanza, and . . . is governed by an overseer."[80] Thus, at last, the Commissioner and Council were discharged of many of the heavy municipal responsibilities they had had to bear ever since 1898, and could now turn to the development of the territory at large, often sadly neglected during these four years.

By mid-1902 great strides had already been made in this direction. In November 1901, after the federal government had responded to a widespread demand for lower transportation costs by ordering the recently completed White Pass and Yukon Route (W.P.Y.R.) to reduce its freight rates, the company acceded.[81] That same month, when Wilson and Prudhomme had asked Council to endorse a petition calling for an elective council, two members of Parliament, and more territorial control over the liquor trade, Commissioner Ross appointed a special Council committee to draft a memorial containing these requests. The committee concurred with the third demand, and reached compromises on the first—by recommending the addition of three elected members—and on the second—by advocating one member in the House of Commons and one in the Senate.[82] In January 1902 Ross left Dawson for Ottawa, promising five elected members for Council and at least one in Parliament, and pledging to see what could be done about another popular goal, the establishment of an assay office in the territory.[83] That he had some success became evident on May 15 when the Governor General gave his assent to two acts of Parliament: one granted the Yukon Territory a representative in the House of Commons; and the other added three elected members to the Yukon Council, placed the wholesale liquor trade under Council's jurisdiction, and made some changes in the restrictions applying to the powers of the Governor in Council and the Commissioner in Council to legislate for the territory.[84] Also, upon his return to Dawson in June, Commissioner Ross said that the federal government would build a mint in 1903, thus providing a use for Yukon gold, and that shortly thereafter an assay office would be opened in Dawson.[85] Ross held in store an added surprise: the fact that the Minister of the Interior planned to replace the royalty on placer gold with an export tax of 2.5 per cent.[86]

Thus, during Ross's first year in office, many of the demands of the press, the defunct Miners' Association, the Citizens' Committee, the Dawson Board of Trade, and the candidates in the territorial election were met. The Commissioner's sympathy with these aims led not only to the satisfaction of goals associated with economic development—through government action to decrease the tax on placer gold, to increase the size of placer claims, and to reduce transportation costs—but also to the partial fulfillment of the desire for more public participation in government—through measures to give the Yukon representation in the House of Commons, to increase the number of elected Yukon councillors, and to grant incorporation to Dawson. Ross might have returned to the Yukon as a conquering hero, but, during his absence, the most significant political issue ever to appear in the territory arose and grew to such proportions that the Canadian press and the official opposition again saw the Yukon as a national problem demanding immediate attention.

CHAPTER SIX

THE TREADGOLD CONCESSION

ON FEBRUARY 13, 1902, while Commissioner Ross was "on the outside," E. C. Senkler, the Gold Commissioner, announced that the federal government had decided to give all abandoned claims on Bonanza, Bear, and Hunker creeks to a hydraulic mining syndicate. The disclosure created a storm of political protest that did not subside for two years. To understand the fight against the "Treadgold Concession," the greatest of all political struggles in the Yukon, it is necessary to turn the calendar back to January 1898.

At that time, the Laurier administration decided to encourage large-scale mining in the Klondike by granting Robert Anderson, an English mining engineer, a lease to conduct hydraulic mining operations on a section of Hunker Creek. The order in council conferring the privileges upon Mr. Anderson read, in part:

> Mr. T. Fawcett, the Gold Commissioner . . . states that the tract [of land] applied for . . . has been passed over by individual prospectors and it is altogether too wide to prospect in search of a pay streak; that a claim of less area . . . would not justify the expenditure necessary to give the experiment a fair trial. . . . The Minister states that he is of the opinion that it is desirable to introduce hydraulic mining in the Yukon District . . . and he recommends the application be granted.[1]

Conditions attached to the application became the bases of hydraulic mining regulations, which, by 1900, provided that all successful applicants for hydraulic privileges were to be given a lease, not exceeding twelve years in duration, with a frontage of one to five miles in length and one mile in depth. "The leases involved an annual rental of $150 for each mile of frontage, the payment of the usual royalty on gold output with an annual exemption of $25,000, the beginning of operations within one year from the date of the lease, and the spending of not less than $5,000 each year from the date of the lease."[2] Many leases or "concessions" were issued in the years after 1898, the most generous of all to a mining syndicate headed by A. N. C. Treadgold, a British mining expert.

After travelling to the Klondike in 1898, Treadgold became convinced that the goldfields offered a marvellous opportunity for capital investment, particularly the hill and bench claims, which could not be worked long without the use of sophisticated hydraulicking techniques.[3] Taking Clifford Sifton into his confidence, he obtained from the Minister a promise that he would be given rights to the richest creeks in the area—Bonanza (and its tributary, Eldorado), Bear, and Hunker—so that he could install an elaborate waterworks system to conduct hydraulic operations. However, Treadgold had to solve a serious problem before he could make formal application for a lease: since his operation would involve dumping tons of waste gravel on the creeks below the hills, small-scale mining along the creek beds would have to cease. In the following excerpts from two of his letters to Sifton, Treadgold indicated the means to overcome the obstacle:

I found considerable difficulty likely to occur on the question of dumping grounds because nearly every one of the gulches on the left side of Hunker and Bonanza has turned out rich for at least three claims from the mouth. I set to work and, in other names, bought creek claims at convenient intervals. I have invested 219,000 dollars in this way and when I have got three more claims on Lower Bonanza there will be no need of expropriation and no chance for blackmailers.

The output is safe to be more than maintained this year and maintained next, but I think that by the end of 1901 you may reduce your royalty (and your expenses too, eh?) for the Klondike, because by then the Yankees on Eldorado and Upper Bonanza will have cleared out and the lowgrade gravels can begin to be treated, if we get the water going all right.[4]

In other words, Treadgold sought to obtain creek claims by misrepresentation and to drive remaining miners out of the Klondike by influencing Sifton to maintain the royalty at 10 per cent.

A question that arises from the forthright manner in which Treadgold communicated with Sifton is whether or not the Minister had interests in Treadgold's scheme other than placing Yukon mining on a permanent foundation and reducing federal expenditures in the territory. Although there is no evidence in the Sifton Papers of the Minister's personal financial involvement, one of the above letters from Treadgold to Sir Clifford did state: "Keep me free and strong and the enterprise is a gainer. That is why I want the concession made out to mere nominees of my own; the enterprise is still at the stage at which *orders must come only from you*."[5] If the Minister of the Interior were the mastermind of the plan, and Treadgold only his agent, then the slowness of the federal government's response to territorial demands throughout Sifton's tenure as a minister of the Crown becomes more understandable, because the venture, if it were to realize large profits quickly, depended upon driving hundreds of placer miners from the Yukon.

The "mere nominees" chosen by Treadgold—M. H. Orr-Ewing and Walter Barwick —apparently unaware of the close association between Treadgold and Sifton, sent a formal submission to the Minister in which they attempted to prove the constitutionality of the privileges sought by their syndicate.[6] Sifton certainly did not doubt the legality of their requests, and, in May 1901, asked the cabinet to approve the syndicate's application for a concession to divert water from several creeks in the Klondike River basin (provided that water was sold to all who needed it) and to enter and work any lapsed claims on Bear, Hunker, and Bonanza creeks. The ministry passed an order in council conferring these rights and offering this justification for them: "Whereas mining now carried on in the Klondike District is, because of the inadequate supply of water necessarily confined to the washing of the richest ground only, comparatively small in area, thus leaving large tracts of gold-bearing gravels unworked ... it is believed that the riches of the ... District can only be properly utilized by such a water supply as that which the ... applicants are prepared to establish."[7] The order was forwarded to Dawson.

Upon receipt of the order in council, E. C. Senkler, the Gold Commissioner, was somewhat confused about the implications of the tenth clause, which gave the syndicate the right to enter and work abandoned claims. Did this term mean that the claims were to be closed to relocation or that they were to be reserved only after Treadgold's representatives recorded them in the usual way? He sent his query to Ottawa, noting that he had temporarily closed the ground.[8] Before he received a reply the Citizens' Committee, at its meeting of July 31 (held ostensibly to discuss incorporation), passed a resolution condemning the Treadgold Concession. Barney Sugrue said that, although most of the government's repressive measures had been removed, this latest action was the worst plague of all; and Joseph McGillvray, a "veteran 49'er," claimed that the government must have been ignorant of the true nature of the privileges granted the syndicate.[9] The *Klondike Nugget* wrote several editorials decrying Senkler's reservation,[10] but the Gold Commissioner, after being ordered to hold all abandoned claims for Treadgold, refused to alter his original decision.[11] However, a month later, after Commissioner Ross had appealed to the Department of the Interior to change its interpretation of clause ten,[12] Senkler was ordered to reopen the claims and to treat representatives of the syndicate like any other miners.[13] The agitation against the Treadgold grant quickly died down as the campaigns for incorporation and municipal offices absorbed the energy of territorial politicians.

Then, on February 13, 1902, came the announcement that the Treadgold order in council had been amended to close all abandoned claims to relocation effective the first day of the previous month.[14] Although the amendment merely restored the interpretation originally placed upon clause ten, it caused an immediate furore, far more pronounced than that of the summer before. The increased magnitude of the protest can be explained in part by the fact that many men, unemployed during the winter lull in economic activity, like nothing better than a good political squabble, but lying deeper than that reason were obvious signs of an impending transition from small- to large-scale mining.[15] Some Yukoners, not yet prepared to accept the inevitability of such a transition, saw the Treadgold Concession as a conspiracy to destroy the prevailing economic system, and, with it, their means of livelihood.

As soon as the terms of the amendment were disclosed, the *Nugget* and the *News* respectively denounced the Treadgold Concession as "an octopus" and "an iniquitous monopoly,"[16] and, the next day, the government organ, the *Yukon Sun*, entered the fray:

Probably the editor of this paper is in a better position than most people of Dawson to fully appreciate the only possible defence that can be offered for the passing of the order in council. . . . It is apparent that there must have been a vast combination of misrepresentations regarding the Yukon formed to assail the authorities in Ottawa to induce them to come to the conclusion that this territory cannot get along without Treadgold. . . . [He] and his associates are horribly anxious to develop this country. They are grieved to think our people are suffering for water. It will be observed, however, that their efforts to develop are confined to districts where other men have found and opened the richest mines on earth. They do not care to strike out for new regions for themselves. . . . [The amended] clause ten . . . is *ultra vires* of the Governor in Council. We know of no power of the Governor in Council to dispose of claims in the manner pursued in this order.[17]

Although the views of the *Sun* were mild in contrast to those of the American-controlled newspapers, they did show, as did the events of the next few days, that the concern expressed was not just for partisan advantage. F. T. Congdon, formerly Legal Adviser and now in private practice, called a meeting of the Yukon Liberal Association to protest the amendment. The meeting passed a resolution (later forwarded to Ross in Ottawa) which called upon the Commissioner, who

has the greatest confidence [of] . . . this meeting, . . . to use all his . . . influence to secure a cancellation of the obnoxious features of the recent order in council, and the order in council relating to such concession, and to relieve this territory from the disastrous consequences certain to ensue if . . . [the] order . . . is allowed to stand in full . . . and that he represent to the government that . . . the insertion of such features [that is, the amendment] . . . could only have been procured by the grossest misrepresentation and fraudulent concealment.[18]

Two days later, on February 17, the Citizens' Committee held a mass meeting, attended by well-known Conservatives and Liberals. Colonel McGregor, the first speaker, exclaimed that soon the Moosehide Indians would be occupying the Administration Building if something were not done to prevent the mass exodus of people that would most certainly result from the amended concession order. Dufferin Pattullo,[19] the Assistant Gold Commissioner, confronted the crowd and attempted to excuse the government, but even he admitted that the new clause ten would hurt the country. The gathering adjourned after a decision was taken to pool the efforts of the Citizens' Committee, the Liberal Association, and the Board of Trade in a common cause to seek revocation of Treadgold's privileges.[20] The next day, delegations from the three groups met as the "committee of twenty" and drafted a telegram to the Prime Minister requesting a delay in the implementation of the order in council until "representatives of the people," to be chosen by the committee, arrived in Ottawa.[21]

Commissioner Ross, in Vancouver on his way to the national capital, said, when interviewed by the press, that the agitation in the Yukon "seems chiefly hot air,"[22] but, whether justified in their concern or not, the Yukoners pushed ahead with their plans for a full-scale onslaught on the federal government. Councillor Prudhomme called upon the Acting Commissioner to convene an emergency session of Council, which would be requested to petition the cabinet; steps were taken to reorganize the Citizens' Yukon Party, the members of which would set aside past party affiliations in order to promote "the good government of the Yukon"; and, the "committee of twenty" chose Barney Sugrue, Arthur Wilson, A. D. Williams, and F. T. Congdon to travel to Ottawa with instructions to secure cancellation of the Treadgold Concession.[23] Although Prudhomme's efforts failed and party harmony did not ensue, the "committee of twenty" did manage to raise sufficient funds to send Sugrue and Wilson to Ottawa.[24] The delegation of two and Commissioner Ross persuaded Sifton that the amendment to clause ten would bring discredit to the government and economic collapse to the Yukon. On April 17 the Minister ordered the Gold Commissioner to throw open all lapsed and abandoned claims withheld from entry because of the provisions of the Treadgold order in council. Four days later, all orders relating to the syndicate's concession were rescinded and replaced by a new one imposing somewhat more stringent conditions upon Treadgold and his associates.[25]

However, in Dawson, modifications were not enough. The amendment of clause ten had struck a spark that ignited the passions of the people. Now the fight would be against the concession *in toto*; no effort would be spared to bring about the complete cancellation of Treadgold's privileges. On April 22 Woodworth convened a mass meeting, at which he condemned Fawcett, Ogilvie, Sifton, and Senkler for the Treadgold Concession, and proposed a resolution asking for cancellation and calling upon the Acting Commissioner to hold a session of Council.[26] A few days later, a mass meeting on Gold Bottom Creek passed a similar resolution.[27] The stage was set for two elections—federal and territorial—later that year.

The unofficial campaign for the federal by-election—perhaps one of the longest in history—began on July 28, when the "opposition" organized, and ended on December 2, when voting took place. Called by the members of the Citizens' Committee and the old Citizens' Yukon Party, the mass meeting held on July 28 was led by Joe Clarke, the secretary of the Citizens' Committee, who nominated the presiding officers, presented a timetable for twenty-seven preliminaries, and selected August 23 as the date for the territorial convention.[28] In the preliminaries, held to select delegates to the convention and to organize election machinery in each district, the "opposition" (which went by no other name) brought the Treadgold Concession forward as *the* issue.[29] While these primaries were being conducted, James Smart, the Deputy Minister of the Interior, visited the Yukon, and was beseeched by the *Daily News* to abolish all concessions as "an act of common justice to the miners, the pioneers and the mainstay of the country."[30] In an interview, Smart said that he regretted the commotion and thought that, although the government had paid too much attention to the advocates of concessions, it was up to Mr. Sifton to decide what was to be done.[31]

Smart was still in Dawson on August 23, and perhaps was able to gauge for his Minister the strength of opposition elements from reports of their convention. Joseph Andrew Clarke emerged from a tempestuous meeting as the opposition candidate for Parliament over his only opponent, C. M. Woodworth, the unofficial leader of the Citizens' Committee.[32] Clarke, aged thirty-five, was a man who liked a good fight, caring not for what he fought, as long as he could contribute all his energy to the cause.[33] His chief shortcoming, and the most important Liberal asset in the campaign that followed, was that he did not know when to stop, often concluding a verbal tirade only after saying things he did not intend. He had a varied and fascinating career behind him. After training in law at the University of Toronto, he joined the N.W.M.P. in 1892; following his desertion in 1893 he was fined and dismissed. He went to Edmonton where he worked hard for the Liberals in the election of 1896, at least enthusiastically enough to warrant his appointment as Thomas Fawcett's stenographer in 1897. After staying in the Gold Commissioner's office for a year, he left to practise law as a solicitor. He attended all Citizens' Committee mass meetings and invariably heaped abuse upon the federal and territorial governments, a pastime which became his occupation in 1901 when he and Barney Sugrue purchased the *Klondike Miner*. Few issues of the paper, which went bankrupt in 1902, were saved, but the following editorial addressed to Commissioner Ross demonstrates the sort of journalism in which Clarke indulged: "The difference between Hon. 'Billy' the VENERABLE LADY [Ogilvie], now of historic memory and our own Jas. H. [Ross] is simply this—William, the Mistake, did not know any better and misgoverned through ignorance and bad advice; J. H. Ross knows full well the difference between right and wrong administration. Liquor Permits . . . and Concessions are . . . samples of his doing from his own free choice, the result of an intellect politically perverted, or—Speak Jas. H., why is it?"[34] Just a month before the convention, Clarke had been acquitted of charges of criminal libel and contempt in his latest sojourn in court.[35] Local Liberals rejoiced at the selection of the boyish-looking professional agitator over Woodworth, the distinguished lawyer, for now they thought they could win—at least with a good man.[36]

Although a better candidate than J. H. Ross would have been difficult to find, the Commissioner was nominated under tragic circumstances. On July 18, having just lost his wife and youngest child when their steamer sank en route to Vancouver, he suffered a paralytic stroke while on his way to Whitehorse, and was unable to resume his duties in Dawson.[37] Nevertheless, whether Ross could campaign or not, the Liberals wanted to place his name—untarnished save for the Treadgold Concession—before the voters of the territory. During September the Liberal Association followed the opposition example and conducted preliminaries throughout the territory, each one pledging delegates to Ross.[38] On September 18, 142 men assembled in Dawson and chose the Commissioner by acclamation.[39] Ross, in a Whitehorse hospital, wired his acceptance with regrets that he would have to leave the campaign to his friends.[40] He resigned from his post of Commissioner on October 1.[41]

The three daily papers aligned themselves for the coming fight: the *Daily News* for Clarke, and the *Klondike Nugget* and the *Yukon Sun* for Ross. The *Nugget*, long a supporter of the Citizens' Committee (except on the issue of incorporation), feigned independence, but said that there was really no choice between Clarke, "the demagogue," and Ross, "the tried statesman" and the "man of action." It attacked the opposition candidate as "a combination of venom and ignorance, tinctured with corrupt instincts which contribute to make him a character both to be despised and distrusted."[42] Early in September the *News* gave Ross credit for his part in the cancellation of the obnoxious features of the Treadgold Concession, but, as the days passed, it began to accuse the former Commissioner of being weak and unknown, and of having to seek a constituency away from the North-West Territories, where he had been defeated in the Assiniboia constituency by Nicholas Flood Davin in 1887.[43]

A sidelight in the campaign was the announced candidacy of William Catto, a Dawson physician and former supporter of the Citizens' Committee, who published one of the bitterest attacks on the government to that time. Among other things, he called the Minister of the Interior "this despicable wretch" and the "Napoleon of the Northwest," and then went on to write: "The Press of Dawson has been indiscreet. Our cause has suffered by its indiscretion. But the indiscretions of the Press are harmless accidents compared with an administration that hangs in the air like an infectious pestilence, to industry, a paralysing poison; to crime, on which it feeds, a nourishing breath."[44] Barney Sugrue, now accused of having the "government faith," was rumoured to be a second Liberal candidate,[45] but neither he nor Dr. Catto allowed his name to stand in nomination.

Paralleling the territorial campaign of 1900, the federal contest was not waged on significant differences of policy. Both Ross's supporters and Clarke pledged to seek total cancellation of the Treadgold Concession and other hydraulic leases, a wholly elective council with widened powers, an assay office for Dawson, better mining laws, and many other things.[46] The only variation came in the platform of the opposition, which promised (not surprisingly) to abolish the party spoils system. (How one member of Parliament could effect so many and such sweeping reforms, neither side indicated.) Thus, again, the issues were the personalities of the contestants and the popularity of the federal and territorial governments. Although this time the cabinet did not announce significant changes in the mining regulations to induce support for its candidate, it did appoint F. X. Gosselin as Assistant Gold Commissioner after a plea from Ross's committee that the only way to win the French vote was to select a French Canadian for the vacancy.[47] The Liberals also made effective use of a rumour that Ross, if elected, would succeed Clifford Sifton as Minister of the Interior.[48] The *News* did its best to deny the truth of the claim by quoting telegrams proving that Ross lay ill in Los Angeles, and countered with more hearsay—that the Liberal campaign committee would announce a rich discovery of gold on the Stewart River just prior to election day, thereby causing a stampede from Dawson and its environs.[49] The passage of time proved both rumours false.

James Hamilton Ross won the election by a margin of 2,944 to 2,065,[50] whereupon the *Nugget* and the *Sun* heralded his victory as the beginning of a new era for the Yukon.[51] The *News*, which a week before had declared that "this election is a fight between the people on one side and Clifford Sifton and his nominee on the other," made an about-face, congratulating the former Commissioner and claiming that he had won on his personality not on Siftonian policy.[52] Later, when the opposition party met to assess the results, George Black, one of Clarke's most ardent workers, was appointed to investigate allegations that aliens had voted.[53] He reported that car-loads of Americans had been brought in from Skagway to cast ballots at Miller Creek and Caribou Crossing. How else, he queried, could Ross have won the former poll by 161 to 15, when thirty-five residents were entitled to vote, and the latter by 109 to 12, when about twenty British subjects were in the district.[54] Years later, Mrs. Black related her husband's memories of the campaign:

Numbers of foreigners were railroaded through a fake form of naturalization and allowed to vote.... [Agents] gave Government supporters large credits on I.O.U.'s or "Tabs" as they were called. ... After the election these were repudiated and unredeemed, and the party responsible and its followers nicknamed "Tabs". In one transaction the agent who went to Skagway with money to hire pluggers, lost his roll at the roulette wheel and had neither money nor tabs to pay the carload of imported aliens who, in the meantime, had voted. When they found that the agent had skipped the country, in their rage they smashed train windows, tore up seats and raised general ruction.[55]

The opposition supporters, although positive they had been duped, decided not to contest the result because the charges were too vague to be proved in court. Instead, they delegated Joe Clarke to go to Ottawa to watch over Ross and to inform the people of the member's attempts to implement the election promises made in his name.[56]

As soon as the by-election results were announced, excitement was transferred to the territorial election set for January 13.[57] Five men were to be chosen for a two-year term: two from Dawson, two from the gold-fields, and one from the south of the territory.[58] The *Nugget* and the *News* both stated their opposition to a campaign fought on party lines, the former because there were no well-defined issues, and the latter because "good men from both sides will be crowded out."[59] Many candidates came forward during the month of December, all but five as independents (that is, independent of any ticket or party).

Most interest was displayed in Dawson, where the first to announce his candidacy was Dr. Alfred Thompson—a physician, member of the Citizens' Committee, and defeated Kid Committee candidate for mayor of Dawson—who said he would run in the city as an independent on his own merits. Although he had been a firm supporter of Joe Clarke, Thompson declared: "It is not to be forgotten that the appointive members are still in the majority and I cannot see that anything would be gained by entering into a radical opposition party."[60] Nevertheless, the opposition group held a convention at which Joe Clarke and Alex Prudhomme, the incumbent Citizens' Yukon Party councillor, were picked to contest the Dawson seats.[61] Twelve others, including a naturalized Japanese Canadian,[62] announced similar intentions, but, when the smoke cleared on nomination day, only seven were in the race: Clarke, Prudhomme, and Thompson; G. K. Gilbert, tin-smith and nominee of the Dawson Trades and Labour Council; W. A. Beddoe, editor of the *Dawson Daily News*, who repudiated Clarke and supported Gilbert and himself; and lawyers C. W. C. Tabor and William Thornburn.[63]

On the creeks, the miners followed tradition, holding preliminaries and then a convention, which chose Arthur Wilson and M. G. H. Henderson. Maxime Landre-ville, a Dawson hotelkeeper; John Pringle, a Grand Forks clergyman; and George

White-Fraser, a miner, completed the slate.[64] In the Whitehorse district, Robert Lowe, a businessman, a Mr. Dixon, and a Dr. Sudgen filed nomination papers.[65] In all, there were fifteen candidates for five Council seats.

Once again, the candidates, attempting to match each other's promises, ran on virtually identical platforms.[66] Almost everyone promised to seek the abolition of the Treadgold Concession, and to prevent further concessions from being granted except on lands suited only to hydraulic mining. An elective council, an assay office, a reduction in taxation, a more effective miners' lien law, and better roads were common to most appeals.[67] Mr. Pringle included an additional promise, one that was soon to become a contentious issue; he pledged to work towards the establishment of a government-owned waterworks, which, he claimed, would be far more satisfactory than any private system provided by capitalists such as those in the Treadgold syndicate.[68] Some contestants had special interests: Gilbert's only promise was to secure an adequate lien law; Clarke's main concern, although he supported all the major planks, was to stop graft and corruption; and Tabor's chief interest was to work towards provincial autonomy.[69]

The newspapers pledged themselves to various candidates, but, this time, did not indulge in bitter criticism of one another. The *Sun*, noting that "Politics makes strange bedfellows," supported Lowe, a Liberal, for Whitehorse, and Thompson, Wilson, and Henderson, "all oppositionists," for Dawson and the creeks. (It did not choose a second candidate for the city.) The *Nugget* advocated the election of Thompson, Tabor, Wilson, and Henderson, while Beddoe of the *News* designated Gilbert, Wilson, Henderson, and himself as the only candidates "for the people."[70] Joe Clarke and Alex Prudhomme received abuse from all three journals. The government organ declared that the most important issue in the election was "to erase" the two men, for, although Prudhomme "is not a bad citizen, he keeps bad company."[71] Beddoe and Arnold George, editor of the *Nugget*, refused to mention Clarke's name in their columns, preferring to refer to him as "the unworthy instrument" or "the most unworthy,"[72] until the *Nugget*, in an editorial the day before the election, called upon the people to destroy "Clarkism" because "Joseph Andrew Clarke . . . is a menace to law, order, and good government."[73]

Nevertheless, Clarke was elected, much to the dismay of the *Sun* and the *Nugget*, both of which were otherwise satisfied with the results. They accused Clarke of deserting Prudhomme by persuading his supporters to vote only for him and not for a second candidate, and the *Sun* claimed that seventy-three of these "plumpers" were residents of Grand Forks, for whom Clarke had provided transportation to Dawson; now, he would have "to prove himself," for, if he did not, he would be "finished" in the Yukon.[74] According to the final election statistics (see Table I), about 93 per cent of the eligible voters exercised their franchise, but the figure is misleading because, owing to the absence of voters' lists, many men voted in both Dawson and Klondike.

Just four days after the election, the *Sun* announced the discovery of rich placer gravels in the Tanana Valley, Alaska,[75] and, although it could not be known at the time, that revelation heralded the end of the relative prosperity the Yukon had enjoyed since 1900 when the economy had made a partial recovery from the recession that ended the gold rush boom. Many men, realizing that the conversion to higher-order techniques of gold production was inevitable, rushed to Tanana, but others, convinced that the Yukon had a future, stayed. To those who remained, the Treadgold Concession and other hydraulic leases—covering vast tracts of unworked gold-bearing land—

TABLE I

FINAL RESULTS IN TERRITORIAL ELECTION, JANUARY 13, 1903*

DAWSON		KLONDIKE	
J. A. Clarke	772	*J. Pringle*	719
A. Thompson	719	*M. Landreville*	656
C. W. C. Tabor	560	*A. Wilson*	594
G. K. Gilbert	367	M. G. H. Henderson	387
A. Prudhomme	320	G. White-Fraser	255
W. Thornburn	80	W. McNamee	43†
W. A. Beddoe	67		
WHITEHORSE			
R. Lowe	180	Spoiled and rejected	212
Dixon	92	Number voting	3,252‡
Sudgen	35	Estimated eligible voters	3,500
		Approx. % voting	93

* Compiled from *Klondike Nugget*, January 26, 1903; and *Yukon Sun*, January 30, 1903. The names of the winning candidates are italicized.

† Although McNamee had withdrawn, his name was not removed from the ballot.

‡ Computed by dividing the total votes for two candidates by two, and by adding the number who voted for only one in Dawson and Klondike to the number of votes cast in Whitehorse.

appeared as greater evils than before. The representative in Ottawa and the five elected members of the Yukon Council were expected to act quickly to secure cancellation of the concessions. Further, it was hoped that the new Commissioner would add his influence to the struggle, especially when it was learned that the cabinet, on the recommendation of Ross and the Yukon Liberal Association, had appointed F. T. Congdon, one of the leaders in the protest movement against the Treadgold Concession.[76]

Congdon, however, was in Ottawa at the time of his appointment, and thus unable to return to the Yukon before the exodus to Tanana brought about renewed agitation against Treadgold. On February 20, 1903, having formed a new Miners' Association, the miners on the creeks appealed to the Yukon Council to send a memorial to the federal government requesting the revocation of hydraulic privileges, the establishment of an assay office, and the creation of a fully elective council.[77] On March 6 the elected councillors from Dawson and Klondike presented an ultimatum to the Acting Commissioner, Major Z. T. Wood: if he did not convene an immediate session of Council to petition Ottawa they would appeal directly to Lord Minto. Wood agreed to inform the Minister of the Interior that four elected councillors desired a meeting but told Sifton that he himself was not so disposed.[78] Ten days later, the members wired Laurier asking for outright cancellation of the Treadgold Concession, to which Sir Wilfrid replied: "Will confer with Ross and everything I think will be satisfactory."[79]

Meanwhile, the Dawson Board of Trade, the Dawson Liberal Club, and the Miners' Association telegraphed separate demands for cancellation, and the Board circulated a mammoth petition throughout the mining districts and the city.[80] Major Wood attempted to calm the troubled waters by announcing the government's intentions to consider the feasibility of installing a publicly owned water system.[81] Commissioner Congdon, interviewed in Vancouver on his way north, intimated that such a project would have to be undertaken, although it would be difficult to prod eastern members of Parliament into acceptance of the scheme.[82] A little later,

Mr. Thibideau, a government mining engineer, said that excellent mineral prospects made a government waterworks eminently worth while.[83]

Nevertheless, agitation did not die down. When Commissioner Congdon arrived in Dawson on April 8, he was greeted by hostility from the *News*, which declared it an outrage that he did not intend to call Council into session immediately.[84] But Congdon had already made known his views on Council:

Unless there is special need for it there will be no session of council until the estimates have been made at Ottawa. Deliberation of council must be on these estimates. I do not approve of convening sessions . . . except when necessary. Many might perhaps conceive the necessity of convening council every few weeks and later regret the session had ever convened. . . . Frequent sessions afford too great a danger for the passage of crank measures that would not be enacted if time was taken to fully deliberate upon them. The best legislation the world over emanates from long sessions convening at stated and not too frequent periods. Upon their adjournment legislation is settled definitely for a given time.[85]

Although Congdon may have been correct, the people had grown accustomed to frequent sessions—weekly under Ogilvie and monthly under Ross—in which councillors acted as scrutineers of administrative activity as well as framers of legislation. Even more disturbing was the Commissioner's appraisal of Council's role in relation to the federal government: although he recognized the right of the local assembly to send memorials to the Governor in Council, he felt that it should "keep to its own business." Elaborating, he said that he personally favoured an elective council and cancellation of the Treadgold Concession, but that these matters were of concern to Ottawa not Dawson.[86] Joe Clarke, incensed over Congdon's decision not to convene Council, addressed an open letter to the Commissioner calling for an immediate session to consider urgent problems requiring both federal and territorial action. The chief executive acquiesced, and set May 7 as opening day.[87]

Before the elected councillors could seek any of their objectives, Council had to deal with certain other matters, most notably the need to organize itself to suit its new composition. It adopted a set of standing orders, patterned after those of Ontario, Manitoba, and the North-West Territories, and gave its committees (standing orders and private bills, finance, mining, public works, civil justice, municipal law, and education) powers similar to those exercised by committees of the Canadian House of Commons.[88] Although Council had followed parliamentary procedure ever since it had ceased to sit in executive sessions, the air of informality now disappeared; with the Commissioner acting as Speaker, strict adherence to the rules ensued. As a reflection of its new status, Council decided to publish its formal proceedings in *Journals*.

Once these details were out of the way, the elected members, not content to consider petitions and a legislative programme, were determined to go beyond local matters to a discussion of the subjects upon which they wished to forward memorials to the federal government. Mr. Landreville, seconded by Mr. Pringle, moved that a committee prepare a memorial requesting the Governor in Council to amend the Yukon Act to provide for a wholly elective council before the expiration of the current terms of the elected members. Mr. Girouard (the Registrar), seconded by Mr. Senkler, then moved that the change come only when "the population, revenue, and conditions of the Yukon Territory justify the introduction of wholly responsible government," whereupon Major Wood, seconded by Mr. Newlands (the Legal Adviser), moved a second amendment, adding the words "and . . . [when] proper provision can be made for carrying on such Government."[89] During debate on the motion as amended, Thompson and Clarke were most adamant in their demands that the original motion be passed. Thompson noted: "Premier Laurier said last December that in two years more [the] Yukon Territory should have an all elected council, and he would be willing to allow it then. And here we have government appointees opposing the idea of the premier." Clarke repudiated the notion, inherent in the amendments, that the Yukon could not afford responsible government: "Only two provinces in Canada spend as much as the Yukon government costs each year, and yet it is said this country could not finance its own way. . . . The Yukon pays for the Yukon. Probably no other part of Canada can boast this. It is beyond reason that we be asked to delay responsible government."[90] The five appointed members did not debate the question, but voted as a solid bloc for the amended motion. Because they were joined by Lowe, one of the elected members, the motion therefore passed by six to four.[91]

Attempting to work towards responsible government in another way—by trying to secure a constitutional change similar to that of 1888 in the North-West Territories when an Advisory Council on Finance had been constituted to assist the Lieutenant Governor—Mr. Pringle moved that a memorial ask the federal government's permission to set up an advisory committee of elected members to sit with the Commissioner during recess to advise him on all matters concerning territorial public expenditures. H. W. Newlands, the Legal Adviser, pointed out that, according to the Yukon Act, all Council members were the Commissioner's advisers, to which Judge Dugas added: "We are disposed to let the elected members advise the Commissioner all they please. He does not have to accept their advice." The motion was tabled.[92] Later, Congdon said that he approved of the advisory board, but made it clear that it would not in any way change the present constitutional arrangement.[93] Although Pringle, Lowe, and Landreville were chosen by the five elected members as their "cabinet,"[94] this body, which had no access to confidential information, played no role whatsoever during the succeeding year.

Before Council adjourned on May 23 other important matters received its attention. Memorials were forwarded to the federal cabinet calling for the establishment of an assay office or an arrangement with the banks to conduct assay operations, and for a cash subsidy or guarantee of bonds to assist a proposed Klondike Mines Railway from Dawson to the creeks.[95] A lien bill, drafted by the Dawson Trades and Labour Council and approved by a mass meeting, was held over until the summer session.[96] However, concern which the elected councillors felt about these matters was insignificant in contrast to that they expressed with respect to the Treadgold Concession. On May 12 Dr. Thompson, seconded by Mr. Pringle, moved that a "Select Committee [be appointed] . . . to prepare a Resolution, setting forth . . . the opinion and wish of the Yukon people, who are absolutely a unit," that the Treadgold Concession be annulled "in toto." The Legal Adviser protested the terms of the motion, saying that "Any advice on our part as a council to Ottawa would be looked on as a criticism. Advice might be given by us on any matter the government has not dealt with and rendered a decision. We have a member in Parliament represented by [sic] the people, direct from the people and the whole of the people there to represent us in this matter. We can safely leave the matter to him to deal with according to the instructions of the people." Mr. Girouard, seconded by Judge Dugas, then moved an amendment striking out the original motion and replacing it with "it is not within our functions to make such a Memorial in this. . . case." Although the Registrar attempted to prevent a division from being recorded, the vote on the amended motion was placed in the *Journals*—

five for and five against. Congdon broke the deadlock by siding with the "yeas."[97] The six appointed officials had thus defeated the wishes of the five representatives of the people.

The *News* was bitter the next day: "We see a legislative body that violates every principle of representative government. . . . The people's representation on the council is a farce, it is an insult to the intelligence of British subjects."[98] The *Nugget*, in contrast, was mild, regretting that the appointed members behaved in the way they did but realizing that etiquette had to be followed.[99] To ascertain whether or not this "etiquette" were correct, Congdon wired the Minister of Justice, asking if Council could consider matters previously dealt with by the Governor in Council. The Minister replied that the question was of propriety not law, "and according to constitutional usage officers appointed by the governor in council could not publicly criticize acts of the governor in council."[100] On the final day of the session Dr. Thompson moved a resolution requesting the appointment of a committee of three men, assisted by counsel, to prepare "the case of the people" against Treadgold. The Commissioner ruled that the opinion of the Minister of Justice prohibited a motion making reference to Treadgold, whereupon Dr. Thompson replaced "Treadgold" with "the concessions." The motion was lost by a margin of eight to two, only Joe Clarke coming to the doctor's aid.[101]

During the session, Judge Dugas, suddenly worried about the growing agitation to cancel the concession, telegraphed the Prime Minister to inquire if the government would object to a Council resolution requesting a royal commission to investigate the Treadgold affair.[102] There is no record of an answer from Laurier, but, after receiving the above-mentioned petition from the Board of Trade,[103] the cabinet announced its intention to constitute a commission to look into the whole question of mining operations and leases in the Yukon Territory. Shortly thereafter, Laurier appointed Judge B. M. Britton of the Ontario High Court, and Mr. B. T. A. Bell, Secretary of the Mining Institute and Editor of the *Canadian Mining Review*, to serve as commissioners.[104]

The *News* decried the terms of reference of the Commission—to decide whether or not the concessions were beneficial—because, it claimed, the real source of complaint was that Treadgold and others had obtained leases by fraud and misrepresentation.[105] The Board of Trade, in a telegraph thanking Sir Wilfrid for the appointment of a commission, asked that the instructions be broadened to include the charges of fraud, but the Prime Minister replied that he could not comply because the complaints were so vague.[106] Arriving in Dawson in August, the commissioners spent the next month conducting hearings in the city and on the creeks to obtain evidence from those who opposed the concessions. Judge Britton reported that he faced great difficulties because "the season was very dry, and there was comparatively little work at mining by individual miners, and so a great many hostile miners thronged the court room and the corridors during the sittings. It required considerable moral courage for any miner voluntarily to give evidence against the expressed opinion of the hostile majority."[107] Furthermore, while the commissioners were in Dawson, stalwarts of the Citizens' Committee called a mass meeting, which passed a resolution strongly condemning the Commission's terms of reference and Judge Britton's methods of conducting the hearings.[108]

Nor did the agitation cease with the departure of the commissioners. Lord Minto wrote the Prime Minister to say that he had received correspondence from Yukoners who were "wholly dissatisfied" with the perfunctory investigation the commissioners had undertaken.[109] J. S. Willison, Laurier's old friend, claimed that no matter what the Commission reported, the appointment of Judge Britton, until recently a Liberal member of Parliament, had been a mistake because the opposition would accuse the government of a "political whitewash."[110] Even before the report was brought down, Willison's prediction was proven correct, for, late in the parliamentary session of 1903, the Conservatives, once again convinced they could embarrass the ministry with scandal in the Yukon, showered abuse upon the government for its appointment of a partisan commision.[111] In October the *News*, in a reflection of the mounting concern over the increasing exodus of people from the Klondike, spread a cartoon over half of its front page showing Dawson and the creeks deserted, except for a few Indians, by late 1903.[112] In that same month, Council, which was precluded from discussing the same issue twice during a session, was prorogued, having passed a compromise lien bill and a watered-down elective council memorial at its summer and autumn sittings.[113]

In December 1903 Congdon convened a special session of Council to approve estimates for public works (recently transferred from the federal Department of Public Works to the territorial administration), to vote supplementary supply for the fiscal year 1903–4, and to consider an amendment to the "Ordinance respecting the Form and Interpretation of Ordinances." He expected the five councillors present—Girouard, Senkler, Wood, Thompson, and Clarke—to proceed rapidly with the business at hand,[114] but Messrs. Thompson and Clarke, irked by their inability to raise the Treadgold Concession and other issues during the second and third sittings of Council in 1903, were determined to bring these matters before the special session. Thus, after Council had transacted routine business on the first two days, the two elected members gave notice of motion of memorials to the federal government calling for cancellation of the concession and for an elective council. Congdon ruled these subjects out of order, claiming that only matters laid before Council by the executive could be entertained at a special session. Then, "with the unexpectedness of a bolt from the blue," Clarke and Thompson announced that they would boycott proceedings—leaving the legislative body without its five-member quorum—until the Commissioner was prepared to hear the "people's" views.[115] Although Landreville was located, his presence did not make a quorum, and twice Council was forced to adjourn. On the second occasion, Girouard reminded the Commissioner that, because it did not devolve upon the chair to ascertain whether or not there was a quorum, Council could proceed with the business at hand until one of its members demanded a count of those present. However, Congdon, who "did not look in very good helath," thought it best to adjourn until the new year.[116] Only a month earlier, the Commissioner had written Sifton: "There would be no trouble in handling . . . a wholly elective council; it would naturally divide on party lines, and in some respects . . . would be easier to handle than the present [Council]. I should have no fear of meeting a wholly elective council."[117] Perhaps he had some doubts now.

On January 2, 1904, Thompson filed a notice of motion calling upon the Commissioner to prorogue the special session and convene a regular one in its place.[118] Two days later, the adjourned sitting of Council was reopened, and J. T. Lithgow, the Comptroller, was sworn as a replacement for H. W. Newlands, the retired Legal Adviser. When the Commissioner ruled Thompson's motion out of order because one day's notice had not been given from the member's seat, the doctor appealed the ruling, but received support only from Clarke. Congdon then requested unanimous consent to suspend the rules in order to pass the supply and interpretation ordinances through all three stages. Thompson and Clarke refused, once more announcing their intentions to boycott proceedings, and, this time, Landreville, petitioned by a mass meeting in Grand Forks to support Thompson and Clarke, signified that he would attend no more meetings.[119] The next day, the Commissioner assumed the chair and, with only Messrs. Girouard, Wood, Senkler, and Lithgow in their places, repeated his request to suspend the rules. Council, though lacking a quorum, did so, and passed the bills before it. Colonel Donald McGregor, in reaction to the behaviour of the appointed members, told the *News* that Council was a sham, ostensibly giving the people a share in government, but throttling that right completely.[120]

However, even without a memorial from Council, the elected Yukon councillors and their supporters won the battle against Treadgold, because the latter, as a result of the heated agitation, could not secure sufficient capital to undertake his project. On June 22, at the syndicate's request, the cabinet rescinded the order in council conferring rights and privileges upon A. N. C. Treadgold, M. H. Orr-Ewing, and Walter Barwick.[121] A month later, Mr. Justice Britton's report, which concluded that hydraulic concessions were beneficial, came as an anticlimax, although it did serve to incense certain territorial politicians to fight against the remaining leases.

From February 1902 to January 1904 the Treadgold Concession was the central issue in territorial politics. Had it not been for the federal government's decision to reserve claims on Bonanza, Bear, and Hunker creeks for the Treadgold syndicate, the press and the pressure groups, content to enjoy the reforms secured during Ross's tenure in office, would have moderated their agitation against those who administered territorial affairs. But following the reservation of these mining properties, renewed discontent led not only to the demand for cancellation of the concession, but also to the expression of other goals such as the creation of a wholly elective council, the establishment of the assay office promised by Ross, and the provision of adequate protection for miners' wages. Although this political pressure brought about the withdrawal of the most obnoxious features of the Treadgold grant, protest against the concession continued, creating a highly emotional setting for the federal and territorial elections of 1902 and 1903 respectively. The heated political climate carried over to the sittings of the Yukon Council, wherein Alfred Thompson and Joseph Clarke, despite the fact that they had not been elected on a common ticket, formed a close liaison to work towards cancellation of the concession and other reforms they had promised to secure. Although their success in Council was limited to the passage of a lien bill and a memorial calling for an assay office, the over-all movement against the Treadgold Concession indirectly brought about its revocation. However, by June 1904, when the cabinet passed the order in council rescinding Treadgold's privileges, few Yukoners were interested because a new conflict, centring around the activities of Commissioner Congdon, was diverting the attention of the political activists.

CHAPTER SEVEN

THE CONGDON MACHINE

FREDERICK TENNYSON CONGDON was an ambitious man. At the beginning of his tenure as Commissioner of the Yukon Territory he possessed almost unlimited confidence in his ability to govern. He saw himself not only as an efficient administrator competent to bury the "Yukon question" as an issue in federal partisan politics, but also an an effective political strategist capable of strengthening the electoral appeal of the territorial Liberal party. However, failing to live up to his own expectations, he committed a series of tactical errors that culminated in dividing the party and, thereby, ensuring his own political defeat.

A Nova Scotian lawyer and newspaper editor, Congdon came to the Yukon at the age of forty-three to assume the position of Legal Adviser, which he held from April to September 1901.[1] He resigned to join F. C. Wade's legal firm, and remained associated with it until his appointment as Commissioner. While engaged in private legal practice, he commenced his Yukon political career as Vice-President of the Liberal Association. Quickly earning a reputation as a dynamic speaker and a shrewd political organizer, Congdon became the acknowledged leader of the territorial party during its campaigns to remove clause ten from the Treadgold order in council and to elect Ross as a member of Parliament.[2] There must have been great pleasure among the ranks of the Liberal Association when one of their own members assumed the duties of Commissioner in March 1903. He would certainly look after their interests.

Once in office, the new chief executive did indeed consider the tending of party fortunes as one of his most important tasks, but his methods of strengthening the Liberal position were to prove unpopular with his former fellow executive officers in the association. On the basis of Congdon's actions, one may conclude that he viewed his political task as twofold: first, to build up a personal machine that could dispense patronage; and, secondly, to weaken the "opposition" group that had so frequently plagued the work of his predecessors. The Commissioner chose a lieutenant, William Temple, to fulfil the first objective. A former railroader who had neither mined nor spent any time in the Yukon, Temple was given an aura of legitimacy through his appointment as "Keeper of the Government Diamond Drill" with the theoretical responsibility of assisting the development of the quartz mining industry.[3] His real duties, however, involved establishing within the civil service a coterie of loyal followers who were to organize the territory for electoral purposes. To achieve the second goal, Congdon and Temple sought to woo into territorial jobs men who heretofore had been prominent in the agitation against the government. Arthur Wilson, Barney Sugrue, and others, perhaps less concerned with principles than personal gain, were given key positions within the administration.[4] The Commisioner seemed to have succeeded not just in neutralizing certain vocal opponents but in actually bringing their influence to bear in the Liberal cause.

C

During 1903, while the Treadgold Concession and other issues (such as the struggle for some measure of responsible government) occupied the attention of Yukon politicians, Congdon and Temple quietly built their machine. Apart from opposition cries of excesses in patronage and press complaints of Congdon's turning against the people,[5] slight attention was paid to what the Commissioner was doing. By 1904, however, from within the ranks of his own party, seeds of discontent had sprouted and soon blossomed into outright antagonism. The issue was patronage.

Professor E. M. Reid, in his analysis of the Saskatchewan Liberal machine before 1929, noted that there were two sides to the party organization: one, formal and ineffective, consisting of a democratic hierarchy in poll, constituency, and provincial associations; and the other, informal and effective, composed of the party's central office, constituency organizers (usually civil servants), and newspapers (rendering support in return for government printing contracts). The first organization was theoretically in charge of conducting election campaigns, but the real work was done by the second through its network for hearing grievances, its suggestions for dispensing patronage, and its control over the communications media.[6] Before Congdon's elevation to the Commissioner's chair, only one organization existed in the Yukon— the Yukon Liberal Association formed after the defeat of Noel and O'Brien in the territorial election of 1900—and it served not only to wage electoral campaigns, but also to advise the territorial administration on appointments and contracts. It was when Congdon's personal machine assumed the latter role that the Yukon then had both formal and ineffective, and informal and effective Liberal organizations. But, because they had not grown up simultaneously, and because the Liberal executive became incensed over the usurpation of its prime means to secure votes and to influence government, friction developed between the leaders of the two organizations.

Congdon's newspaper policy brought the disagreement between the two sides to public attention. Although the *Yukon Sun* had been loyal to the government on all issues—with the exception of the Treadgold affair—the Commissioner decided that he had to have a newspaper completely subservient to his will. He therefore directed Temple to establish a rival government organ, the *Yukon World*, and to hire as editor W. A. Beddoe, the former agitator, opposition campaigner, and editor of the *Dawson Daily News*.[7] On February 27, 1904, the *News*, now edited by publisher Richard Roediger, reported that the Liberals were a "house divided" over the issue of newspaper patronage. The next day the *Yukon Sun*, despite the fact that it was steadily losing government contracts, declared that there was complete harmony in the Liberal fold. However, when political tempers approached the boiling point a few days later, the breach could no longer be concealed.

On March 5 the Liberal Association held an *in camera* session to heal the party wounds. The anti-Congdon forces apparently secured some concessions from the Commissioner's friends because they held back a resolution requesting the dismissal of Congdon in favour of one declaring the existence of party harmony.[8] Nevertheless, dissatisfaction remained, for, shortly thereafter, Dufferin Pattullo, Treasurer of the association, wrote Sifton, imploring him to order the Commissioner to keep patronage with the *Sun*, and W. F. Thompson, the newspaper's editor, informed the Minister that his newspaper was "finished unless . . . [you] put your trust in the true Liberals of the Yukon, and not in the civil servants who are after more government money. . . . That trust will never be betrayed."[9] Congdon, realizing that Sifton would hear of the discontent, told the Minister: "Political agitation in the Yukon is never worthy of attention, especially when it occurs in the winter when men often have nothing to do but make trouble."[10] But a *News* editorial, attacking "King Congdon" for using the *World* as the Official Gazette in violation of an ordinance conferring that privilege on the *Sun,* gave forewarning of what was to come when it declared that the only thing in the Commissioner's favour was that he was splitting the government party in a federal election year.[11]

On April 6 the Liberal Association passed resolutions condemning interference by government employees in the affairs of the Liberal party, recommending abolition of certain "unneeded" positions in the territorial administration, and revoking the membership of civil servants in the association. T. W. O'Brien was re-elected President, and Pattullo replaced F. M. Shepard, a government stenographer, as Secretary.[12] The newly-elected executive telegraphed the Prime Minister, asking him either to investigate Congdon's maladministration or to recall him immediately.[13] Although Shepard called another meeting for April 8, open only to those to whom he gave tickets, his plans were upset by 300 Liberals, who, after pushing their way into the Pioneer Hall, passed resolutions praising Laurier, condemning Congdon and the *World,* and ordering Shepard to give the association's records to Pattullo. Refusing to comply, Shepard walked out of the meeting with thirty-four other men. The Commissioner's supporters adjourned to a closed meeting at which they formed the Yukon "Territorial" Liberal Association, elected a slate of officers, and passed a unanimous vote of confidence in Congdon.[14] In Grand Forks the following night, the Bonanza Liberal Club drafted a petition to the Prime Minister relating events at the Dawson meeting and demanding Congdon's dismissal.[15] A week later, while the Commissioner attended a hockey game, the Yukon Liberal Association and the Yukon Territorial Liberal Association held meetings—the former in open session and the latter behind closed doors—at which they passed resolutions denouncing one another.[16]

Sir Wilfrid Laurier, 4,000 miles from the Klondike, must have been thoroughly confused by the sudden barrage of letters and petitions he received from the feuding territorial Liberals. Only gradually did reasons, other than newspaper patronage, emerge to explain the schism. J. C. Noel, Auguste's brother and the Crown Prosecutor, wrote the Prime Minister to explain the squabble from the point of view of the "Territorial" Association: "This year the expenditure had to be curtailed and Mr. Congdon, not having as much patronage as could have been disposed of two years ago, therefore he is in the impossibility to satisfy the exigencies of some of our friends who are hungry and he is held by them responsible for that state of affairs." Moreover, he continued, Protestants within the party were disappointed with Congdon's doing "what was right for the Catholics and the Government" by paying nuns in the separate school who did not hold teaching certificates and by refusing to grant extra funds to the Presbyterian Good Samaritan Hospital. Another difficulty arose from the fact that the Commissioner "don't drink," and never served liquor in his house. The cabinet, Noel concluded, must stand with Congdon "or the situation will be lost" because Tom O'Brien, "who is neither liberal nor conservative but who is Tom O'Brien," leads nothing but a "gang of bums."[17] The other side of the story came shortly thereafter, when Sir Wilfrid received a letter from Dufferin Pattullo repudiating the Territorial Association's vote of confidence in the Commissioner as the expression of a few who could not afford to pass up government favours.[18] Laurier replied to each submission, telling Noel that Congdon clearly "broke the law in paying Catholic teachers and in refusing patronage to the Protestant hospital," and asking Pattullo to re-establish harmony, an easy matter, Laurier thought, because the division seemed to be over patronage not public questions.[19]

However, the gap was too wide to bridge, and controversy continued to rage. Pattullo wrote the Prime Minister again, this time to refute the suggestion that the conflict was over a matter of petty patronage. He agreed that patronage might be the basis of the difficulty, but the appointment of Wilson, Sugrue, and Beddoe, "three oppositionists . . . [raises] a very broad principle as to whether or not old time Liberals are to put up a fight and the very men who have opposed them reap the rewards." The party does not feel, he said, that it should be dictated to by an autocratic Commissioner, a man who had shown himself "to be unreliable, impolitic, . . . weak and wholly lacking in ordinary judgment."[20] To Pattullo's conclusion, that both organizations would field candidates in the federal election, Laurier replied, "unless you bury the hatchet, it will mean a loss to the government of a very safe seat."[21] Noel, too, wrote another letter, in which he explained that Congdon had been forced to appoint unqualified teachers if the school were to continue to operate.[22] Sir Wilfrid answered: "Congdon knows his business and, for my part, I have absolute confidence in him," except that he must not pay uncertified teachers, for, if it ever became known that he did, it would be a severe blow to separate schools.[23] Later, the Commissioner defended his actions, noting that he had been unaware that the teachers were unqualified when the school term had started, and that patronage to the Good Samaritan Hospital had been reduced because this institution was keeping some indigents after they were well enough to be discharged.[24]

By May 1904 Congdon's supporters were being called "Tabs" to denote the presumed role of the Commissioner in refusing to pay bribery debts after the Ross election campaign; and his opponents were being styled "Steam Beers" to indicate the position of leadership of Tom O'Brien, the local beer manufacturer.[25] The two factions held separate meetings on May 6, and, while the "Tabs" "spent the evening singing and listening to stories and in drinking punch," the "Steam Beers" discussed specific grievances. Patullo, Congdon's most vociferous opponent, accused the Commissioner of leaving him $2,500 in debt by revoking a contract with him to publish a government year-book. Another speaker complained that Congdon had backed down on a promise to pay him to draw up the new ordinances for Council, while W. F. Thompson, editor of the *Sun*, claimed that he was ordered to remove his newspaper office from government property so that a new firehall could be erected.[26] It was obvious now that the two Liberal camps would contest a federal election bitterly opposed to one another.

The opposition forces in the territory did not sit back and watch the Liberals destroy themselves, but took the initiative to build a strong and efficient organization capable of defeating both prospective Liberal candidates. By 1904, however, the Citizens' Yukon Party had given way to the Yukon Conservative Association, pledged to support not only reforms for the Yukon but also the entire platform of Opposition Leader Borden. The transformation had begun the previous summer, when, at a mass meeting called to denounce the Britton Royal Commission, it was resolved "that in the opinion of this meeting the Yukon Territory has been betrayed in every important particular by J. H. Ross, and the deliberate intention to repudiate election pledges by our member, we hereby ask Mr. Ross to resign his seat and seek again the suffrages of the Yukon Territory upon his seat and the government's record." Unlike the resolution of the Citizens' Committee mass meeting of 1900 calling for the dismissal of Ogilvie, this one, tantamount to a petition of recall, was not repudiated by those who called the meeting.[27] Although the Conservatives in the crowd decided to organize for the next federal election, by December it seemed that no formal steps would be taken in this direction, especially when Joe Clarke again offered his candidacy, saying that he would not run for the Conservatives. Instead, he would welcome all Yukon advocates to his cause whether they were Tories, Grits, Australians, Britishers, or nationalized citizens.[28]

With or without Clarke, however, Dr. Thompson and George Black were determined to organize a Conservative party, and during January 1904 they spoke to gatherings in Caribou, Granville, and Sulphur Creek to explain their purpose to the miners.[29] Early in February they called a mass meeting in Dawson at which C. M. Woodworth (who, four years earlier, had described himself as a Liberal) delivered the keynote address, denouncing Wilson and Sugrue for taking government jobs and noting that the Conservatives were alone in opposition now that the Liberal agitators had shown their true colours. The meeting set up a city Conservative association—the first Tory organization in the territory—elected officers, and ratified a constitution which outlined the purpose of the association as follows: "to spread the principles and promote the interests of the Conservative Party in the City of Dawson particularly and throughout the Yukon Territory in general, and to aid by all lawful means in its power the election to the House of Commons of Canada as member for Yukon a supporter and member of that party."[30] During the next few months, similar organizations were formed in Granville, Caribou, Gold Bottom, Whitehorse, and Bonanza.[31] When the Caribou Conservative Club was founded, Joe Clarke indicated his willingness to support the Conservatives and to step down as a candidate for parliamentary honours if Dr. Thompson could be induced to run.[32]

In April representatives of the community Conservative associations met in Grand Forks to establish a territorial party. C. M. Woodworth, again the main speaker, attacked the Laurier ministry for its Yukon policy and administration from 1897 to 1904. The last good government, he said, was the Conservative regime under Constantine.

We [have] tried repeatedly to remedy the situation by electing opposition Grits and to run elections without organization. Both were dismal failures. We [will] nominate no more unknowns, but will join hands with the great Conservative party on the outside that has fought our battle so well, and organize so thoroughly that defeat would be impossible, then we [will] roll back beyond our borders forever the corruption and misgovernment that has been a disgrace to Canada and the British flag.

The meeting passed resolutions condemning Landreville, Pringle, and Lowe for deserting the people during Council deliberations, and Ross for his failure to fulfil the election promises made in his name. Among officers elected were George Black and Joe Clarke.[33] The Conservatives were ready to fight the "Tabs" and the "Steams" whenever writs for the federal general election were issued.

Of the two Liberal groups, the "Tabs" were the first to make preparations for the election, holding a secret meeting on June 25. After voicing approval of the manner in which Laurier, Sifton, Congdon, and Ross had worked on behalf of the territory, the men present chose J. H. Ross as the standard-bearer of the Yukon Territorial Liberal Association. The move was seen by the *News* as a means to heal party wounds because the "Steams" would not turn down the popular Ross, despite the fact that the former Commissioner had been too ill to attend any sessions of Parliament.[34]

However, if the "Tabs" sought to reconcile their differences with the "Steam Beers" they were disappointed, for, on the day the Yukon Liberal Association held its convention, Ross telegraphed his decision not to seek re-election.[35] Delegates from eleven districts gave the nomination to Thomas Kearney, a Grand Forks merchant, over a Dawson businessman, after Duff Pattullo withdrew in favour of Kearney. They drafted a programme calling for a consolidated mining code, a better lien law, an assay office, cancellation of concessions controlled by men who had not lived up to their contractual obligations, an all-Canadian railroad to the Yukon, non-interference by civil servants in partisan political matters, and dismissal of unnecessary government employees.[36] Although those in attendance also expressed confidence in the Prime Minister, Pattullo sent Sir Wilfrid a confidential letter, in which he said that the "Steam Beers" would soon publicly blame the federal government for Congdon's maladministration if the Commissioner were not removed. Again, Laurier appealed to Pattullo to work towards a reconciliation of the two factions,[37] but, now that the "Steams" had nominated a candidate and adopted a programme—both unacceptable to the "Tabs"—re-unification was impossible.

During July and August, usually quiet months in Yukon politics, hostility between the two groups continued to grow. The "Steams," incensed over their lost battle to keep patronage with the *Sun*,[38] became even more outraged when Congdon's appointees on the Board of Licence Commissioners—including Temple and Auguste Noel—revoked the licences of thirty-five saloons.[39] After the Dawson Liberal Club accused the commissioners of political favouritism, Pattullo wrote Laurier, claiming not only that well known "Steams" and Tories had lost their licences, but also that several houses of ill repute had been given permission to dispense liquor.[40]

The Prime Minister, weary of the petty squabbling, did not acknowledge Pattullo's letter, but began to worry when H. J. Woodside, a former editor of the *Sun* and now an employee in the Customs Department, sent him a long communication containing specific charges against Congdon. Woodside, who, in his earlier correspondence with Sir Wilfrid, had been fair and reasonable in his estimation of the territorial administration, said he had believed that Congdon would make an admirable successor to Ross—indeed, in many ways, the Commissioner had proven himself capable—but his weaknesses for money and converting opponents had blackened his image. Woodside complained that Congdon still owed $20,000 to election workers in the 1902 campaign; that he was vindictive towards any civil servant who did not submit to his organizing tactics; that Beddoe, a "despicable wretch" fired from the *News* for attempting to blackmail explorer J. B. Tyrrell, was running a vile newspaper; and that Temple did no work for his $350 per month "except to promote newspapers, organize civil servant Liberal clubs, breed trouble, scandal, and . . . split the Liberal party of the Yukon, as well as earn the contempt of all honest men."[41] The Prime Minister told Woodside that the whole affair confused him, but that the "impression left on my mind is that, though the Commissioner may have made mistakes, it is . . . a greater mistake on the part of those who do not share his views to magnify them and to increase the irritation caused thereby."[42]

The controversy was ideally suited to the purposes of the Conservative party, and, when Council met late in July 1904, Thompson and Clarke did their best to drive the wedge even deeper between the two feuding factions. Shortly after the session opened, Joe Clarke delivered a blistering attack on the Board of Licence Commissioners, following which he moved an amendment to the Liquor Ordinance to provide for an appeal from the Board to Council. During the ensuing debate, J. T. Lithgow, the

Comptroller, freely admitted that the liquor licensing system was used for political ends: "I think the probabilities are that the commissioners will refuse to license when the applicants are not in friendly sympathy with the government, and that in cases where applicants take an aggressive and offensive part against officials of this government the probabilities are that they will lose their licences." Clarke's amendment was defeated by a margin of six to two.[43] Later in the session, Council did pass an amendment (to the Liquor Ordinance) which legalized dancehalls and placed them under the supervision of the Board of Licence Commissioners.[44]

Clarke also brought up the issue of government aid to hospitals, asking: "Why is the Good Samaritan hospital given less patronage than St. Mary's?," to which Congdon replied: "It is not a matter of patronage. Each hospital receives exactly what it earns under the Ordinance for care and treatment of indigents, who select their own hospital." Later, a return ordered by Clarke showed that the Catholic hospital had been given more than twice as much public assistance as the Presbyterian one during the previous year.[45] When the senior member for Dawson demanded to know the details of the printing contract that the Commissioner had entered into with Duff Pattullo to produce the Yukon year-book, Congdon answered that an order had been placed with Pattullo but that it had been revoked before a contract was signed.[46]

Congdon's policy with respect to the Official Gazette came under even heavier fire. On July 27 Mr. Lithgow read a second time a bill which proposed to establish the office of King's Printer, "completely under the control of the Commissioner," to be responsible for the superintendence of printing Council *Journals* and *Ordinances*, the Official Gazette, and other territorial publications. Joe Clarke objected to the new bill, which to him seemed to transfer the authority over the Gazette from Council to the Commissioner. Although he also denounced Congdon for transferring government notices to the *World* without consent of Council and in violation of the 1901 ordinance which had established the *Yukon Sun* as the Official Gazette, Clarke went on to suggest that now it would be best to call tenders for government printing; the government newspaper, he felt, could survive without its excessive "milking" of the government. Congdon replied that the well-established precedent giving the executive complete discretion to choose the Official Gazette placed him fully within his rights to transfer patronage from the *Sun* to the *World*. He also rejected the demand to call for tenders, saying that as long as the majority in Council favoured British institutions over American ones he would not consider giving the "American reptile press" one dollar of business. Clarke proceeded to chastise the Commissioner for abusing Americans, the majority in the territory, especially at a time when Canada was encouraging aliens of all nationalities to come to the country. Dr. Thompson took the floor and claimed that he could prove that the government was paying $3.50 a column inch for the Gazette, which, if published in the *News*, would cost only one cent an inch. The *News* reported that the Commissioner, after "looking incredulous for a moment," said that the government had to be run on government principles, which most certainly precluded printing anything in the *News*.[47]

On the motion to read the bill a third time, Clarke and Thompson again waged a vigorous fight, this time moving an amendment to refer the piece of legislation back to committee of the whole for revisions that would provide "that all contracts for public printing be let by contract open to public tender and competition and to the lowest bidder, that the Yukon Gazette be abolished and the offer of the *Dawson Daily News* be accepted, and that no discrimination or prejudice shall be recognized against any establishment doing business in the Yukon so long as [it] complies with the laws of Canada." The amendment was lost on division, and the bill was given third reading.[48]

The opposition members also sought to embarrass Congdon by requesting the appointment of a special committee "to ratify and legalize all . . . proceedings and acts as were had and passed in the absence of a quorum of the Council at a special session held in January, 1904." In the ensuing debate, after Girouard pointed out that the Speaker was not called upon to ascertain the number of members present, Joe Clarke ridiculed the Registrar by saying that Congdon, if he so desired, could then conduct proceedings by himself. After it was ruled that the words "in the absence of a quorum" were out of order, the motion was defeated six to two.[49]

During the 1904 session Clarke and Thompson were even less successful than they had been in the previous year in their attempts to induce Council to prepare memorials on subjects requiring federal action. The first such matter they brought to Council's attention was the need to secure an adequate miners' lien law. The one passed in 1903 had been declared *ultra vires* by the Territorial Court because it dealt with public lands which were under the jurisdiction of the Governor in Council. After Clarke proposed a memorial requesting cabinet enactment of a lien provision, a committee, constituted to consider the advisability of drafting such a petition, recommended taking the present Lien Ordinance to the highest court in the land to determine its validity. The Dawson members opposed the suggestion because it would leave mine labourers without protection, but their second motion to memorialize Ottawa was defeated on division.[50]

Although the Treadgold Concession had been cancelled, rancour against the 200 remaining hydraulic leases persisted, and was perhaps more pronounced because of the tenor of the Britton Report. When Thompson attempted to secure Council support for a memorial asking for the cancellation of all concessions fraudulently obtained or improperly retained, F. C. Senkler, the Gold Commissioner, attacked him for trying to embarrass the federal and local governments, and (interpreting the Yukon Act rather narrowly) reminded him that all councillors were elected to aid and assist, not to obstruct, the Commissioner. A Senkler amendment stating the impropriety of a memorial on the subject was passed by the usual division.[51] Earlier in the session, in reply to Thompson's renewed demand for a government water system to replace the abortive concession policy, Judge Dugas had countered: "you will never get it."[52] The *World* accused the doctor and his fellow member from Dawson of socialism, but, replied the *News*, were they any more socialistic than the federal Opposition Leader who was advocating government ownership of a second trans-Canada railroad?[53]

The struggle for some measure of responsible government continued unabated from the previous session, but resolutions requesting the Laurier administration to provide the Yukon with a wholly elective council and Congdon to constitute an advisory committee on finance were defeated by the official majority augmented by the votes of elected councillors Landreville and Lowe. When the former motion was discussed, Judge Dugas offered two objections: first, the constitutional change was unwarranted at a time when economic conditions were declining and many people were leaving the country; and, second, an elective council would be most irresponsible if it were composed of men like "the N.W.M.P. deserter." To the first argument Dr. Thompson replied that a council responsible to the people would prevent the sort of dissatisfaction that had caused hundreds to leave the Klondike for the Tanana. Moreover, he said, responsible government should depend not on gold production and people, but on principle. To the second, Clarke claimed that he had been young and irresponsible at the time of his desertion, but was now much older and wiser. Then he exhorted Landreville and Lowe to support the motion: "Are you men or are you dogs, to lie down like curs at the bidding of this man Temple! Will you sit supinely by and allow yourselves to be placed in the attitude of sycophantic hypocrites, kissing the hand that slaps you in the face, hurrahing for the crowd of grafters that are doing their best to put this Territory and every man in it out of business?"[54] Judge Dugas moved an amendment, "that in the opinion of this Council the present time...is most inopportune for the presentation of such a memorial," which was carried by a margin of six to two.[55] Clarke's motion for an advisory board, similar to the one the Rev. John Pringle had proposed in 1903, was defeated after the appointed members repeated Dugas's arguments against an elective council.[56]

On August 23, when Council prorogued after the liveliest session in its history, Dr. Thompson moved a vote of thanks to the other councillors for the courtesy they had extended him during his two-year tenure. Joe Clarke felt that "there was no thanks due," and announced his retirement from public life and the Yukon; shortly thereafter he departed for Ontario.[57]

That same day, Council had given third reading to a bill which, when brought into force, became a new source of tension within the feuding Liberal party. The Dawson city charter was amended to allow the residents of the city to vote in a new plebiscite to decide between the mayor-council and appointive commission forms of government. In passing the measure, Council acceded to the wishes of many Dawson merchants, who, dissatisfied with the high taxes they were obliged to pay under conditions of economic recession, had petitioned the assembly for the plebiscite.[58] Shortly after prorogation, Congdon began preparing for the forthcoming plebiscite, but, on September 6, he was obstructed by City Council. The municipal body, which the Commissioner later described as a "hot-bed [of] agitation and movements adverse to the Government," dismissed the City Clerk, whose responsibility it was to issue certificates to eligible voters.[59] The next day, the mayor, who was also Congdon's Chief Preventive Officer, reinstated the Clerk against the wishes of the Council majority, and the territorial administration seized City Hall, barring its doors to all aldermen.[60] Duff Pattullo, one of the city councillors, crawled into the building through a window, and later reported that the Clerk was altering the voters' list to disfranchise all those who favoured retention of the present local institutions.[61] On September 13, the day the vote was taken, Mr. Justice Craig of the Territorial Court declared that, although requested to do so, he could not issue an injunction restraining the Commissioner from proceeding with the plebiscite. However, the judge did say that City Council had been fully justified in removing the City Clerk, and that the mayor had had no right either to reinstate the official or to refuse to convene a Council meeting. Furthermore, the Clerk's voting certificates were invalid because they had been prepared within too short a period of time.[62]

Late that evening, after the vote had been tabulated, W. F. Thompson telegraphed the following press release to the newspapers of Canada:

At the request of ten per cent of the taxpayers of the city, the Congdon Administration forced through the Yukon Council a bill compelling the city to submit a plebiscite to the people to decide if they wanted to retain the city's charter. . . . [Then], after a shameless exhibition of the most barefaced jobbery ever manifested in Canada; after the dictum of the Superior Court Judge that the election under the circumstances would not be legal; after a united protest by the press and people; the local

c*

Administration of the Yukon Territory to-day stole from the people of Dawson their city charter in an election forced upon the people by the Commissioner of the Territory with the illegal issue of voting certificates to people who had no right to vote. By the disfranchisement of several aldermen, the city attorney and a majority of the taxpayers, the Congdon government was able to appropriate the city charter and to throw the city government into the hands of the Territory by a vote of 288 to 92, a total of only 380 votes cast out of at least 3440 taxpayers. . . . Conditions here constitute a reign of terror.[63]

Thompson's views were exaggerated, but some of the essential facts were true. Although many of those who were disfranchised (if, indeed, any were) would probably have voted against the mayor-council system and brought about its defeat anyway, the manner in which the plebiscite was conducted was most improper, if not illegal. Congdon most certainly did break the law in its aftermath, for he refused to appoint a three-man commission, choosing, instead, to govern Dawson from the Commissioner's office.[64] In a letter to Sifton, expressing great satisfaction at the outcome of the plebiscite, Congdon added: "I hope you will have paid no attention to the ravings wired out by that idiot Thompson. He is a drunken dope fiend."[65]

Despite the hostility the plebiscite aroused, Congdon, just a week after its occurrence, informed Laurier that the Liberals would retain the Yukon seat with ease in the federal election. "I am glad to hear it," replied the Prime Minister, "but who shall the man be? We need a strong candidate."[66] The answer to his query came on October 27, when the Commissioner telegraphed Sifton to say that he had been given the nomination, which he would accept if given permission.[67] Two days later, consent having been granted, the "Tabs" selected Congdon in a closed convention. That same day, Congdon forwarded his resignation to Sir Wilfred with a cover letter thanking the Prime Minister for his support and expressing hope for a "right royal vindication" on December 16, the day fixed for the Yukon election.[68] The *News* reported that William Temple had resigned from the civil service to devote his full time to the campaign.[69]

Seemingly undaunted in his correspondence with Ottawa, Congdon must have felt a little less optimistic two weeks before his candidacy was announced, when Conservative delegates, selected in preliminaries in all parts of the territory, met in Grand Forks to give their nomination to the popular Yukon councillor, Dr. Alfred Thompson.[70] The Conservative cause had been hurt by C. M. Woodworth's departure to practise law in Vancouver,[71] and perhaps even by the loss of Joe Clarke, but the organization built by Thompson, Black, Woodworth, and Clarke during the previous eight months was strong and ready to fight both the "Tabs" and the "Steam Beers." The platform adopted by the convention was similar to the one earlier drafted by the "Steams" except that it pledged support for a government water system and to the national Conservative programme.[72]

Meanwhile, at the national level, the Laurier ministry was returned to power on November 3 with a larger majority in the House of Commons than it had secured in the two previous electoral contests. "Big Alex" McDonald, an ardent "Tab" despite his former espousal of the Citizens' Committee cause, wrote the Prime Minister, offering congratulations and noting that the victory in the general election would enhance Congdon's chances of success.[73] Joe Clarke must have feared the same thing, for he wired the Thompson campaign committee to say that he would return to the Yukon to help bring about the defeat of the former Commissioner, who had to be beaten "at all costs."[74] Following the announcement of the Dominion results, the campaign in the territory began to gain momentum. Each of the three candidates held mass meetings and conducted a personal canvass among the voters. It was obvious that the only real issue before the electorate was Congdon's administration of territorial affairs.

For this reason, it was not surprising that the "Tabs" called a mass meeting to discuss the various charges laid against their candidate in the hope that the "silver-tongued orator" would refute all of them.[75] However, when the chairman called the meeting to order, he announced the most ludicrous rules of debate that ever governed a political meeting in the Yukon. The chair, he said, would entertain only personal attacks against the Commissioner and would not tolerate any discussion of political matters. Dr. Thompson, who had come prepared to discuss his election platform, refused to speak, but Tom O'Brien, Duff Pattullo, and other "Steam Beers," on behalf of Kearney, took the opportunity to criticize Congdon's methods of political manipulation, although not his personal honour. Pattullo was particularly bitter, charging Congdon with prostituting the public service to purposes political and forming a machine for political blackmail.[76]

The day after this mass meeting, Congdon's chances of victory weakened when Thomas Kearney and Alfred Thompson withdrew as candidates of the Yukon Liberal Association and the Yukon Conservative party respectively, and the two organizations were merged to form the Yukon Independent Party (Y.I.P.). The combined executives renominated Dr. Thompson to run on the "Steam Beer" platform minus the plank pledging support to the Prime Minister. On November 18 only two candidates— F. T. Congdon and A. Thompson—filed nomination papers.[77]

Coming as it did after two years of heated political controversy over the Treadgold Concession and the Congdon machine, the campaign was the most impassioned in the history of the territory. The contestants hurled stinging epithets at one another, and the two newspapers—the *News* and the *World*—battled each other far more fiercely than had the *News* and the *Nugget* during the 1900 territorial campaign. At first, Congdon's organization worked well: road crews were larger than ever before; the Licence Commissioners were making promises and threatening saloon keepers; and Temple was occupied in falsifying voters' lists.[78] Suddenly, however, it became apparent that the machine had gone too far—patronage was one thing but corruption was a far different matter. On December 1 the lists of eligible voters were posted in accordance with the provisions of the statute governing Yukon elections, but, within an hour, none could be found. They had been "stolen." Four days later, Thompson committeemen wired Ottawa, complaining that they had not seen the voters' lists. The Secretary of State telegraphed the Chief Returning Officer, ordering him to furnish Thompson's agents with complete election lists. The election official refused to comply with the Minister's wishes, and, only by capturing individual enumerators, did the Y.I.P. obtain fragments of the lists.[79] Mrs. George Black, in her reminiscences, recalled that the Chief Returning Officer was almost lynched by an angry mob before Y.I.P. supporters intervened, and that the N.W.M.P. maintained a twenty-four-hour guard duty on Judge Dugas, who had appointed the election officials.[80] Finally, on December 13, just three days before the election, a Dawson enumerator confessed that he had been expected to do all in his power to keep Y.I.P. supporters from voting. William Temple and other "Tabs" were formally charged with conspiracy to defeat the Election Act.[81]

Whatever chances Congdon had had of winning were lost by the exposé of Temple's corrupt methods. Thompson defeated the former Commissioner by 600 votes, and the *News* declared that the margin would have been 1,500 had it not been for the manipulation of the electoral machinery by supporters of the losing candidate. Conservatives and "Steam Beers" paraded the streets of Dawson to celebrate their victory over the machine, but they had won only the first battle of the war, for the "Tabs" announced that they would seek to reinstate Congdon as Commissioner and would file counter-charges against the Thompson committee in the hope of securing a controversion of the election.[82]

Nothing much came of the conspiracy cases, because, at the suggestion of the Department of Justice, they were dropped in March 1905.[83] John Grant, a "Tab" saloon-keeper, filed another suit against Thompson later in 1905, but it was thrown out by the Territorial Court, a decision later sustained by the Supreme Court of Canada.[84] However, the campaign for Congdon's reappointment lasted for five months after the federal election. On December 19 Congdon's friends informed Sir Wilfrid that their candidate had been defeated because bribed deputy returning officers had allowed Thompson supporters to stuff ballot boxes after the polls closed. Re-appoint Congdon, they urged, because he, at last, had removed the Yukon question from federal politics.[85] The former Commissioner himself asked to be reinstated, and then left for Ottawa in company with Auguste Noel.[86]

Meanwhile, Major Wood, the Acting Commissioner,[87] was determined to do his part to quash the machine while he remained in authority. The Major disliked Congdon intensely for the reason he outlined in a letter to F. C. Wade prior to the election: "win or lose [Congdon] will see that . . . I leave the Yukon . . . [because] the police have in certain measure prevented Temple from carrying out his Tammany schemes; for instance we stopped gambling and thus put an end to his receiving 'protection' money from this class."[88] Once the contest was over, Wood sent a lengthy report of Congdon's activities to Fred White, the Comptroller of the N.W.M.P., who passed the communication on to the Minister of the Interior. The Acting Commissioner revealed his story of how the city charter was revoked to permit the machine to reopen gambling, of how the election was rigged to disfranchise Thompson's supporters, and of how Temple had boasted that the administration would spend $170,000 on roads when the appropriations for that purpose were exhausted. In January 1905 Wood dismissed Temple, Sugrue, and a host of other Congdon appointees.[89]

Congdon's friends kept up their pressure to win back the Commissioner's chair for their leader, but Laurier, having read Wood's account of the machine's tactics, did not answer their demands. Nevertheless, it was difficult to find a man who would calm the troubled waters. Tom O'Brien, in the name of the Yukon Liberal Association, asked that E. S. Busby, the Collector of Customs, be given the appointment (H. J. Woodside, now in Winnipeg, agreed), but it was obvious that the "Tabs" would have nothing to do with Busby, who had consistently opposed Congdon's efforts to organize his department.[90] "Big Alex" McDonald, in a letter asking for Congdon's reinstatement, wrote Laurier: "in the name of Catholics, I implore you not to appoint Busby."[91] J. E. Girouard offered his services, claiming that it was time the French Canadians had one of their own in command in the Yukon.[92] A third suggestion was tendered by a Vancouver Liberal, who recommended W. W. B. McInnes, a former member of Parliament and then a member of the British Columbia Legislative Assembly; other letters were sent in support of McInnes, including one from J. H. (now Senator) Ross.[93] However, the Prime Minister and the Minister of the Interior, content to allow Wood to handle territorial affairs until agitation died down, refused to make a quick decision.

While the "Tabs" were campaigning for Congdon's reappointment, members of the Yukon Independent Party eagerly prepared for the territorial election. Deciding not to contest the election in Whitehorse, party members began to organize in the four new constituencies created by a recent amendment to the Council election ordinance—North Dawson, South Dawson, Klondike, and Bonanza.[94] They agreed to allow each of the "Steam Beer" and Tory wings to nominate a candidate for one of the Dawson ridings, and to hold joint conventions to choose contestants for the creek constituencies.[95] Only one obstacle stood in the way of continued harmony in the hybrid party—Joe Clarke. Joe had returned from the "outside" to help Thompson defeat Congdon, and had spent most of his time organizing Y.I.P. forces in Whitehorse. Because he was credited with sharply reducing the "Tab" majority in the southern town, the Y.I.P. tendered him a banquet on his return to Dawson. George Black, the main speaker at the affair, noted that Clarke's cry had always been "Yukon for Yukoners," and, as a result, Joe had been somewhat reluctant to join the Conservatives. Now, Black continued, all who espoused that dictum were united in one great party, thus fulfilling Clarke's most precious dream. Although Clarke was offered his choice of constituencies in which to run, he was not as certain as Black that the Y.I.P. was a dream come true.[96] Soon after the reception, he made it clear that he would have no part of the liaison with the "Steam Beers."

The first convention, held in Grand Forks, chose miner Charles Reid, a "Steam," over miner John Gillespie, a Conservative and Clarke's personal choice, to run in Bonanza. After protesting the twenty-nine to twenty-eight vote, Joe and all his followers left the meeting and renounced their affiliation with the Y.I.P. When the Tory wing of the party met in the territorial capital to select a candidate for North Dawson, Clarke was nominated, but he refused to allow his name to stand. Merchant N. F. Hagel, President of the Dawson Conservative Association, was eventually chosen over a defeated aspirant in the 1903 election, C. W. C. Tabor. There was no rancour in the other conventions, which chose T. W. O'Brien and George Black to contest South Dawson and Klondike respectively. On February 9 a Y.I.P. executive meeting formally ratified the selection of the four candidates.[97]

Clarke meanwhile sponsored another convention in Grand Forks, at which John Gillespie was nominated, and announced his own intention of opposing Tom O'Brien in South Dawson as a representative of the "Independent Labour Party."[98] Thus, midway through February the election campaign began to take on the appearance of a contest between Clarke and the Y.I.P., no "Tabs" having announced their candidacy. Nor had the election date itself been set; Wood was hoping to leave the matter to the new Commissioner who was to have been chosen in March.[99] However, when no appointment was forthcoming because Clifford Sifton, for nine years Minister of the Interior, had resigned in protest over the provisions of the Saskatchewan and Alberta autonomy bills,[100] the Acting Commissioner was instructed to conduct the election himself. He therefore announced that voting would take place on April 12.[101]

Little public interest was displayed in territorial politics during the month of March. The candidacies of several men were rumoured, including those of "Tabs" Henry Macaulay, Barney Sugrue, Arthur Wilson, and W. A. Beddoe.[102] However, when nomination papers were filed, it became evident that the "Tab" threat had not materialized, because Henry Macaulay, nominated to run against Hagel in North Dawson, was the only one of Congdon's supporters to seek election.[103] O'Brien and Clarke in South Dawson and Reid and Gillespie in Bonanza were left free of further opposition, while George Black and incumbent Robert Lowe were declared elected by acclamation in Klondike and Whitehorse respectively.[104]

In the short campaign that ensued, many election planks had a familiar ring— an elective council with increased powers and a comprehensive mining code— while others were new—an employers' liability ordinance[105]—but, on the whole, there were fewer and less grandiose promises than in previous territorial contests. Two basic issues emerged. The first, a rare occurrence in the Yukon, was division over principle, all candidates but Macaulay favouring a federal miners' lien statute: the "Tab," echoing Congdon's argument when Arthur Wilson had first introduced a lien bill to Council, said that the capitalist and the merchant deserved consideration equal to that shown the labourer.[106] The second issue, more in keeping with the general pattern of territorial elections, concerned personalities: most attacks centred on Congdon, but some of the candidates, particularly those who ran in Dawson, were strongly abused as well.[107]

The contest between O'Brien and Clarke was particularly bitter, although one-sided. Clarke accused the "Steam Beer" President of defrauding the people in the tramway affair, of being implicated in the importation of aliens to vote for Ross in 1902, and of being "secretly against" the people. The Y.I.P. candidate used his opponent's own excuse for deserting the N.W.M.P. to defend his part in the tramway scandal—it was "ancient history." With respect to the Ross election, the entire scheme to stuff the ballot boxes had been engineered by a certain Mr. Jackson. O'Brien chose not to attack Clarke, preferring to concentrate on Congdon, whom he condemned for ruining the territorial brewing industry and for all the other misdemeanours so frequently mentioned before.[108]

In the words of Major Wood, "the Yukon Council elections . . . created little, if any excitement or interest."[109] Probably no more than 70 per cent of the voters went to the polls to elect Macaulay in North Dawson, O'Brien in South Dawson, and Gillespie in Bonanza.[110] Thus, Council, in the years 1905 and 1906, would consist of the appointed members, three representatives of the Y.I.P. (Black, Gillespie,[111] and O'Brien), one "Tab" (Macaulay), and a consistent supporter of the territorial administration (Lowe). The *News* expressed satisfaction at the results except in North Dawson, where, it claimed, a hundred "Tabs" had voted illegally,[112] but, apart from the newspaper's apprehension over how Macaulay might act, few people seemed to care about the outcome.

Joe Clarke, however, was concerned. He was never more bitter than when he telegraphed the Prime Minister to complain that he had suffered injustice at the hands of Major Wood, the Acting Commissioner, whose "semi-military dictatorship" had brought about his (Clarke's) defeat by a margin of 414 to 358.[113] When Sir Wilfrid asked the defeated incumbent to forward specific charges, Clarke replied that Chief Detective Welch, "Major Wood's political heeler," had intimidated voters and had herded the police vote to the polls in South Dawson.[114] Furthermore, Wood was betraying the federal government by appointing "Steam Beers' to the positions left vacant by the dismissed "Tabs." Clarke concluded his submission by telling the Prime Minister that "the interest of your government . . . is identical with my own. . . . Protect the Yukon from the biggest gang of political grafters that ever tried to hold up a government, namely, the Yukon Steam Beer Grits." Clarke brought the charges of intimidation of voters before the Territorial Court, but the case was dismissed when the judge ascertained that all Welch had done was to warn a hapless voter, told by Clarke that he could vote in two polling stations, that he could not do so.[115]

J. C. Noel, "Tab" leader now that most members of the machine had left the territory, also wrote Laurier, claiming that Macaulay's victory had vindicated Congdon's record, that the disreputable O'Brien had won only because the "Tabs" preferred him to Clarke, and that people were most sorry they had voted for Thompson in the federal election. Therefore, he said, Congdon must be reappointed, a conclusion reached by another "Tab," who added that it would be a good lesson to government officials who had dared to rise up in rebellion.[116] For the first time, the Prime Minister replied that he could not reinstate Congdon, although, in a letter to Auguste Noel, Sir Wilfrid promised to name the former Commissioner to the territorial bench if either Dugas or Craig resigned.[117] Laurier wrote Auguste Noel two further letters, in which he disclosed that W. W. B. McInnes would be appointed Commissioner, and that Congdon would be given back his old job as Legal Adviser on the firm understanding that he would not be able to practise law privately and that he would not be able to dispense any government patronage.[118] On May 27, 1905, an order in council formally named William Wallace Burns McInnes Commissioner of the Yukon Territory,[119] thereby signifying the final demise of the Congdon machine. The Yukon had not heard the last of Frederick Tennyson Congdon, but his machine was never reassembled.

The appointment of McInnes terminated the most colourful phase of territorial politics in the decade after the gold rush. During the period examined in this chapter the chief executive of the Yukon Territory fashioned a personal political machine, sanctioned official intervention in party politics, violated two territorial ordinances,[120] defied the wishes of representatives elected by the people,[121] and allowed his lieutenant to support gambling in contravention of the Canadian Criminal Code and to use public revenues to further political ends. These actions, in addition to the schism in the territorial Liberal party, the formation of the Yukon Conservative Association, the conduct of two election campaigns, the instance of judicial interference in politics,[122] and the attempt to recall the territory's member of Parliament, created an unusual political environment. Under these circumstances, the general movement for political and economic amelioration made no headway. Demands raised at the beginning of Congdon's tenure—for an elective council, a consolidated mining code, a government water system, and cancellation of hydraulic concessions—remained unmet at the time of the Commissioner's resignation. Now that Congdon had been defeated, some territorial politicians could turn again to the struggle to secure the reforms they desired.

CHAPTER EIGHT

THE NEW ADMINISTRATION

IN 1905 the Yukon Territory moved into a new political setting, with McInnes succeeding Congdon as Commissioner and Frank Oliver replacing Clifford Sifton as Minister of the Interior. Furthermore, Alfred Thompson was in the House of Commons to represent the territory, and J. H. Ross, having fully recovered from his illness, was in the Senate where, although he officially represented Saskatchewan, he retained a keen interest in Yukon affairs.[1] Men involved in territorial politics anxiously waited to see if the changes would bring about new government attitudes to the problems they sought to solve.

Commissioner McInnes arrived in Dawson on July 4 and was greeted by the members of the Yukon Council and an enthusiastic welcoming committee headed by Colonel Donald McGregor. The tenor of the reception was in sharp contrast to that of the one for F. T. Congdon, who had returned three days earlier to be met only by a few "Tabs."[2] On July 7 the Canadian Club of Dawson sponsored a banquet in honour of the incoming chief executive, who, according to the *Dawson Daily News*, made a "big hit" when he spoke to the 200 invited guests (not one of whom was a "Tab"). After lauding the work that Laurier, Oliver, and Thompson were doing for the Yukon, McInnes stated that the civil service would be kept out of territorial and federal politics; that the laws governing elections would be altered to prevent the abuses that had occurred in the past, that the nature of the Yukon Council would be changed in accordance with democratic principles; that the hydraulic concessionaires would have to live up to their agreements or their leases would be cancelled; and that the feasibility of a government water system would be investigated. He also quashed a current rumour that the Yukon would be annexed to British Columbia by saying that the territory should aim at becoming a province itself.[3]

The Commissioner was well pleased with the way in which his tenure began, writing Sir Wilfrid: "the people of the Territory are behind your government, although some . . . [have been alienated by] your representatives here . . . [because of] the latter's coarse political manipulation and a series of acts incredibly petty and impolitic." All factional strife would be overcome by a sound administration operating "on good business principles."[4] Although J. C. Noel reported that McInnes was making a good impression and was doing his best to reconcile "different elements here," the Commissioner's position was not a pleasant one, for Congdon (whom Laurier had beseeched to help McInnes) took an immediate dislike to his successor and stated his own unwillingness to remain in his present position.[5] In November Dr. Thompson, back in Dawson after his first session of Parliament, asked the Prime Minister to remove Congdon because the latter was blatantly interfering with the government of the territory. Sir Wilfrid replied that he had no other place for the Legal Adviser, and that it remained a mystery to him how a man with such ability and good intentions "had not been a complete success."[6]

Thompson, himself, had made a most favourable impression upon his constituents and upon the Liberal government during his first few months in Ottawa. Even before he took his seat, the new member of Parliament secured promises from the Prime Minister that the government would introduce a consolidated mining code, conduct a hydrographic survey to determine the practicability of a public water system, and abolish the royalty on quartz gold and copper.[7] On June 7 a representative of the Yukon people spoke to the Canadian House of Commons for the first time when Dr. Thompson addressed the chair on a motion to go into committee of supply. After explaining his election as an independent, he said: "I find, Mr. Speaker, in discussing with private members and gentlemen in this House that there is an immense dearth of information in regard to the Territory which I have the honour to represent." He proceeded to give an excellent and thorough account of the history, geography, and climate of the Yukon, and the social and economic conditions therein, concluding this part of his speech by stating: "We are a territory and as such we must come to this federal Parliament for absolutely everything pertaining to our territory and to our one industry." Then, he suggested specific reforms such as a consolidated mining code to increase certainty among investors; abolition of the export tax on placer gold to put the Yukon on a competitive basis with Alaska; a workable lien law to protect the miners; an assay office to eliminate the costs of selling gold to the banks; and removal of the tax on liquor in order to place the Yukon liquor trade on the same basis as that in other parts of Canada.

Finally, Thompson discussed the two issues that most deeply concerned him—the hydraulic concessions and the composition of the Yukon Council. With respect to the former, he said:

This land in the very heart of our gold-bearing district is locked up; the government gets no revenue out of it, the people get no employment, and the men who own the concessions play the part of the absentee landlord in Ireland. . . . This question of concessions is affecting the Yukon Territory, I believe, more than anything else. It has damped the ardour of the people there. They find it difficult to go on and prospect with these blankets covering the Territory.

Judge Britton had concluded that the Yukon badly needed a better water supply for placer mining, but because the concessionaires were not furnishing it, could not the state, Thompson asked, follow the example of Australia and provide it? With respect to the Council, he stated:

I submit that there is no principle so deeply embedded in the heart of the Anglo-Saxon as that of responsible government. When you trace the history of the race . . . you will find running through it that one bright thread . . . They want the right to elect their own representatives to govern themselves. . . . In the Yukon, . . . [although] we are 4,000 miles removed from here, there is in our breast the same sentiment which has animated this race from its dawn . . . to the present day. . . . [At present], the Dominion government always holds the power [on the Yukon Council] . . . because it controls the five nominative members and the Commissioner against five elective members. . . . I know all [the appointed councillors] . . . very well, and I know them all to be estimable gentlemen. They are Canadians down to the ground and good citizens, and in the main have done good work. But every one of these derives his sustenance directly from the federal government and, being human, must necessarily be biased at times and biased against the interests of the people. . . . What I ask is that we should give the people of the Yukon the right to elect ten members of their Council and let the Commissioner preside as at present. . . . Trust the people every time; grant them responsible government, and they will show themselves worthy of it. . . . I do not ask for provincial government . . . because we are not prepared for that, [but] I do ask that we . . . be given that government which . . . [the North-West Territories have enjoyed from 1897 to the present].

If such a system could not be granted immediately, he concluded, it would be better to replace the appointed officials with local citizens than to retain the current composition of the assembly.[8]

Sir Wilfrid answered Dr. Thompson himself. He said that, although the authority to make mining regulations had been vested in the Governor in Council so that changes could be made rapidly, perhaps the time had come to ask Parliament to pass an act embodying all of them. He also concurred in the recommendations for a lien law and an assay office, but stated that the government could not abolish the export tax on placer gold or the duty on imported liquor. The former was necessary to provide revenue to offset expenditures in the territory and the latter was required to restrain excessive consumption of liquor. With respect to the hydraulic concessions, he said that although the government motive—to provide a plentiful water supply—had been good, the policy had been a mistake and no further leases would be granted. As far as Council was concerned, the Prime Minister asked:

> Is the government . . . derelict in its duty . . .? It is only eight years since the Yukon was discovered [sic] and brought into civilization. . . . My hon. friend will agree with me that it would have been extremely unwise if we had given to this new population coming in from all parts of the world representative institutions. . . . That [the Council] must be made elective at an early date goes without saying, that it must be made elective almost immediately I am quite prepared to consider also, but I submit that if it should be done to-day, it should not have been done before, and that the government has not been remiss in the character which it has given to the institutions of the Yukon.[9]

R. L. Borden, the Leader of the Opposition, concluded the debate by urging immediate self-government for the territory and by rebuking the cabinet for not making such a provision three or four years earlier.[10]

Thompson did not return to the Yukon empty-handed, for, in addition to the promises he had secured from the Laurier ministry, the *News*, on August 11, announced that the government had passed an order in council doubling the size of placer claims, reducing the fee for free miners' licences, and making several other minor changes in the mining regulations. About two weeks later Frank Oliver arrived in Dawson to become the first federal minister ever to set foot in the Yukon Territory. He was given an office in the Administration Building, and spent a busy three days listening to the grievances and suggestions of hundreds of people.[11] Oliver reiterated that the concessionaires had to act quickly to fulfil their obligations or they would be compelled to forfeit their leases, and, in an interview with Colonel Donald McGregor, agreed that something would have to be done to prevent a recurrence of the petty political squabbling that had been the curse of the country. Thompson and Black arranged a mass meeting for the Minister on September 1, and presented him with a petition in which 300 men requested that he prolong his stay one more day so he could attend the gathering. Oliver, probably wisely in view of past reports of mass meetings, offered an apology for not remaining, but aroused the suspicion of some when, on August 31, he attended a smoker tendered him by the "Tabs."[12] Nevertheless, his mission was a decided success because, at last, many agitators were convinced that Ottawa was concerned about the affairs of the Yukon.

The harmony that prevailed during Oliver's sojourn in the territory—partially due to Dr. Thompson's success in Ottawa—carried over to McInnes's first session of Council. Some rancour was displayed by Black, Gillespie, and O'Brien towards the abuses produced by the Congdon machine,[13] but, for the most part, the *News*' prediction that the reform sentiments of the Commissioner would usher forth a new epoch in the political history of the Yukon seemed to be justified.[14] Indeed, Council approved many measures it had refused to consider under Congdon's tenure, including memorials requesting the federal government to provide a lien law, to cancel concessions, to improve postal facilities, to bring a consolidated mining code before Parliament, and to initiate the development of an adequate water supply.

The question of securing protection for miners' wages was the most contentious issue of all. After Mr. Lithgow gave notice of introducing a bill on the subject, the Commissioner noted that the federal government would in all likelihood prepare either a bill or an order in council to provide for miners' liens, because the old ordinance had been declared *ultra vires*.[15] George Black then moved that a committee be appointed to memorialize the government to take immediate action, pointing out that federal candidates from all factions had promised to do something about the problem. Henry Macaulay amended the motion to make it optional whether or not the committee prepared a submission, after which he repeated the argument he had used during the election campaign—that the merchant as well as the labourer needed protection. T. W. O'Brien disagreed, saying that the merchant was protected because he did not have to part with his goods until he had either money or security, whereas the worker gave his labour before he received remuneration. The division on the motion as amended produced a deadlock—Messrs. Girouard, Senkler, Wood, and Macaulay voting for it, and Messrs. Black, O'Brien, Lithgow, and Lowe against. McInnes, however, voted against the amendment, and the original motion was carried on a reversal of the same division.[16] The *News* commented that it was "the first time a Commissioner of this territory has voted with the people of this territory in lo, these many moons."[17] Later in the session, the committee appointed to draw up the memorial was authorized to sit after prorogation, with instructions to prepare a draft of a lien law.[18]

Compromises were reached on the memorials requesting cancellation of hydraulic concessions and the installation of a water system. Black's original motion—to petition the federal government to revoke the leases of all concessionaires who had obtained them through fraud and misrepresentation, or who had violated their terms —was amended by Mr. Senkler, the Gold Commissioner, who moved that the references to "fraud" and "misrepresentation" be deleted; the amendment was passed by a margin of six to three, Gillespie being absent and Lowe supporting the appointed members.[19] Black withdrew another motion—to ask the government to install a gravity water supply at public expense—after Lithgow amended it to read that the Council would support such a scheme, whether financed privately or publicly, if the government's hydrographic survey proved it feasible; Lithgow's amendment was passed unanimously. It was further agreed that a special committee of Council would be appointed to sit after prorogation to gather "all evidence, facts, information, or data relating to the benefit to be derived from a general water system."[20] Both resolutions represented great strides for the elected members who, for three years, had sought to secure the withdrawal of the concession policy and its replacement with a more satisfactory alternative.

Even less controversy centred around the resolutions to petition Ottawa on a consolidated mining code and an improvement in the postal service, both of which passed unanimously.[21] With respect to the former, it was decided to constitute a committee of Council, similar to the one on a miners' lien law, to sit after the session to prepare a comprehensive outline for a federal statute. The only total defeat suffered by the elected councillors (minus Lowe) in their campaign to use Council to secure action by the Laurier ministry was on a motion to prepare a memorial requesting a fully elective legislative body.[22] For the fifth consecutive year, the appointed members refused to recommend the constitutional change, even after the Prime Minister himself had signified his approval of it.

For two reasons the session was a marked success from the standpoint of those who sought federal reforms. First, the appointed councillors displayed a change of heart. Although the elected members appreciated the sudden willingness of their official counterparts to advise Ottawa on policy matters, George Black did chastise the appointed councillors for being inconsistent—only a year before they had refused to petition the cabinet on any issue. Girouard defended himself and his colleagues by saying they had never opposed memorials on principle, but had objected only to those they believed unnecessary.[23] Second, and as a result of this change, positive steps were taken towards the realization of several goals long held by territorial politicians. In the months that followed prorogation, the special committees on the lien law, the mining code, and a water system conducted public hearings and drafted comprehensive memorials favourable to all three.[24] On February 1, 1906, Commissioner McInnes departed for Ottawa, promising that the lien law draft and the mining code would be accepted with virtually no changes, and that he would attempt to induce the cabinet to agree to the construction of a publicly owned waterworks.[25]

Before his departure, the Commissioner took action with respect to the mining concessions, beginning in November 1905 with an investigation of one particular lease to see whether or not its contractual obligations were being fulfilled. After a series of hearings, McInnes ordered the lessee to cease certain objectionable practices on penalty of forfeiture.[26] Meanwhile, the *Dawson Daily News* had decided to reopen its case of "the people *v.* the concessions," and for several weeks displayed evidence purporting to show that most of the leases had been obtained by misrepresentation and that much of the ground they covered was lying idle.[27] McInnes then promised that no further concessions would be granted, and hinted that there was a chance some would be cancelled.[28]

A few days after the Commissioner left for the national capital, George Black called a mass meeting to discuss reforms that Dr. Thompson would be asked to seek in the forthcoming session of Parliament. The Yukon member, the main speaker at the meeting, stated openly that several leases would be revoked because Sir Wilfrid Laurier was sick of the agitation that they had caused. He said he was most pleased with the work Council had done in drafting memorials, and promised that he would assist the Commissioner in persuading the government to implement their terms. Furthermore, he would strongly urge the ministry to confer responsible government on the Yukon, and to establish an assay office in Dawson. Several other men spoke, including Joe Clarke, who delivered a vindictive attack on Laurier, Oliver, and McInnes for doing nothing to prevent the growing exodus of population. The meeting then turned to a matter it considered most urgent—the composition of the Yukon Council. A rumour had been circulating that the Department of the Interior planned to implement, as a substitute for an elective council, Dr. Thompson's suggestion that Council officials be replaced by local citizens. The Young Men's Liberal Association, part of the "Steam Beer" faction, had already passed a resolution condemning the scheme and recommending a wholly elective council, and those assembled at the mass meeting decided to send a similar petition to the government. They also constituted a continuing committee on the matter with powers to protest the rumoured change if the government formally announced it and to call further mass meetings to recommend an elective council.[29]

Thompson and McInnes worked as a team in Ottawa, and before long the fruits of their endeavours became apparent. On April 6 the *News* received a telegram from Dr. Thompson, saying that the Minister of the Interior would cancel several concessions and would give to the lessees only a few claims in compensation for the work they had done on the land granted them. A month later, the government announced the revocation of six leases, stipulating that the compensation would be granted only if the syndicates involved accepted the cancellation within sixty days.[30] Many of the lessees took the government decision to the courts, but on January 9, 1908, the Supreme Court of Canada handed down thirty-two decisions unfavourable to the concessionaires.[31] For nearly a decade many Yukoners had fought the Laurier government's policy on hydraulic mining, and, at last, they emerged victorious. Two more sources of heated agitation were stemmed when the drafts of the lien bill and the mining code were passed by the Governor in Council and Parliament respectively.[32]

Thompson and McInnes tackled other problems as well. After the Board of Trade appealed, in February, for an investigation of freight rates on the White Pass and Yukon Route (virtually the rates the company had imposed in 1901, during more prosperous times), the Commissioner and the Member of Parliament exerted pressure on the government to force the company to revise its rate structure.[33] They made some headway, for in August 1906 two members of the Board of Railway Commissioners held a public inquiry in Dawson into the White Pass rates.[34] Thompson and McInnes also did their best to persuade the cabinet and members of Parliament that a government water system would be a great boon to the territory.[35] Although this mission was unsuccessful, by the end of the year there were encouraging prospects for the construction of several private systems—to be built without special privileges such as those conferred upon Treadgold in 1901.

Despite the fact that Oliver, McInnes, and Thompson were creating a new political atmosphere in the territory, one major goal of political protest remained unattained. On May 8, after reading the petitions of the Young Men's Liberal Association and the mass meeting, Robert Borden, the Opposition Leader, asked the ministry about its intentions to grant Yukoners an elective council. Oliver was non-committal in his answer, saying that he thought interest in the matter had petered out.[36] Four days later, at a Board of Trade meeting in Dawson, the Minister's statement was brought up for discussion, but, because the February mass meeting had appointed a committee to seek the constitutional change, the Board decided not to take a stand on the issue itself.[37] Shortly thereafter, the committee called a second mass meeting to prove to the federal government that interest had not abated and that an elective council was the greatest current need of the Yukon. Harry Landahl, a member of the committee and Secretary of the Board of Trade, said:

There have been 100 mass meetings here on public questions, and all have endorsed the proposition for an wholly elective council. Every candidate for parliament has stood on such a platform. The premier went so far as to promise the wholly elective council. All the present appointive members . . . are tired of the job. All ask to be relieved. Therefore, we step on the toes of no one in urging an all elective council. We have fought and begged for this reform and we might as well keep it up . . . especially now that there is a wrong impression needing correction.[38]

Only sixty-three people turned out for the mass meeting—a far cry from days past—

to hear such stalwarts of political activity as Colonel McGregor, Joe Clarke, and George Black exhort the government to grant a fully representative council. Clarke was in his usual form when he proclaimed: "The Yukon Council has no more power than this mass meeting!" Black presented the committee's resolution, which gave several reasons for the desired constitutional change: the Prime Minister and every Yukon candidate for Parliament had promised it; several petitions requesting it had been sent to Ottawa; and the territory was self-supporting. The meeting agreed to send copies of the petiton to Laurier, Oliver, Borden, and Thompson.[39]

On June 12 Dr. Thompson read the resolution to the House, noting that, although the population was decreasing, the great majority of the inhabitants of the territory were adult males prepared to accept more responsibility for the governing of their affairs. The people, he said, do not desire autonomy, but they do want representative institutions similar to those which "prevailed in the North-West Territories previous to the passage of the Autonomy Bills—a system of government under which their local affairs shall be attended to purely by local representatives in a legislative assembly." Borden supported Dr. Thompson, declaring that there was no reason to delay the establishment of popular government, particularly now that the new mining code would lend stability to the area.[40] Later, Oliver pointed out that the people had abandoned municipal government in Dawson, a fact which seemed to indicate a lack of interest in representative institutions. Although Thompson replied, telling the Minister that the citizens of Dawson had given up their local government only because it was too expensive,[41] he could secure no further promises from the government benches, and the issue was allowed to lapse.

In Dawson, Commissioner McInnes was warmly received when he returned from Ottawa in June, but shortly thereafter, when he convened Council for its annual session, the Y.I.P. councillors once more exhibited their determination to keep the issue of an elective council alive. They began with a motion to petition the government of Canada to establish a board, which would sit with the Commissioner during recess and advise him on all matters of public expenditure. After this motion was defeated, they presented another requesting that the cabinet introduce an amendment to the Yukon Act to provide for a wholly elective council. It, too, was lost on division, the vote in both cases being seven to three, with the appointed members and Lowe receiving support from Macaulay, the "Tab" representative.[42] Just a year before, the latter had sided with the Y.I.P. members, but now he claimed that "the country is going back, not forward," and that responsible government, which would undoubtedly accompany an elective council, would be too expensive.[43]

Apart from a motion, supported only by Black and Gillespie, calling upon the Governor in Council to revoke all hydraulic leases not cancelled earlier in the year,[44] the remainder of the session was quiet and harmonious. Unanimous consent was given two bills designed to alleviate problems that had heretofore plagued the territory.[45] One empowered the Commissioner to seek advisory opinions on the legality of proposed ordinances from the Territorial Court, thereby making unnecessary the expensive litigation that had followed previous legislation such as the 1903 miners' lien ordinance. The other made provision for voters' lists for Council elections, so that abuses that had accompanied the three previous territorial contests would not be repeated.

An interesting sidelight to Council's activities in 1906 was its promotion of a scheme to make more plentiful the supply of water on gold-bearing creeks, a plan which, if successful, would have proven far cheaper than the installation of a water system.[46] On March 1 the *News* reported that C. M. Hatfield, a well-known American rain maker, would be brought to the Klondike to use whatever means he had at his disposal to increase the rainfall. A board of seven—three to be chosen by Hatfield, three by the territorial government, and one by the other six—would decide whether or not more rain than usual had fallen, and, if so, Hatfield would be given $10,000, half from the territorial treasury and half from miners on the creeks. The rain maker and his assistant arrived early in June and, refusing to tell anyone what their process was, set up elaborate equipment about thirty miles from Dawson. During the July session of Council, the appropriation of $5,000 was unanimously approved, but less than a week after prorogation, the board of seven decided that there had been no appreciable increase in rainfall, and, thus, that the contract had not been carried out. The territorial government paid $1,153 to Hatfield in full settlement of its liability. The next year, in a Commons debate on the granting of an elective council to the Yukon, George Foster asked:

[What] . . . has made it impossible to carry out what otherwise would have been carried out—the giving of autonomy, in the way of power to elect their own Council, to the people of the Yukon? Maybe it was because the operations of that celebrated member of the administration, or high officer of the administration, the Dawson rainmaker did not turn out as well as the government thought he would, or well enough to justify the appropriation that was made. That was a disappointment, a sore disappointment. But I protest against such a thing as that operating to keep the people of the Yukon from having the right to elect their own council at as early a date as possible.[47]

His insinuations were questionable, for the charlatan had duped every member of Council, not just those elected by the people.

With the exception of the Hatfield episode, everything had gone well for McInnes during his first year in office, at least on the surface. But behind the scenes, a bitter struggle for power was gradually developing into a repetition of the troubles that had harassed the territory during Congdon's régime. Laurier received his first indications of what was to come when the Commissioner wrote him in June 1906, complaining that the *World*—ostensibly the government paper—had been running a series of articles which, signed by "Dawson," severely attacked the police. McInnes was certain that "Dawson" was "none other than Congdon," who, along with his immediate "party friends," hated the police because of the alleged support given Dr. Thompson by Major Wood in the 1904 election. The attitude of the "Tabs," he continued, was "largely due to social rivalries between certain leading families of both factions the 'Tabs' and the 'Steam Beers' and to ill-advised acts of administration, which were not calculated to cement our friends." However, McInnes concluded that the trouble would disappear because the *News* had just purchased the *World*.[48]

But the trouble was just beginning. C. H. Wells, President of the Yukon Territorial Liberal Association, wrote Laurier to condemn the manner in which McInnes was behaving. He began by noting that "straight" Liberals had wanted Congdon reappointed Commissioner, and were most upset when McInnes received the position and began to criticize his predecessor. Although Congdon and J. C. Noel had asked Wells and others to keep peace, the President felt that the time had come when they must speak up, because, despite a pledge not to do so, McInnes had transferred government printing patronage from the *World* to the *News*, thereby putting the loyal paper out of business, and had dismissed many loyal Liberals from the civil service. "His

vulgarity, insincerity, dishonesty, disregard of all interests but his own, open drunkenness, and notorious immorality have made him a stench in the nostrils of the community." Wells also forwarded a petition from the "Tabs" asking for McInnes'
dismissal and the reinstatement of loyal Liberals.[49]

After the Prime Minister questioned the Commissioner about the resolution and
Wells' charges, McInnes answered that he had heard nothing of either until they were
mentioned by Laurier and that he would like to come to Ottawa to discuss them
privately.[50] On November 1 the "Tab" Vice-President held a meeting at which the
earlier resolution was repudiated, and Wells was chastised for using the party name
in such an "unwarranted and unworthy manner."[51] Dr. Thompson also wrote in
support of the Commissioner, as did Duff Pattullo on behalf of the "Steam Beers,"
who, at a public meeting, had endorsed the Commissioner's regime wholeheartedly.[52]
When Wells wrote again, he claimed that McInnes himself had prompted the testi-
monials, and that the "Tab" meeting of November 1 was unauthorized by the true
Liberals of the territory.[53]

For the second time in two years, the Prime Minister was confronted by a strange
conflict among his followers in the Yukon, but on this occasion he was hearing more
than mere petty complaints from those who were not in receipt of government
patronage. McInnes' comments on "Tab" persecution of the police became somewhat
more understandable when Laurier received a letter from Fred White, Comptroller
of the Royal North-West Mounted Police, reporting that Major Wood wished to be
relieved of his Yukon command because he was placed in the middle of a struggle
between two opposing forces led by Judge Dugas and the Commissioner. Apparently
the senior judge of the Territorial Court had been severely critical of the Major's
attempts to suppress gambling, and had threatened to relax his enforcement of the
gambling law unless Wood authorized a raid on the dancehalls. McInnes, however,
favoured the dancehall interests, and was doing his utmost to prevent the police
from interfering with their operations.[54]

Early in November McInnes announced his intention to travel to Ottawa and,
before he departed, was tendered "the most elaborate and successful banquet ever
given in the Yukon," at which several speeches were made praising him and declaring
that he had been the greatest of all Yukon commissioners. The chief executive also
spoke, paying warm tribute to the loyal work of the civil service, to the honesty of
the press, and to the comparative harmony that now prevailed in the territory. The
Yukon, he said, "has really awakened to second and new life."[55] In December, after
he had seen the Prime Minister, McInnes wrote Lithgow, the Comptroller, to say he
had decided to resign in order to run in the forthcoming provincial election in British
Columbia.[56] The circumstances surrounding the resignation remain a mystery, although it is known that Sir Wilfrid was most concerned that charges against McInnes'
personal conduct would reach the floor of the House of Commons.[57] A few months
later, the government received another resignation—F. T. Congdon, who had remained in the service throughout McInnes' regime, gave up his position as Legal
Adviser and moved to Ottawa.[58]

During McInnes' year and a half as Commissioner, he, Alfred Thompson, and
Frank Oliver had done much to quell agitation against the federal and territorial
governments. Through their efforts, steps had been taken to open vast tracts of land
hitherto controlled by hydraulic concessionaires, to stabilize the mining regulations,
and to protect the wages of mine labourers. However, certain goals and problems

remained: no provisions had been made for an elective council, or for a water system, and the controversy over dancehalls and gambling—a confidential matter until the end of 1906—had the potential of a major public scandal. Signs pointed towards continued political conflict in the Yukon.

CHAPTER NINE

THE END OF AN ERA

ON HIS WAY "outside" in November 1906, W. W. B. McInnes remarked to a school teacher en route to the territorial capital: "there's no one left in Dawson. Everybody's leaving. I mean *everybody*."[1] The population exodus, rapid at the time of the Nome and Tanana discoveries, was becoming more pronounced than ever; the Yukon was approaching the end of an era founded on the gold rush and characterized by social, economic, and political unrest. Soon the territory would settle down to become a land forgotten by the rest of Canada. First, however, certain developments moderated much of the discontent that had permeated the community.

Following McInnes' resignation in January 1907, territorial politicians, for the fourth time in the short history of the territory, sought to exert some influence over the federal government's choice of a Commissioner. On January 5 the *Dawson Daily News*, now supported by the patronage of the territorial administration, announced that people were rushing to join the "bandwagon to give [J. T.] Lithgow [the Comptroller] the Commissionership." Ten days later, Lithgow's supporters convened a mass meeting "to select" a Commissioner. Before that topic was discussed, Colonel McGregor delivered an address in which he reviewed the history of mass meetings and the successes they had achieved, and Joe Clarke, on crutches as the result of a defeat in a boxing exhibition the previous night, "hobbled up [to the stage] to give his usual abuse." When a vote was taken on Lithgow, ninety-four opposed and seventy-five approved his choice, the majority of the 500 present not bothering to vote. The meeting broke up without recommending a successor to McInnes.[2]

On February 4 one Thomas Babcock called another mass meeting, at which four resolutions were "unanimously" approved by a large and representative assembly in the Pioneer Hall.[3] One resolved that "this meeting reiterates the expression given at the mass meeting held by the promoters of J. T. Lithgow's campaign for the commissionership in the A.B. Hall, and which was so misreported in the press of Dawson, and we say again that the appointment of Mr. J. T. Lithgow . . . [would bring about] a continuation of the unfortunate and unhappy McInnes regime." The other resolutions condemned the amalgamation of the *News* and the *World* as a means to apologize for the government and to misrepresent facts; requested that government employees be forbidden to interfere in territorial politics; and recommended the establishment of a new political party to represent the people of the Yukon. The "Tabs" also met, and, disapproving of Lithgow's candidacy, suggested that one of F. T. Congdon, J. E. Girouard, C. A. Dugas, A. Noel, and J. C. Noel receive the appointment.[4]

Private citizens also protested against Lithgow. The Rev. John Pringle, who, during 1903–4, had represented Klondike on the Yukon Council, and who had drafted the Babcock meeting's resolution on the Comptroller, wrote the Minister of the Interior:

I am ashamed to think that the impression will go abroad that the people of the Yukon are willing to have such a man as Lithgow as commissioner, much less to request the government to appoint him. His life here has been a public scandal, and while, if he were a private citizen, I should have nothing to say except to himself, as a public official and one evidently seeking the highest position in this territory *in the people's gift*, he is open to the judgement of every citizen.[5]

In March the Presbyterian clergyman began to write open letters to the press of Canada regarding the appointment of a Commissioner. The following appeared in the *Toronto News:*

[Give] . . . us a [commissioner] to whom a drunken orgy will be but an incident among other common-place incidents; who has no moral ideals, or has ceased to regard them; who will prostitute the moral and material interest of the people to private or party exigencies; who will lead a lewd life before the people whose interests he is appointed to serve; who is by habit . . . allied to the lowest elements of our social life . . . and discontent will persist and grow. . . . But give us a clean, sane, upright man, who will frown upon vice . . . and he will effect the contentment of the great mass of our people.[6]

Although Pringle's campaign was the beginning of a larger one against vice in the territorial administration, his private crusade had gone on for quite some time before.

In 1900, after being asked by some Maritime Liberals to write an account of the administration in the Yukon, the clergyman, who was not in the territory at the time, painted a glowing account of the progress the government had made since the gold rush. His statements were used extensively during the federal general election campaign of that year, but, a year later, when Pringle was transferred to Grand Forks, he began to feel some doubts about what he had written. On May 27, 1902, he wrote the Prime Minister and other cabinet ministers, declaring his support of the Liberal party but decrying the abuses he had witnessed in the Klondike. Although Ross had improved conditions, many officials, Pringle claimed, began to perpetrate excesses, particularly that of allowing gambling to reopen while the Commissioner was in Ottawa.[7] Laurier did not answer the communication. Three years later, after the Thompson–Congdon election, Pringle wrote again, complaining of loose morality in the administration and of flagrant corruption in both the 1902 and 1904 federal elections. "Things have gone from bad to worse under Mr. Congdon's administration. He has shown such a lack of moral strength in his relation to the public service and the public interests while commissioner, and his relations to the political interest of our people, before his appointment, and since his resignation to run for Parliament, that there has been a general uprising against him." Pringle referred specifically to the amendment of the liquor ordinance legalizing dancehalls as an example of Congdon's "lack of moral strength."[8]

This time, the Prime Minister responded, saying that all charges "will receive immediate attention from the departments concerned."[9] Pringle's letter was given to Congdon, who wrote a lengthy memorandum in reply to the complaints, claiming that "I had no more to do with any corruption . . . than Mr. Pringle, . . . [and] Mr. Pringle knows this," and stating that the clergyman's motive in writing was personal animosity owing to his failure to secure the Liberal nomination for the 1904 election. "With regard to the dancehall ordinance, it is somewhat surprising that neither in Council of which Mr. Pringle was a member, nor upon the public platform has he ventured publicly to condemn that which he now desires secretly to criticise."[10] In actual fact, Pringle had not attended the 1904 session, although, in a debate on liquor regulations in 1903, he had said: "While I may be an extremist on the liquor question,

I am opposed to any kind of legislation that runs too far ahead of public sentiment."[11] Thus, he had placed himself in the position, perhaps to advance his political career, of privately abhorring vice, yet of publicly tolerating it.

In 1906, on learning of Congdon's memorandum, Pringle asked the Minister of the Interior to send him a copy, but Oliver replied that he was unaware of the existence of such a document.[12] Then, on July, 31, 1907, dissatisfaction with this and other government responses provoked Pringle to write again to Sir Wilfrid: "Dancehalls and bawdy houses are the natural concomitants of the presence in our administrative life of unashamed male prostitutes. I have resolved, if this continues as at present, to state the case in the plainest terms in the eastern press, without regard to the notoriety and discomfort which such disclosures may bring to myself."[13] Actually, he had begun his campaign of newspaper criticism a few months earlier when he wrote his open letter asking for a "clean, sane, and upright commissioner," implying thereby that previous chief executives and the main aspirant for the position (Lithgow) did not meet these qualifications. Now, however, he started to cite specific charges of immorality against Yukon officials, singling out Lithgow and J. E. Girouard.[14]

Before Pringle wrote his July letter, the government had appointed Alexander Henderson, formerly Attorney General of British Columbia and a county court judge, as Commissioner of the Yukon Territory.[15] Soon after his arrival in Dawson, Henderson announced that he would work towards "the moral and material betterment" of the Yukon, and would begin by inducing Council to abolish dancehalls.[16] In reading Pringle's heretofore general attack on administrative morality, the new Commissioner had probably noted the clergyman's reference to these Klondike institutions: "Nor is it to be overlooked that the legalizing of the added attraction [prostitution] in these . . . houses is an injustice to those who are in the legitimate liquor business, and a discrimination—I am almost ashamed to write this—against the much less dangerous houses in Klondike City."[17] The Council Henderson had to face was changed in composition from the one McInnes had met, for, in the interval between the appearance of Pringle's first letters to the press and the new Commissioner's arrival, there had been another territorial election campaign, one in which abolition of dancehalls was an issue.

The election, on April 16, was the quietest the Yukon had ever experienced. Robert Lowe was re-elected by acclamation in Whitehorse, and all other candidates (see Table II) were nominated as independents, with the exception of George Black, who

TABLE II

FINAL RESULTS IN TERRITORIAL ELECTION, APRIL 16, 1907*

NORTH DAWSON		BONANZA	
J. O. LaChapelle	160	T. Kearney	129
J. A. Clarke	120	R. Gillespie	93
G. Vernon	28	R. L. Ashbaugh	49
SOUTH DAWSON		KLONDIKE	
John Grant	158	G. Black	335
F. Lowe	126	J. McGrath	226
A. Lobley	117		

* Compiled from *Dawson Daily News*, April 30 and May 1, 1907. The names of the winning candidates are italicized.

was chosen by a convention of the Yukon Independent Party.[18] However, despite the absence of formal affiliations, LaChapelle and Ashbaugh were supporters of Black, and Lobley and Gillespie of Joe Clarke, Black and Clarke having failed to reconcile the differences between them that had first appeared in the 1905 election.[19] The old rift in Liberal ranks was apparent as well in the nominations of "Tabs" Vernon and Grant "Steam Beers" F. Lowe and Kearney, although the two factions opposed one another only in South Dawson.

Unlike previous territorial campaigns, the 1907 contest lasted only two weeks, during which just one public meeting was held for the candidates. An elective council, better mail services, and reduced freight rates, none of which became contested issues, were the sole federal reforms sought by the Council aspirants; the only local matters raised were the abolition of dancehalls and the inauguration of a nine-hour working week, both advanced by Clarke and Lobley and either criticized or ignored by their opponents. As always, personal abuse dominated proceedings.[20] The *News*, the only newspaper still publishing in Dawson, made only one editorial reference to the campaign when it declared its support for Black and LaChapelle,[21] a stand which, in the light of the claim of the February 4 mass meeting that the paper was whitewashing the government, was surprising because the two men were basically anti-administration candidates.

The results of the contests, in which 57 per cent of the eligible voters participated, are given in Table II.[22] Two "Steam Beers" (Lowe and Kearney), two Black Conservatives (Black and LaChapelle), and one "Tab" (Grant) secured election. The *News*, however, felt that party affiliations and issues had been insignificant: "In all districts the vote was small. There was no public question before the voters in which the whole of the community was interested and upon which it might be divided in opinion. . . . The people voted for their friends."[23] If the *News* were correct, the 1907 election demonstrated the phenomenon of "friends and neighbours voting" observed by Professor V. O. Key, Jr., in many Democratic primaries in the southern United States.[24]

When the new Council met, Henderson, true to his prime objective, persuaded Judge Dugas to propose an amendment to the liquor ordinance prohibiting dance-halls from serving intoxicants and from having connections with licensed premises.[25] The judge, apparently obstructed by McInnes in his previous efforts to curtail the activities of dancehalls, took great relish in guiding the bill through Council. Although he met strong opposition from Robert Lowe, who proposed a motion to defer action on the matter until 1908, and from Lithgow, who requested an amendment to give dancehall proprietors time to make preparations, the bill was passed on division.[26] After the ordinance was given assent, the "M & N" and "Floradora" music halls continued to operate on a "temperance basis," but the former soon closed down owing to poor patronage.[27]

Mr. Pringle, however, was still not content, and, even though Oliver promised to ask Henderson to investigate all charges laid against Lithgow, Girouard, and any other official in the employ of the government,[28] the clergyman's letters to the "outside" press continued. On November 8 the Commissioner, reporting that Pringle would not agree to an informal investigation, requested the appointment of a commission with full powers to summon and protect witnesses, but Oliver replied that the Inquiries Act could not be construed to allow a formal investigation of charges of private misconduct.[29] The matter was dropped from the official point of view after

Henderson wired the Minister: "I can unhesitatingly affirm that the Yukon including Dawson is as moral in all respects as any other part of Canada"; the telegram was printed in several Canadian newspapers.[30] In January 1908, Pringle unleashed another of his tirades, stating that the laws against prostitution and gambling, and the liquor ordinance were not being properly enforced.[31] As if in reply, Mr. Justice Craig, mentioning no names, condemned those who made statements reflecting upon moral standards in the territory, and the Dawson Board of Trade passed a resolution specifically denouncing Pringle's activities.[32] When the clergyman subsequently accused the Board of bending to the wishes of Henderson, the President of the Board and the Commissioner promptly denied this charge.[33] Finally, on March 29, after delivering his last sermon in the Klondike, Pringle departed for the "outside."[34]

However, the furore he had created was far from over. On June 2 George Foster, in possession of a return of all correspondence between Pringle and the federal cabinet, brought the whole affair before the House of Commons. Using the 1902 letter and those that followed, he proceeded to demonstrate what he claimed was government negligence in not correcting the abuses of which Pringle had complained. Many Liberal and Conservative members spoke to rebut and to augment what Foster had said, but probably the best reply to opposition criticism came from a Liberal Member of Parliament who noted that, if moral and administrative conditions were as bad as Foster maintained, Dr. Thompson, elected as an independent and not as a friend of the government, would have spoken on the subject during his four years in the House.[35] Thompson had no chance to speak in the debate, for, confident of a pending dissolution, he had left for the Yukon in March.[36]

Back in Dawson, Pringle's behaviour became a major issue during Council's deliberations in July. Dr. LaChapelle, seconded by John Grant, moved:

That this Council expresses in the strongest terms its regret that Mr. Pringle should have entered upon a deliberate campaign of exaggerated calumny and slander and should now be so industriously engaged in villifying those with whom he lately associated in pretended amity and esteem and from whom he has received for ten years past, support, maintenance and comfort; [and] that this Council expresses its approval of the action of the Commissioner in forwarding [the] telegram [to the Minister of the Interior] and its belief that the Yukon Territory and Dawson will compare favorably with any part of America and with any town in the respect paid to law and order, the regard for morality and observance of all social, commercial, legal and religious conventions, decencies and amenities.

In proposing the motion, LaChapelle said that, although he would have supported Pringle "if he had roasted the government on other things," the crusade had been more damaging to the reputation of the people of the Yukon than that of the administration. George Black disagreed, and declared that, as a result of "this motion to purify the Liberals," his fellow Conservative had allowed himself to become a tool of the government. The debate reached a climax when John Grant exclaimed that "Mr. Pringle is a puritanical hypocrite and a coat of tar and feathers would fit him better than the praise which has been accorded him on the outside." The member for South Dawson then introduced an affidavit, signed by a prostitute, alleging that the clergyman had behaved improperly. Black succeeded in having the document withdrawn, but failed to persuade Council to defeat the motion of censure. On division, only Black voted against it. Ena Girouard was not present at the session, because, following the criticism he received at the hands of Mr. Pringle, he had resigned his office of Registrar to resume his law practice in Arthabaskaville.[37]

By the end of 1908 the Pringle crusade had disappeared from public interest, but not before the clergyman, in a sense, had the last word. At the general meeting of the Presbyterian Church of Canada, he was honoured with a resolution praising his "fearless denunciation of vice."[38] The Pringle affair was a strange episode in the history of the Yukon because it occurred not during the gold rush and its aftermath when "vice" was commonplace, but at a time when the territory had lost much of its earlier frontier character. Nevertheless, Pringle did manage to bring the dancehall era to a close, for the last of the "dens of iniquity"—the "Floradora," unable to sustain its business by selling soft drinks—closed its doors early in 1908.[39]

While social conditions in the Yukon occupied public attention, significant changes were taking place in the economic life of the territory. The agitation against the hydraulic concessions had been successful, but the simple techniques of gold mining unavoidably gave way to more advanced methods of extraction. The transformation, first noticeable in the final months of Ross's regime, had advanced to such a stage by 1908 that the *Canadian Annual Review* reported: "The glamour of the Yukon has passed, the days of the individual miner and the romance of great fortunes picked up in a week, have altogether gone. In ... [the past year] it was a question of organized mining on a large scale with large companies and much capital. ... Dredge-working, hydraulicking, and the efforts of applied science in quartz mining [have] replaced the placer diggings."[40] Strangely enough, A. N. C. Treadgold, once looked upon as the symbol of a vicious plot to ruin the country, was instrumental in bringing about the transition to large-scale mining, which, if it did not sustain the economy at previous levels, did effect an increase in gold production (see Appendix B), and thus prevented a complete collapse. He persuaded the Guggenheim interests in New York to invest in the Klondike, and in 1906 the Yukon Gold Company was formed with a capitalization of $17.5 million.[41] By means of the consolidated mining code passed by Parliament that year, the Guggenheims and other smaller interests were able to group claims in order to begin hydraulicking and dredging operations.[42] Furthermore, they constructed ditches and dams, which provided sufficient water and hydro-electric power to make operations worthwhile in the years to come.[43] The problem of transportation to the creeks was solved by the construction of Klondike Mines Railway Company. Its principle promoter and first general manager was Tom O'Brien, the former Yukon councillor, who years before had been the villain of the Grand Forks tramway scandal.[44]

Some Yukon residents, mostly in the business community, were unwilling to admit that the days of profitable individual mining had come to an end. In August 1908 a group of Dawson merchants prominent in the Board of Trade met to found the "Merchants' and Miners' Association." Declaring that the Klondike was the last region in the world where a man could reap mineral wealth "without expensive machinery or workings costing large sums," the organizers opened offices in Dawson and on the creeks to distribute free information about mining opportunities, particularly in areas where claims lay deserted. However, despite an initial outburst of enthusiasm, the members must have soon realized the futility of their task, for the association had ceased to function before the year ended.[45]

The year 1908 brought to an end the persistent agitation of the press, pressure groups, and political parties for a wholly elective Yukon council—a goal which had been sought ever since Lord Minto's visit to the Klondike in 1900. Dr. Thompson had raised the issue again early in the 1907 session of Parliament. After assuring the House that he was not requesting complete provincial autonomy he demonstrated that the matter was not a partisan one when he read a petition from the Yukon

Liberal Association calling for the constitutional change. With respect to the present Council, Thompson said:

It is not sufficiently representative. . . . The five members who are appointed draw salaries as occupants of various positions under the government, and they are, therefore, necessarily not as closely in touch with the people as would be men who were elected directly by the people. This is the only territory in all this vast Dominion which has not full and complete autonomy, the only portion of Canada that has not directly representative institutions. . . . I submit to the government the propriety of widening the Yukon Council so that it will be composed hereafter of men who directly represent the people from the various portions of the territory, and I can assure you, Mr. Speaker, and this government, and the people of this country, that if that boon is given it will not be abused.

Frank Oliver replied: "we may take it for granted that the pending 1907 election will be the last that will be held in the Yukon where a council not fully elective will be chosen."[46]

After prorogation, Dr. Thompson, in an article on the government of the Yukon, noted that the territory would soon have an elective council, which, when constituted, would render "the government . . . not only . . . representative, but responsible as well."[47] However, if he meant "responsible government" in the British sense of the term, he must have been disappointed when the Minister of the Interior introduced a bill to amend the Yukon Act in May 1908. When given assent, the amendment created a separation of powers through its provisions to remove the Commissioner from Council, to make a council of ten members fully elective, and to give each, respectively, a monopoly over executive and legislative powers. The Commissioner, granted the powers of reservation and disallowance over Council legislation, was to continue his administration of federal responsibilities on advice from Ottawa, and to retain his supervision over employees of the Canadian and Yukon governments; the representatives of the people, prohibited from considering financial legislation not recommended by the chief executive, were to have control—but no initiative—over the public purse, power to conduct their proceedings as they saw fit under their own speaker, and freedom to legislate on non-financial matters. The act also provided a three-year term for Council, but gave the Commissioner power to dissolve it and call a new election at any time.[48]

Although it has been suggested that the constitutional change was inspired by American institutions,[49] that assumption is incorrect. The new formal relationship between the Commissioner and the Council was similar to that between the governor and the legislature in any British system of government. The anomaly, a separation of powers, arose from the actual relationship prescribed between the two institutions: the chief executive was barred from the proceedings of a council that was made fully representative but not responsible. When the time came in other evolving British constitutions for the governor or some other representative of the metropolitan government to cease deliberating with the legislature, a link was always provided by the establishment of an embryonic cabinet that was permitted to exercise, fully or partially, executive powers delegated to it. By not allowing for the development of cabinet government, the framers of the amendment created a hybrid system half-way between two British constitutional patterns. Thus, it may be concluded that, although the new arrangement was based firmly on British rather than American precedents, it did represent a departure from tradition in so far as it failed to make all the changes required to advance the government of the territory from one constitutional stage to another.

Once before, a federal ministry had drafted a constitution similar to the one provided for the Yukon in 1908. In 1888, faced with persistent demands from political activists in the North-West Territories, the government of Sir John A. Macdonald had found it expedient to grant a fully elective legislature without conferring responsible government. However, at that time, a plea from a private member prevented the adoption of a separation of powers and led to the creation of an advisory council on finance, which served as a bridge between the Lieutenant Governor and the Legislative Assembly and allowed for the gradual emergence of a cabinet.[50]

Unfortunately, no one in 1908 was able to persuade the Laurier cabinet that the proposed amendment to the Yukon Act was inconsistent with a system of government based on the Westminster model. George Foster attempted to do so:

It seems a little peculiar to have the people elect their own representatives to do their legislation and then have the whole of the administration vested in some one appointed by the Crown. . . . We elect our representatives and we have a Governor General, but he does not do the administration. The representatives act through a cabinet, and they really do the administration and legislation, of course divided off by a sharp . . . division between the two. . . . [But] here you have a gulf between the two. The people . . . can only go as far as legislation.[51]

In the upper house, Senator Lougheed pointed out another difficulty:

[Suppose] . . . the commissioner . . . as the representative of the federal government . . . and the elective council . . . would not be able to agree . . . as to the expenditure of supplies, what would be the result? The result will be that there is no body such as the cabinet responsible to the assembly itself, because the members who are elected to represent the entire territory will naturally maintain whatever policies they may decide upon, even against the commissioner. The commissioner is then vested with authority to . . . dissolve the assembly, and to bring on another election. . . . Can my hon. friend give the Chamber any information as to why the government stopped short in adopting the same system of government which we have in the other [sic] provinces of Canada?[52]

Senator R. W. Scott, the Secretary of State, replied:

It would be rather a farce—perhaps that is too strong a word—to invest a community of that kind with powers given to a province. The population of the . . . territory is less than 10,000. Surely it would be making a toy of government if you were to give all the ceremonial incident to the constitution of a province to a community of that number.[53]

Oliver had given virtually the same answer, although in less colourful terms, to Foster in the House of Commons.[54]

It is true that the Yukon by 1908 did not warrant the establishment of responsible government: the population had dwindled from over 27,000 in 1901 to less than 10,000; gold production had fallen rapidly since 1900; federal subsidies to the territorial treasury had mounted year by year in proportion to other revenues;[55] and the civil service (under the regimes of McInnes and Henderson) had been reduced to a skeleton of its former self.[56] However, the bizarre form of government granted by the 1908 amendment proved more unsatisfactory than the previous arrangement. In the years that followed, the major difficulty confronting the system was the absence of any leadership provided in, and accountable to, Council. Apart from non-financial bills, which, as everywhere, were few, all pieces of legislation came before the Council on the initiative of the Commissioner, who, if they were defeated, was not compelled to resign. If a stalemate were reached, the only solution was compromise, the chief executive being armed with the weapon of threatening dissolution and the councillors with that of refusing supply. Accountability was also missing in territorial elections, wherein, even if the candidates ran on party tickets, the voters could not determine

D

responsibility because incumbents lacked the power to achieve positive goals and were thus free of the rigidities imposed by party platforms and whips. Furthermore, the absence of direct confrontation between the Commissioner and Council meant that, apart from written questions directed to the chief executive by the Speaker, there was no free flow of information—so vital to the working of responsible government—concerning the feasibility of certain projects and the nature of administrative activities. Of these three problems, the first (at least, to a degree) and the third had not existed under the old constitutional scheme.

Partly because they could not foresee the problems that would arise, but mostly because of apathy, the men who fought so hard for an elective council and an increase in popular control over government did not seem upset by the compromise Oliver and his colleagues effected. Even Dr. Thompson, who was not in Ottawa when the amendment was debated, said he regretted that the changes had not been more sweeping, "but it is better to have half a loaf than none at all."[57] His attitude was symbolic of a gradual change that had occurred in the political life of the Yukon— the fiery reforming zeal of the early days was gone. Fifty years were to pass before the territory made further progress towards responsible government.

As 1908 drew to a close, the Yukon experienced an election campaign that also seemed to symbolize that change. The prize at stake was the seat in the House of Commons, because, following dissolution of the third Parliament under the Laurier ministry, Alfred Thompson had decided not to seek re-election.[58] Like the two previous federal contests, the 1908 campaign took place in the dead of winter, and the political climate it produced was almost hot enough to offset the icy blasts of that intemperate season. But there was a difference—the major goals (which admittedly were never electoral issues) had disappeared, and in their place only the name-calling was left. For a campaign of personal abuse, four better candidates than F. T. Congdon, Robert Lowe, George Black, and Joe Clarke would have been hard to find.[59] Congdon, who had since returned from Ottawa, was the "Tab" nominee, and the other three represented the "Steam Beers," the Conservatives, and the Clarke Conservatives respectively. Such matters as better mail services, abolition of the export tax on placer gold, investigation of the remaining concessions, and cheaper transportation facilities were raised, but, for the most part, the campaign amounted to Congdon versus the other three, and Black versus Clarke. All the "dirty linen" surrounding both Congdon's regime as Commissioner and the break-up of the Liberal and Conservative parties was aired again and again.[60] The reasons for the intra-party conflicts had disappeared, but the squabbles themselves persisted. Like the lone prospectors and miners still on the creeks after the transition to large-scale mining, the candidates were living in the past.

On January 19, 1909, some three months after Sir Wilfrid Laurier had been returned for a fourth consecutive term of office, the people of the Yukon exercised their franchise. Despite a bitter campaign on the part of the press and other candidates against him, Frederick Tennyson Congdon won the day,[61] and did so without the flagrant corruption for which he had been blamed in the elections of 1902 and 1904. The people had spoken, and, shortly thereafter, Joseph Andrew Clarke, an embittered man, left the territory for the last time—a fitting climax to a decade of political agitation.[62]

It may seem questionable to infer from the course of history in a region that a particular time marked a turning point in its development, but occurrences during the years 1907 and 1908 do seem to represent the end of an era in the Yukon. The closure of licensed dancehalls, the introduction of large-scale mining techniques, and the grant of a fully representative council all wrought significant changes in the life of the territory. Events in the succeeding eleven years re-enforced these changes and made their initial impact irrevocable. A brief glance at this next period will serve to conclude and place in perspective the story of the political aftermath of the Klondike gold rush.

CHAPTER TEN

STAGNATION AND DECLINE

THE SOCIAL, economic, and constitutional transformation that had occurred in the Yukon by the end of 1908 brought about a dramatic alteration in the nature of territorial political conflict. In the years that followed, the impact of continued economic uncertainty, technological change, and population decline, together with that of external events, made the victories achieved through earlier political agitation seem irrelevant to new conditions. By 1920 the wealth of the Klondike, even though augmented by the profits of copper and silver mining elsewhere in the territory,[1] proved insufficient to support the governmental structures that had grown up in response to the gold rush.

On New Year's Day 1909 the editor of the *Dawson Daily News* exclaimed that the "Yukon territory stands on the verge of its most successful era. With triumphs in material wealth at which to point with pride during an eleven years of active production which have passed, the country has a future which will pale into insignificance the output of the first decade." Perhaps his optimism was genuine for short-run economic prospects were indeed encouraging: gold production had risen in 1908 for the first time since 1900, and a spokesman for the Grand Trunk Pacific Railway had indicated recently that his company would at last provide an all-Canadian route to the Yukon.[2] However, despite the fact that gold output increased steadily (if slowly) until 1914, the territorial economy failed to make satisfactory advances. Moreover, the plans to build a railway, which might have given lumber, coal, base metals, and other products from the Yukon access to southern markets, were doomed to oblivion in the aftermath of the Canadian recession of 1913 when the Canadian Northern and Grand Trunk railway systems began to suffer financial collapse.

As the result of a net loss of people through migration and a high number of deaths in relation to births (phenomena closely associated with economic stagnation), the population continued to decline rapidly. Probably the sharpest decreases occurred in the period after 1913 when gold production fell each year and many men left the Yukon to help meet Canada's manpower requirements for World War I.[3] By 1921 there were only 4,157 residents (including 1,475 Indians) in the territory, less than one-half the number recorded ten years earlier.[4]

There was a qualitative change in the population as well. The smaller nucleus of permanent residents, all more mature after the rush and no longer imbued with that spirit of egalitarianism which tends to accompany a frontier situation, had become more stratified socially, so that men who once might have led political movements seemed content with membership in Dawson's upper social circle. Exclusive literary societies and a gay round of parties, dances, and receptions replaced earlier forms of entertainment, including the mass meeting.[5] Perhaps the change was partly due to the increasing role women were playing in what had been a man's country. Certainly their impact was apparent in 1920 when, newly enfranchised, they were powerful enough to secure passage of a plebiscite binding Council to pass an ordinance that prohibited the sale of intoxicating liquors except for medicinal purposes.[6] The result must have horrified some people who remembered the Klondike in its "wide-open" days at the turn of the century.

From 1909 to 1918 the only significant political activity apart from election campaigns and Council sessions centred around the freight rates of the White Pass and Yukon Route. Although the company had reduced its charges in 1907, some territorial residents still thought them exhorbitant. In June 1909 a mass meeting petitioned the Board of Railway Commissioners to take action against the W.P.Y.R., and, later that year, the Dawson Board of Trade, following a well-established precedent, formed a "citizens' committee" to keep the issue before the public and the federal government.[7] The committee held several meetings, but, apart from merchants, it did not attract many enthusiastic recruits to its cause. The grounds for complaints seem finally to have been removed in 1911 when the W.P.Y.R. acted on orders from the Board of Railway Commissioners and made substantial reductions in freight rates and passenger fares over the Canadian sections of its line.[8]

In keeping with the trend established in the territorial election of 1907 and the federal one of 1908–9, candidates in the later period did not use electoral campaigns to place before the public important goals for territorial development; in common with all previous contests, they succeeded more in generating heat than in shedding light. Only the federal elections of 1911 and 1917–18 aroused much interest in the populace. In the first one, the traditional deferred balloting in the territory actually came as an anticlimax to the general results, for on September 22, 1911, one month before they were to choose a member of Parliament for the Yukon, voters in Dawson read in the *News* that Laurier's Liberals had been defeated and were to be replaced in office by Borden's Conservatives. Mrs. Laura Berton recalled her impressions of the event:

What celebrating there was that night. . . . Within an hour of victory the Tories had every possible party worker (and some impossible ones) slated for coveted jobs so long held by the enemy. These jobs included everything from commissioner to ditch digger. The election results had hardly been posted before Liberal jobholders were leaping aboard the winter stage and leaving the Territory forever, many of them without even going through the formality of resigning. The next stage (or so it seemed to me) was jammed with Conservatives pouring back into the country. . . . George Black and all the others who had left . . . more than a year before on the last boat, ostensibly forever, were now preparing to return in triumph.[9]

Alexander Henderson had already resigned as Commissioner a few months before, but his temporary replacement, Arthur Wilson (who had left the ranks of the "opposition" to take a government job during Congdon's regime), and several other Liberal appointees did lose their positions.[10] But, while the Conservatives were at last able to benefit from Yukon patronage, the "pork barrel" was much smaller than in the days of Liberal rule. Of the few jobs available, George Black received the biggest prize—the commissionership.[11]

Flushed with the success of their party, the territorial Tories quickly organized to ensure that the Yukon seat in the House of Commons would be theirs as well. Alfred Thompson was persuaded to come out of political retirement to face the incumbent, F. T. Congdon.[12] While the two candidates conducted their campaigns on federal issues—primarily, of course, reciprocity—their supporters delivered lively speeches of personal abuse. Thompson was accused of failing to fulfil his mandate in the

House of Commons between 1904 and 1908, and Congdon was condemned again for his behaviour as Commissioner during the years 1903–4. T. W. O'Brien, who supported Thompson in the absence of a "Steam Beer" candidate, still complained that Congdon had ruined his brewing company eight years before.[13] In the end, on October 23, the doctor won fairly easily, probably more as a result of the Conservative victory a month earlier than of any platform differences or attacks on his opponent.[14]

Early in 1918 Thompson and Congdon faced each other in another deferred election, this one in unusual circumstances: World War I had entered its fifth year and Canadian unity had just been severely strained by an electoral campaign fought over the issue of conscription. Yet, despite the gravity of these international and national troubles, the contest in the Yukon degenerated into a farce. Not only were there no policy differences—that was usual—but both men ran as Unionists in support of Prime Minister Borden. In most other federal constituencies, the sitting member, providing he supported conscription, was chosen as the Unionist candidate irrespective of his previous party affiliation. The exceptional situation in the Yukon arose from Congdon's curious, though not surprising, behaviour. After the sweeping Unionist victory, the former Commissioner, who had intended to contest the election as a Laurier Liberal (against conscription), decided that his chances of victory would be better if he ran in the name of the "People's" Unionist Association.[15] Claiming that Dr. Thompson's nomination by the "Territorial" Unionist Association had represented only Tory opinion, Congdon declared that he was the only candidate truly committed to non-partisan government in a time of crisis.[16]

Virtually devoid of argument over future policies or territorial problems, the campaign consisted of repetitious insinuations by the two men against one another. Thompson, accused by Congdon of receiving personal government favours, denied the truth of all such charges, and went on to attack his opponent's former views on conscription as unpatriotic and anti-English. He also repeated his claim of 1911 that it was in the best interests of the Yukon to be represented by a government supporter, and predicted that Congdon, if elected, would not dare desert his old political mentor, Sir Wilfrid Laurier. Congdon in turn defended himself against allegations of disloyalty and dishonesty, and, although condemning the Conservative government of 1911–17 for its corruption and inefficiency, affirmed his loyalty to the new Unionist administration.[17]

Confronted with a rather absurd choice, voters in the Yukon went to the polls on January 28 and cast 54 per cent of their ballots for F. T. Congdon.[18] Nevertheless, four months later, Alfred Thompson was declared their Member of Parliament by a vote on division in the Canadian House of Commons. That odd turn of events occurred as a result of the rather difficult problem of distributing the votes of Yukon soldiers for and against Borden's government between two men who both claimed to be Unionist candidates. After an initial period of confusion, the Commons, by a majority decision, chose to assign Thompson the Unionist ballots and Congdon the Laurier Liberal ones, thereby turning the doctor's defeat of 110 into a victory of 10.[19] Thus, although politics may have been quieter in the 1910s than they were in the 1900s, they were certainly as bizarre.

Ironic as it may seem in view of the intensity of the struggle that had culminated in 1908 with the constitution of a fully representative Yukon Council, little interest was evinced in the four territorial elections that took place between 1909 and 1918. Party politics, always present (at least informally) in legislative proceedings but seldom in electoral contests, were introduced by the "Tabs" in the 1909 campaign and adhered to by both the Liberals and Conservatives in 1915 and 1917, although not in 1912. Nevertheless, major policy differences were not presented to the voters, mostly (as has been noted above) because of the absence of any provisions (legal or conventional) placing responsibility upon the councillors for government actions, past or future.[20]

In Council itself, the movement for some degree of responsible government did continue for the first two sessions after the election of 1909. Unfortunately, the full story of the campaign, spearheaded by George Black, to give a committee of councillors a share of the Commissioner's powers over recruiting, promoting, and dismissing personnel in the territorial establishment cannot be recounted in this short survey of events in the second decade of the Yukon's existence. It is sufficient to note that the attempt failed in 1911 when the federal cabinet in effect disallowed legislation that, among other provisions, would have dismissed the Territorial Treasurer and replaced him with another man.[21] After this failure to secure an executive role for Council or a committee of its members, the territorial legislature, apart from sending memorials to the federal government on a few issues, ceased to act independently.[22] Even when George Black, a self-declared champion of the people's rights, became Commissioner in 1912, no advance towards self-government was made. (Black's only major innovation was the addition of an element of vice-regal ceremony to the proceedings of Council through his delivery at the beginning of each session of a formal address outlining the administration's programme.[23]) Thus it may be said that 1911 marked the end of the crusade in the Yukon for increased popular control over public affairs.

To digress briefly, it may be noted that, although the size of Council varied considerably as time passed and economic conditions changed,[24] it was not until 1960 that steps were taken to introduce a greater measure of responsibility into the governmental system. This time, the changes came not at the behest of the people, but from the action of federal authorities concerned about the stultifying impact of the gulf between the executive and the legislature. Two innovations were introduced: an advisory committee on finance was constituted to give the elected members some influence, if not control, over the expenditure of territorial revenues; and the restriction barring the Commissioner from Council deliberations was removed to enable the councillors to obtain information, advice, and assistance from the man whose over-all responsibility it is to implement their legislation.[25] Late in 1966 certain territorial politicians began to re-echo the demands of their early twentieth-century forerunners for responsible government and provincial status; however, at the time of writing (1968), they had not secured any definite promises of federal government action.[26]

Although the struggle for responsible government had receded into the background after 1911, it did come as a shock to residents of the territory to read in the *News'* editions of March 23 and April 5, 1918, that Arthur Meighen, the Unionist Minister of the Interior, had decided to abolish the Council and the office of Commissioner, to close several government buildings in Dawson, and to cut the federal grant to the territorial administration from $320,000 to $185,000. Yukoners were by this time accustomed to the gradual measures being taken to reduce the size and scope of public services, but no one seemed aware that economic deterioration and population decline had occurred much more rapidly than had efforts to cut back territorial expenditures and institutions to a level consonant with economic and social realities. Commissioner Black, who might have directed a strong complaint to Meighen, had left the Yukon in

1916 to serve in the war overseas.[27] The Gold Commissioner, G. P. Mackenzie, who was acting as chief executive, could not provide any information about the proposed changes to bewildered Yukon councillors who had just convened for their annual session. Uncertain even of their legal position, they telegraphed the following message to the Minister of the Interior: "Members of the Yukon council request that before drastic changes are made in the government and administration of the territory that the Yukon council be given opportunity to express an opinion regarding the same, as this council is uninformed as to the changes or those proposed to be made."[28] They did not receive an immediate reply, and for days it appears that the only details concerning federal intentions came from a correspondent who telegraphed dispatches to the *Dawson Daily News*. His first report, indicating that the territorial administration would be moved to Ottawa, was later contradicted by another which added that the existing Council would be replaced by a nominated one.[29]

Then, on April 8 the cabinet introduced a bill to amend the Yukon Act to Parliament, where the territory was temporarily unrepresented because of the controversy following the federal election earlier in the year. The bill proposed giving the Governor in Council powers to abolish the present Council, to constitute an appointive body in its place, and to do away with any offices created under the provisions of the act.[30] In effect, the Minister of the Interior would be given a free hand to remould the governmental structures of the territory.

For one month, political activity in the Yukon began to take on the appearance of campaigns years before, but this time the people involved were on the defensive. On April 12 the *News*, in an editorial noting that the Yukon was making the highest per capita contribution to the war effort of all Canadian provinces and territories, decried the proposals to remove representative institutions and to decrease the federal appropriation by 40 per cent.[31] Not long afterwards, the mass meeting again came into prominence when a group of businessmen invited the public to attend a meeting which would "suggest larger grants than has been intimated the Yukon will receive." At the gathering, addressed by, among others, Congdon, a "citizens' committee" was constituted and a telegram sent to Meighen imploring him to defer a final decision on the Yukon estimates until a longer message was sent to him.[32] A few days later, a petition, pointing with pride to the territory's participation in World War I, was sent to the Minister asking him to increase proposed expenditures in the territory so that satisfactory roads and educational facilities could be maintained. A further petition pointed out that the closure of public buildings would have a most damaging effect upon commerce in Dawson.[33]

As the agitation continued to grow, Council found its work paralysed: it could not approve a budget until it received word from Ottawa on whether it still had a right to deliberate and on whether its appeal for a smaller reduction in federal subsidy had been met. On April 14 councillors did learn from the correspondent of the *News* that they were still legally entitled to legislate for the territory, but they had to wait until April 30 before receiving a message from Meighen which indicated that the grant could not be raised above the $185,000 originally promised.[34] Acting on the advice of the Gold Commissioner, Council began to conduct the painful process of reducing estimates and finding alternative means of revenue. Then on May 4 the news came that the federal cabinet, as soon as the enabling legislation was passed, definitely intended to abolish the Council and the office of Commissioner in favour of a simple form of government by the Gold Commissioner, perhaps assisted by an advisory committee of

Yukon residents and civil servants. In response, Council unanimously passed a memorial—to be forwarded to the Prime Minister, the Leader of the Opposition, and all Ministers—requesting that the present representatives be allowed to fulfil the final year of their mandate and that the number of councillors should then be reduced from ten to five. The submission concluded: "any other form of government than that of representative government would be unsatisfactory and repugnant to the people of this territory, the large majority of whom are British subjects."[35] After prorogation, the *News* commented with a note of remorse that the "Yukon council yesterday closed its deliberations for the session, and apparently that notable body never again will be assembled."[36] Having received scanty attention in the two Houses of Parliament, the amendment bill was given royal assent shortly thereafter.[37]

Despite the initial concern that it generated, the issue of retrenchment became dormant until the winter of 1918–19 when Mr. Mackenzie, the Gold Commissioner, and Dr. Thompson, the Yukon's Member of Parliament, held several lengthy conferences with Meighen. The resulting compromise was reasonably satisfactory to the residents of the territory who by now were expecting the worst: the Minister agreed to continue utilizing government buildings in Dawson, to allow the present councillors to complete their terms of office, and to retain a fully representative council, albeit of only three members; however, several public offices, including that of Commissioner, were abolished, and the Gold Commissioner was constituted chief executive of the territory.[38]

Although this confrontation between the people in the Yukon and the federal government did save representative institutions and momentarily slow down the pace of administrative contraction, it did not slacken the course of economic decline. Referring to the Dawson of 1920, Mrs. Berton wrote: "there was no doubt at all that we were living in a decaying town. The population had sunk to eight hundred, though there were buildings enough for ten times that number."[39] On the creeks of the Klondike basin and in other areas of the territory, there were similar symptoms of economic and social disintegration. The malady was to last for many years.

CHAPTER ELEVEN

CONCLUSION

IN 1897–98 expectations of fortunes in glittering gold brought about a sudden influx of people to the Canadian north. The men and women who participated in the Klondike gold rush joined those already in the Yukon to found a community, which, like any other, required institutions to maintain order and provide public services. After examining the provisions made for the government of the Yukon, this study has discussed the struggle of people in the Klondike to secure some measure of control over the administration of their public affairs and over the course of their economic development.

At the time of the gold rush, the Laurier ministry, unfamiliar with the problems of a placer mining camp and faced with poor communications facilities between Ottawa and the gold-fields, framed some ill-advised policies which, together with ineptitude on the part of officials appointed to administer these policies, bred discontent among certain segments of the population. Unrest, persisting even after the creation of a separate Yukon Territory with a government empowered to satisfy local needs, was magnified when the gold rush boom gave way to a prolonged period of economic recession.

As early as 1898, the discontent mushroomed into overt protest, which, in turn, led to the organization of political structures and to the formulation of positive goals. From then until at least 1907, pressure groups, political parties, and newspapers joined in a campaign to achieve certain reforms associated with two broad, interrelated aims: the attainment of some measure of direct influence over the actions of public authorities, and the inducement of government to aid economic development. To realize the first (itself a means to securing the second), a demand for representative institutions arose and continued to be voiced. However, the nature of specific ends related to the second general aim changed markedly as time passed. At the outset, appeals like those for an abolition of the royalty on gold, an increase in the size of placer claims, and a cancellation of monopoly concessions over placer ground were negative and designed to lessen official intervention in the territory; later, as economic conditions deteriorated, requests for such things as a government waterworks, an assay office, a lien law, and a consolidated mining code were positive and directed towards increasing the responsibility of government for territorial welfare. Certainly no particular date marked the alteration in emphasis—often positive and negative demands were made simultaneously—but there was a gradual trend towards seeking active public assistance to foster development in the Yukon.

Although politics were characterized by much petty bickering, there was a surprising degree of unanimity among territorial politicians on the goals they enunciated. Where they differed most was on how to elicit action from the government: some, usually Liberals before coming to the Yukon, conceived broad support for Laurier's ministry, although not necessarily for the administration in the territory, as the best way to obtain what they desired; others, Conservatives and individuals of a personality type that thrives on opposition, chose dissent as their means. The former group used personal submissions to cabinet ministers (and presumably to territorial administrators), election platforms, non-partisan interest groups (such as the Board of Trade), and occasionally mass meetings to urge specific reforms from, while still voicing general approval of, those in authority. The latter utilized mass meetings, protest movements, election campaigns, and letters to the press and to Conservative politicians "on the outside" in order to embarrass the government and thus achieve their objectives.

Both groups were dominated by men in business and the professions, people who had a strong desire to make for themselves and their families a permanent home in the Yukon and who had experienced an educational and environmental background that equipped them, better than miners or prospectors, for public life. From 1901 to 1909 all candidates for the seat in the House of Commons, as well as 71 per cent of the aspirants for election to the Yukon Council and 82 per cent of the councillors elected were drawn from these strata (see Appendixes C and D). Some leaders in pressure group activity, such as Colonel Donald McGregor and "Big Alex" McDonald, were involved in mining, but usually on a large scale. The various citizens' committees and the Board of Trade were dominated by lawyers, doctors, and merchants, and even the Miners' Association and its successors relied heavily on men from Dawson to present their views.

It is difficult to assess exactly what these leaders and their followers accomplished through political activity, although the evidence does suggest that the campaigns of territorial politicians were almost solely responsible for the attainment of representative institutions and were successful in at least speeding up changes in official economic policies. Whether the goals sought were justified in the light of social and economic realities is another question. Certainly, given the isolation of the territory from the rest of Canada, a strong argument existed in favour of placing more responsibility for territorial affairs in the hands of Yukon officials and of giving the residents a greater voice in the formulation of policies for their particular needs. However, there was much wishful thinking about the potential impact of changed laws and mining regulations and of public investment upon the economic climate of the territory. It seems inconceivable that more rapid government action in meeting popular requests would have done more than slightly retard the pace of economic decline. Still, it must be remembered that people in the Yukon, determined to exercise every opportunity to prevent the collapse of their community, had not the advantage of hindsight. Early in the century few of them would have been willing to predict that the Klondike would be virtually deserted by 1920.

APPENDIX A

POPULATION OF THE YUKON TERRITORY BY CITIZENSHIP,
1901 AND 1911*

Citizenship	1901	1911
American	6,720	1,776
Austro-Hungarian	90	128
Belgian	28	13
British subject (by birth)		
British Isles	2,416	1,199
British Possessions	253	140
Canadian (white status)	4,861	2,361
Canadian (Indian status)	3,303	1,489
British subject (by naturalization)	2,034	126
Dutch	9	6
Danish	54	56
French	141	59
German	232	209
Greek	2	12
Italian	61	52
Japanese	73	72
Norwegian and Swedish	442	476
Russian	112	61
Other	67	233
Unknown	6,321	44
	27,219	8,512

* Figures for 1901 were compiled from *Census of Canada*, 1901,
vol. I, Table VI, pp. 412–13, and Table XIV, pp. 446–47; for 1911,
from *ibid.*, 1911, vol. II, Table XVII, pp. 442–43, and Canada,
Census and Statistics Office, *Special Report on the Foreign-born
Population*, p. 60.

APPENDIX B

GOLD PRODUCTION IN THE YUKON, 1885–1918*
(by approximate value in thousands of dollars)

Year	Value of gold production	Year	Value of gold production
1885 } 1886 }	100	1902	12,000
		1903	10,600
1887	70	1904	9,400
1888	40	1905	7,200
1889	175	1906	5,300
1890	175	1907	2,900
1891	40	1908	3,200
1892	88	1909	4,000
1893	176	1910	4,600
1894	125	1911	4,700
1895	250	1912	5,900
1896	300	1913	5,300
1897	2,500	1914	4,600
1898	10,000	1915	4,400
1899	19,000	1916	4,000
1900	22,300	1917	3,300
1901	17,400	1918	1,900

* Compiled from *C.S.P.*, 1898, no. 30a, *Gold Production in the Yukon, 1885–1897; ibid.*, 1904, no. 34, *Report of the Britton Commission on Hydraulic Mining*; Canada, Department of the Interior, *The Yukon Territory: Its History and Resources*, 1909, p. 41; and *Dawson Daily News*, March 3, 1919. Only the approximate values of annual gold production are known because many mine owners did not report their total output to the collectors of royalty. A different set of estimates, based on production during government fiscal years, may be found in H. A. Innis, *Settlement and the Mining Frontier*, p. 219.

APPENDIX C

Occupation	No. of candidates	%
Professional	14*	36·9
Business	13†	34·2
Mining	7‡	18·4
Labouring	3§	7·9
Unknown	1‖	2·6
Total	38	100.0

* Clarke (3), Black (2), Noel, Thompson, Tabor, Thornburn, Pringle, Beddoe, Sudgen, LaChapelle, Ashbaugh.
† R. Lowe (3), O'Brien (2), Prudhomme (2), Landreville, Hagel, Macaulay, Vernon, F. Lowe, Grant.
‡ Wilson (2), Gillespie (2), Henderson, Reid, McGrath.
§ Gilbert, Lobley, Kearney.
‖ Dixon.

APPENDIX D

Yukon Councillors Elected, 1901–8, by Occupation

Occupation	No. of councillors	%
Professional	6*	35·3
Business	8†	47·0
Mining	2‡	11·8
Labouring	1§	5·9
	17	100.0

* Black (2), Pringle, Clarke, Thompson, LaChapelle.
† R. Lowe (3), Prudhomme, Landreville, O'Brien, Macaulay, Grant.
‡ Wilson, Gillespie.
§ Kearney.

NOTES

CHAPTER ONE

1 See Pierre Berton, *The Klondike Fever*, pp. 105–7; H. A. Innis, *Settlement and the Mining Frontier*, p. 183; and S. R. Tompkins, "The Klondike Gold-Rush—A Great International Adventure," *British Columbia Historical Quarterly*, vol. XVII, no. 3, 1953, p. 229.

2 In 1824 Russia and Great Britain signed a treaty creating an arbitrary boundary between their lands in the north. The Klondike River and its tributaries lay to the east of the boundary in British territory. (Canada, Department of the Interior, *The Yukon Territory: Its History and Resources*, 1916, p. 2.) The Russian territory, known as Alaska, was purchased by the United States in 1867, while the British lands were ceded to Canada in 1870.

3 J. W. Dafoe, *Clifford Sifton in Relation to His Times*, p. 155.

4 Innis, *Settlement*, p. 178.

5 Berton, *Klondike Fever*, pp. 146–70, 244–87. The most common routes to the Klondike were from Dyea through the Chilkoot Pass, and from Skagway through the White Pass, to the head of navigable waters leading to the gold-fields. Some stampeders, however, tried other routes, most of which were extremely hazardous. (See *ibid.*, pp. 201–43.)

6 These estimates of the number of people who took part in the gold rush are Pierre Berton's (*ibid.*, p. 417).

7 See Innis, *Settlement, passim.*

8 See Berton, *Klondike Fever*, pp. 288–332, for an excellent description of Dawson and the surrounding area during the height of the rush era.

9 See Appendix A, "Population of the Yukon Territory by Citizenship, 1901 and 1911." The exact composition of the population by nationality during 1898–99 is unknown, but sources perused indicate that the proportion of Americans was higher than in 1901, the year of the first official census.

10 Innis, *Settlement*, p. 207. "A 'lay' is a part of an alluvial claim let out by its owners to two or more miners on condition that [they] . . . pay all expenses connected with the mining and washing of the gold, the owner receiving half the gross output and paying all the royalty on the whole gross output."

11 Innis (*ibid.*) estimates that most people brought in from $750 to $1,000 each.

12 *Canada Sessional Papers* (hereafter cited as *C.S.P.*), 1900, no. 13, *Annual Report of the Commissioner of the North-West Mounted Police for 1899*, s. II, p. 55. See also *Klondike Nugget*, issues of 1899 and 1900.

13 Canada, Census and Statistics Office, *Census of Canada*, 1901, vol. I, p. 5; *ibid.*, 1911, vol. I, p. 169; and Canada, Dominion Bureau of Statistics, *Census of Canada*, 1921, vol. I, p. 3.

14 See Innis, *Settlement*, pp. 213–16.

15 "Report of Commissioner J. H. Ross for 1901–02," *C.S.P.*, 1903, no. 25, *Annual Report of the Department of the Interior for 1901–02*, s. VII, p. 3.

16 See Innis, *Settlement*, pp. 222–25. For figures of gold production, see Appendix B, "Gold Production in the Yukon, 1885–1918."

17 Innis, *Settlement*, pp. 260–62.

18 *Ibid.*, p. 222, and *Yukon Sun*, issues of January 1903.

19 Innis, *Settlement*, pp. 252, 263–64.

20 See Appendix A. The percentages for 1901 and 1911 are based on the proportion of Americans in the total population minus those people whose nationality was undetermined. The percentage for 1900 is based on a rough census taken by the North-West Mounted Police, which showed that 9,534 out of 16,107 persons were Americans (*Klondike Nugget*, May 3, 1900).

21 The percentage of women in the total population of the Yukon Territory was only 15 and 23 in 1901 and 1911 respectively (*Census of Canada*, 1901, vol. I, p. 16, and 1911, vol. I, p. 169).

CHAPTER TWO

1 British order in council, June 23, 1870.

2 See L. H. Thomas, *The Struggle for Responsible Government in the North-West Territories*, pp. 4–5. Although Britain ceded the islands of the Arctic to Canada in 1880, the question of sovereignty over them remained somewhat uncertain thereafter (see Gordon V. Smith, *Territorial Sovereignty in the Canadian North: A Historical Outline of the Problem*, p. 5).

3 For an account of the early history of the Yukon, see Canada, Department of the Interior, *The Yukon Territory: Its History and Resources*, 1907, pp. 1–16, and 1916, pp. 1–12.

4 *Ibid.*, 1907, p. 10.

5 William Ogilvie, *Early Days on the Yukon*, p. 144.

6 W. C. Bompas to the Chief Commissioner of Indian Affairs, May 9, 1893, Annex "B" to Privy Council Order (hereafter cited as P.C.) 2344, November 29, 1893.

7 P.C. 2344, November 29, 1893. For an illustration of government fears, see Memorandum from Fred White, Comptroller of the North-West Mounted Police, to the Prime Minister, February 3, 1897, Laurier Papers, vol. 791a, p. 224428.

8 Bompas to the Superintendent of Indian Affairs, December 9, 1893, Annex "C" to P.C. 1201, May 26, 1894.

9 C. H. Hamilton to T. M. Daly, Minister of the Interior, April 16, 1894, Annex "A" to P.C. 1201, May 26, 1894.

10 P.C. 1201, May 26, 1894. The Comptroller's advice is contained in Annex "D."

11 Both the White memorandum and the final paragraph of the order in council suggest this function, for it was not thought that the originally proposed force of six men could take possession of the district.

12 See "Report of Inspector C. Constantine re the Yukon District," *C.S.P.*, 1895, no. 15, *Annual Report of the Commissioner of the North-West Mounted Police Force for 1894*, pp. 70–85.

13 See *C.S.P.*, 1896, no. 15a, *Supplementary Report of the Commissioner of the North-West Mounted Police Force for 1895*, p. 7. These men were appointed by authority of P.C. 1492, June 1, 1895.

14 P.C. 2640, October 2, 1895.

15 Pierre Berton, *The Klondike Fever*, pp. 24–25.

16 *Supp. Rept. of N.W.M.P. for 1895*, pp. 7–15. See also H. Steele, *Policing the Arctic*, p. 28.

17 *Supp. Rept. of N.W.M.P. for 1895*, p. 74.

18 P.C. 1444J, May 15, 1896.

19 See Ogilvie, *Early Days*, for an authoritative account of the discovery of gold in the Klondike.

20 See "Extracts from Reports of William Ogilvie," *C.S.P.*, 1897, no. 13, *Annual Report of the Department of the Interior for 1896*, s. II, pp. 48–55.

21 See J. A. Smart, Deputy Minister of the Interior, to Constantine, May 3, 1897, Constantine Papers, vol. 3, "General Correspondence, 1844–1908," n.p.

22 P.C. 1190, May 21, 1897.

23 "Excerpts from Reports of Thomas Fawcett," *C.S.P.*, 1898, no. 15, *Interior Dept. Rept.*, *1897*, s. II, p. 74.

24 See opinions of Fawcett's character in Wade to Sifton, April 10, 1898, Sifton Papers, vol. 54, p. 37550; and in Ogilvie to Sifton, September 28, 1898, file 2-0-1 (Whitehorse), "Placer Mining Regulations," n.p.

25 "Excerpts from Reports of Thomas Fawcett," p. 81.

26 P.C. 2468, August 17, 1897. See also "Report of the Deputy Minister of the Interior," *C.S.P.*, 1899, no. 15, *Interior Dept. Rept.*, 1898, p. xiv.

27 See P.C. 2326, July 29, 1897, and P.C. 2461, August 16, 1897, for changes in mining regulations. By the end of 1897 the N.W.M.P. force consisted of eight officers and eighty-eight N.C.O.s (H. Steele, *Policing the Arctic*, p. 37).

28 S. B. Steele, *Forty Years in Canada*, p. 312, and H. Steele, *Policing the Arctic*, p. 39. See also pp. 30–53 in the latter for a detailed description of N.W.M.P. activities in 1897–98.

29 Canada, House of Commons, *Debates* (hereafter cited as H. of C. *Debates*), 1898, col. 1578.

30 *Ibid.*, col. 4795.

31 *Ibid.*, col. 7014, and 1906, col. 7039.

32 Canada, Department of National Defence, *Note on the Yukon Field Force*, pp. 2–4.

33 H. M. Kersey, a leading participant in the syndicate, to Sifton, December 20, 1897, Laurier Papers, vol. 59, p. 18936; and Kersey to Laurier, January 23, 1898, *ibid.*, vol. 63, p. 20060.

34 P.C. 192, January 26, 1898.

35 H. of C. *Debates*, 1898, cols. 228 and 546. See also Henry Borden, ed., *Robert Laird Borden: His Memoirs*, p. 54.

36 Canada, Senate, *Journals*, 1898, p. 103, and H. of C. *Debates*, 1902, col. 4960.

37 J. W. Dafoe, *Clifford Sifton in Relation to His Times*, p. 155.

38 P.C. 2468, August 17, 1897.

39 H. of C. *Debates*, 1899, col. 6058, and Mills to Laurier, June 1, 1899, Laurier Papers, vol. 113, pp. 34092–94.

40 P.C. 2468, August 17, 1897.

41 See Dafoe, *Sifton*, p. 180, and H. of C. *Debates*, 1898, col. 582. The date of Walsh's arrival in Dawson is recorded in *ibid.*, 1899, col. 824.

42 *C.S.P.*, 1898, no. 38b, *Letters and Reports from Major Walsh*. See also Dafoe, *Sifton*, p. 158, and H. of C. *Debates*, 1898, cols. 583–84.

43 Wade to Sifton, March 30, 1898, Sifton Papers, vol. 54, pp. 37519–21. Wade's appointment was made under the provisions of P.C. 2520, August 26, 1897.

44 Tappan Adney, *The Klondike Stampede*, p. 437.

45 See below, pp. 15, 23.

46 Thomas Fawcett to William Ogilvie, October 3, 1898, file 2–0–1 (Whitehorse), n.p. A discovery claim, granted to the first person staking on a creek consisted of a 200-foot frontage, twice the width of an ordinary claim.

47 Wade to Sifton, March 30 and April 10, 1898, Sifton Papers, vol. 54, pp. 37522, 37539, 37545–46.

48 *Klondike Nugget*, July 9, 1898.

49 The only significant amendment to the Placer Mining Regulations proclaimed by Walsh provided an appeal from the Gold Commissioner's rulings on claim disputes to the District Court. ("Report of Major J. M. Walsh," *C.S.P.*, 1899, no. 15, *Interior Dept. Rept.*, 1898, s. IV, p. 337.) Most complaints against the regulations centred around the royalty, which hurt many miners because it was imposed on gross rather than net output. Walsh did exempt some mine owners from the royalty because either mines were not in working order or claims had been renewed before the royalty came into effect (*ibid.*, p. 321), but he was later charged with favouritism in the manner in which he allowed exemptions. (*C.S.P.*, 1899, no. 87, *Report of the Ogilvie Commission of Inquiry*, p. 9.)

50 Interview with T. Hebert, N.W.M.P. dog-driver during 1897–98, Dawson City, August 8, 1963.

51 The account that follows is based primarily on Fawcett to Ogilvie, October 3, 1898, file 2–0–1 (Whitehorse), n.p.

52 Walsh was commonly called "Commissioner."

53 This phase of the Dominion Creek episode was mentioned several times in the House of Commons, but the straight facts were best presented by C. Fitzpatrick, the Solicitor General, in H. of C. *Debates*, 1900, cols. 6388–93.

54 Major Walsh denied all charges in an affidavit (Walsh to Sifton, July 4, 1900, Sifton Papers, vol. 91, pp. 71150–53).

55 Ogilvie to Laurier, March 22, 1899, Laurier Papers, vol. 105, p. 31575.

56 *Klondike Nugget*, July 12 and 20, 1898.

57 Fawcett was given the position of "Chief of Surveys for the Yukon Territory" at a smaller salary than he had received before (P.C. 2368, October 7, 1898). He left the territory in March 1899 (*Klondike Miner*, March 10, 1899).

58 Ogilvie to Laurier, March 22, 1899, Laurier Papers, vol. 105, pp. 31573–74.

59 Laurier to Sifton, August 12, 1898, Sifton Papers, vol. 46, pp. 30767–68.

60 *Ibid.* (telegram), pp. 30761 and 30763.

61 Sifton to Laurier (rough draft of telegram), undated, *ibid.*, p. 30763 (my italics).

62 Cited in H. of C. *Debates*, 1899, cols. 767–68.

63 Sifton to Laurier, August 25, 1898, Laurier Papers, vol. 84, p. 25978.

64 Henry P. Pullon-Bury to Laurier, September 5, 1898, *ibid.*, vol. 85, p. 26224.

65 Laurier to Pullon-Bury, October 3, 1898, *ibid.*, p. 26226.

66 Girouard to Laurier, September 23, 1898, *ibid.*, vol. 86, p. 26689. Girouard was appointed under the terms of P.C. 1776, July 4, 1898.

E

67 P.C. 2371, October 7, 1898.

68 *Rept. Ogilvie Commission*, p. 5. Clement replaced F. C. Wade by P.C. 2432, October 17, 1898. Wade, originally Registrar of Lands, served as Legal Adviser to the Yukon administration from July 7, 1898 (P.C. 1792) to the date of Clement's appointment.

69 *Rept. Ogilvie Commission*, p. 8. Shortly after Ogilvie decided that complaints regarding incidents occurring after August 25 could not be considered by the Commission, he wrote Sifton requesting the appointment of another commission to investigate charges up to July 31, 1899. Sifton took no action. (Ogilvie to Sifton, February 28, 1899, file 1029 [Dawson], "Royal Commission re Charges against Yukon Officials," Interior Department Records of Field Offices in the Yukon Territory, n.p.)

70 *Rept. Ogilvie Commission*, pp. 7–8. See also *Klondike Nugget*, issues of February and March 1899.

71 W. F. Dawson, *Procedure in the Canadian House of Commons*, p. 134.

72 H. of C. *Debates*, 1899, cols. 701–800 and 801–85.

73 *Ibid.*, cols. 5945–6047 and 6053–91. Although the opposition accused Ogilvie of white-washing the actions of government employees, F. C. Wade, one of the officials accused of misbehaviour, wrote to Sifton: "The Commissioner incidentally disclosed what we knew from many sources that he had used every possible effort by acting as an amateur private detective and in other ways to obtain charges against us. . . . This sort of conduct one might be justified in regarding as undignified and contemptible, but, as a matter of fact, I am glad that he did exhaust every effort" (Wade to Sifton, May 30, 1899, Sifton Papers, vol. 74, p. 55182).

74 H. of C. *Debates*, 1899, cols. 6124–65.

75 *C.S.P.*, 1899, no. 87a, *Evidence Taken before the Commissioner Appointed to Investigate Charges of Alleged Malfeasance of Officials of the Yukon Territory*, pp. 253–68.

76 H. of C. *Debates*, 1899, cols. 6226–45, 6248–56, 6267–76.

77 *Ibid.*, col. 6275.

78 *Ibid.*, col. 6278.

79 *Ibid.*, 1900, cols. 938–1005, 4926–50, 4967–5018, 6356–6428, 7136–72, 7658–7727, 8527–8647.

80 Dafoe, *Sifton*, p. 209.

81 H. A. Innis, *Settlement and the Mining Frontier*, p. 183.

82 Adney, *Stampede*, p. 433.

CHAPTER THREE

1 See Frederick Haultain to Sifton, January 11, 1898, *C.S.P.*, 1898, no. 51a, *Correspondence between Ottawa and Regina respecting Liquor Permits*. For an account of the political events leading to the achievement of responsible government in the territories, see L. H. Thomas, *The Struggle for Responsible Government in the North-West Territories*.

2 H. of C. *Debates*, 1898, cols. 1747–48.

3 "Report of Major J. M. Walsh," *C.S.P.*, 1899, no. 15, *Annual Report of the Department of the Interior for 1898*, s. IV, p. 323.

4 Walsh to Constantine, March 5, 1898, Constantine Papers, vol. 3, "General Correspondence, 1884–1908," n.p.

5 "Rept. of Walsh," p. 323.

6 *Klondike Nugget*, July 16, 1898.

7 See C. C. Lingard, *Territorial Government in Canada*, pp. 23–24.

8 The Yukon Act, *Statutes of Canada*, 1898, c. 6.

9 H. of C. *Debates*, 1898, col. 6729.

10 Yukon Act, sects. 3–5.

11 P.C. 1790, July 7, 1898; and P.C. 1850, July 19, 1898. Gradually, a territorial civil service grew up separate from the federal one.

12 P.C. 1790, July 7, 1898.

13 Yukon Act, sects. 6 and 8.

14 See The North-West Territories Act, *Revised Statutes of Canada*, 1898, c. 50, sects. 13–14.

15 See The British North America Act, *British Statutes*, 1867, c. 3, s. 92.

16 Yukon Act, sects. 7–8.

17 *Ibid.*, sects. 10–11 and 14–17.

18 See Thomas, *Struggle*, pp. 1–72 and 83–85. From 1881 to 1905, when Keewatin was incorpo-rated in the reconstituted North-West Territories, the arrangement of having the Lieutenant Governor of Manitoba oversee territorial affairs proved satisfactory because many of the more important centres of population in the territory had been absorbed by the province of Manitoba in 1881.

19 See *ibid.*, pp. 73–145, for an account of the politics of the territories from 1876–88. For a detailed examination of the provisions of the North-West Territories Act of 1875, see *ibid.*, pp. 73–77. For a brief discussion, see Lingard, *Territorial Government*, p. 4.

20 See R. G. Robertson, "The Evolution of Territorial Government in Canada," in J. H. Aitchison, ed., *The Political Process in Canada*, p. 140.

21 See J. N. E. Brown, "The Evolution of Law and Government in the Yukon Territory," in S. M. Wickett, ed., *The Municipal Government of Toronto*, p. 199.

22 *C.S.P.*, 1899, no. 87a, *Evidence Taken before the Commissioner Appointed to Investigate Charges of Alleged Malfeasance of Officials of the Yukon Territory*, pp. 88–89.

23 H. of C. *Debates*, 1899, col. 6016.

24 P.C. 1775, July 4, 1898.

25 P.C. 1813, July 7, 1898.

26 P.C. 2432, October 17, 1898; and P.C. 2369, October 7, 1898.

27 Pierre Berton, *The Klondike Fever*, p. 369.

28 *C.S.P.*, 1900, no. 33u, *Report of Commissioner Ogilvie for 1898–99*, p. 13.

29 *Ibid.*, p. 2.

30 Although exaggerated, the following comments of Judge Dugas reflect the general opinion of Ogilvie: "He is a good man, meaning well, but entirely lacking in administrative capacity. In all his dealing with the public, he . . . reminds me of the girl in that song the 'Chimes of Normandy' who 'never says yes and never says no.' He seems anxious to please everybody and pleases nobody." (Dugas to L. O. David, June 29, 1899, Sifton Papers, vol. 64, p. 46760.)

31 S. B. Steele, *Forty Years in Canada*, p. 329.

32 See *ibid.*, p. 322; *Rept. of Ogilvie*, 1898–99, pp. 13–14 and 23; and *Klondike Nugget*, July 15, 1899.

33 See *Klondike Nugget* for accounts of Council sessions. See also Brown, "Government in Yukon," p. 200.

34 *Ordinances of the Yukon Territory* (hereafter cited as *Ordinances*), 1898, cc. 1, 7 and 8, 11. The last ordinance was later disallowed (P.C. 734, April 14, 1899) because the restrictions on the sale of intoxicants were not as severe as those of the corresponding North-West Territories ordinance (P.C. 718, April 14, 1899). It was replaced by another ordinance, stricter in its control over the retail liquor trade (*Ordinances*, 1899, c. 29). Only one other ordinance was disallowed during the period under discussion—"An Ordinance respecting the Legal Profession," *Ordinances*, 1898, c. 4 (P.C. 734, April 14, 1899).

35 *Rept. of Ogilvie, 1898–99*, p. 32.

36 *Klondike Nugget*, February 15, 1899. Shortly after the franchise was granted (*ibid.*, November 16, 1898), the *Nugget* began to attack the proprietors vigorously for charging tolls on the sled road (see December 28, 1898, and succeeding issues). Later, the paper took them to court, where it was ruled that the tolls had been collected illegally. Council then revoked the contract. The story is particularly noteworthy because T. W. O'Brien later served as President of the Yukon Liberal Association and twice sought an elective seat on the Yukon Council, the first time unsuccessfully.

37 *Ibid.*, July 15, 1899.

38 *Rept. of Ogilvie, 1898–99*, p. 7. See also p. 9.

39 "Report of Commissioner Ogilvie for 1899–1900," *C.S.P.*, 1901, no. 25, *Interior Dept. Rept., 1899–1900*, s. VII, p. 3.

40 Canada, Department of Agriculture, *Statistical Yearbook for 1899*, p. 455.

41 *C.S.P.*, 1900, no. 1, *Report of the Auditor General for 1898–99*. See also the Auditor General's reports for the years 1899–1908.

42 *Ordinances*, 1898, cc. 5 and 9; and 1899, cc. 7, 29, and 31.

43 G. S. Fleming, "The Yukon Telegraph Service," *Dawson Daily News*, August 17, 1917.

44 Ogilvie to Laurier, December 24, 1898, Laurier Papers, vol. 94, pp. 28568–69. Wade was appointed Crown Prosecutor by P.C. 146, February 13, 1899.

45 Wade to Sifton, April 15, 1900, Sifton Papers, vol. 74, p. 55169.

46 Ogilvie to Laurier, December 24, 1898, Laurier Papers, vol. 94, p. 28567; and S. B. Steele to Henry Harwood, February 22, 1899, *ibid.*, vol. 102, p. 30685.

47   Girouard to Laurier, December 25, 1898, *ibid.*, vol. 95, pp. 28940–44; and Clement to Sifton, March 8, 1899, Sifton Papers, vol. 59, p. 41680.

48   P.C. 2272, October 24, 1899. Girouard, however, was still practising the next year (*Dawson Daily News*, May 2, 1900).

49   Ogilvie to Laurier, March 22, 1899, Laurier Papers, vol. 105, p. 31573.

50   P.C. 426, March 29, 1899. See also H. of C. *Debates*, 1899, col. 6037. Dugas, perhaps as an assertion of judicial independence, did not give up his claims, and described them in a letter—which fell into the hands of Laurier and Sifton—written five months after the order in council had been promulgated (Dugas to L. O. David, June 29, 1899, Sifton Papers, vol. 64, p. 46756).

51   Clement to Sifton, December 4, 1899, Sifton Papers, vol. 59, p. 41734 (my italics).

52   Girouard to Laurier, September 23, 1898; October 18, 1898; and December 23, 1899; Laurier Papers, vol. 86, p. 26689; vol. 89, pp. 27266–68; and vol. 134, pp. 40158–63.

53   P.C. 156, January 23, 1900.

CHAPTER FOUR

1   Based on a perusal of newspaper accounts.

2   *Klondike Nugget*, August 3, 1898.

3   *Ibid.*, July 12, 1898.

4   *Ibid.*, July 16, 1898.

5   *Ibid.*, August 3 and July 20, 1898.

6   *Ibid.*, August 10, 1898. The petition was not forwarded until August 25.

7   *Ibid.*, August 13, 1898.

8   *Ibid.*, September 7, 1898.

9   *Ibid.*, October 5, 1898.

10   *Ibid.*, July 16, 1898. Although in an official report of his activities as Chief Executive Officer of the Yukon district, Major Walsh recommended that a council of four appointed officials and four elected representatives be established to assist the Commissioner ("Report of Major J. M. Walsh," *C.S.P.*, 1899, no. 15, *Annual Report of the Department of the Interior for 1898*, s. IV, p. 332), the present author found no records indicating that it was read by any of the men pressing for representation.

11   *Klondike Nugget*, July 27, 1898.

12   *Ibid.*, September 10, 1898.

13   *Ibid.*, September 17 and 28, 1898.

14   *Ibid.*, September 24, 1898.

15   *Ibid.*, October 1, 1898.

16   *Ibid.*, October 5, 1898.

17   *C.S.P.*, 1899, no. 87, *Report of the Ogilvie Commission of Inquiry*, p. 8.

18   See W. F. Thompson, editor of the *Yukon Midnight Sun*, to Ogilvie, March 22, 1901, file 2286 (Dawson), Interior Department Records of Field Offices in the Yukon Territory, n.p.

19   *Klondike Nugget*, December 26, 1898.

20   *Klondike Miner*, February 3, 1899.

21   *Klondike Nugget*, May 6, 1899.

22   See *ibid.* and *Klondike Miner*, issues of December 1898 to February 1900.

23   *Klondike Nugget*, March 25, 1899.

24   *Ibid.*, January 11 and 14, and May 27, 1899.

25   Pierre Berton, *The Klondike Fever*, p. 326.

26   *Dawson Sunday Gleaner*, July 23, 1899.

27   *Ibid.*, October 1, 1899.

28   *Ibid.*, December 10, 1899, and *Klondike Nugget*, December 16, 1899.

29   The *Dawson Daily News* began operations late in 1899, but the author was unable to obtain access to issues published before January 1, 1900.

30   P.C. 4257, March 30, 1899.

31   The Yukon (Amendment) Act, *Statutes of Canada*, 1899, c. 11.

32   Canada, Senate, *Debates*, 1899, p. 914.

33   *Ibid.*, pp. 915–16.

34   *Klondike Nugget*, November 25, 1899.

35   *Dawson Daily News*, February 8, 1900.

36 *Ibid.*, February 13, 1900. On the day the mass meeting was held, W. H. P. Clement, the Legal Adviser, wrote Sifton: "That blatant ass Woodworth is trying to stir up an agitation for representation on the Council but there is no interest in the matter" (Clement to Sifton, February 12, 1900, Sifton Papers, vol. 78, p. 58854). He was soon proven wrong.

37 *Klondike Nugget*, February 24 and April 21, 1900.

38 *Ibid.*, February 24, 1900.

39 *Ibid.*, February 28, 1900.

40 *Ibid.*, March 1, 1900.

41 *Ibid.*, March 2, 1900.

42 *Ibid.*, March 7, 1900.

43 *Ibid.*, March 9, 1900.

44 *Ibid.*, March 17, 1900. Superintendent A. B. Perry replaced S. B. Steele on Council in September 1899; the Gold Commissioner, E. C. Senkler, was appointed at the same time (P.C. 1989, September 5, 1899).

45 *Klondike Nugget*, March 24, 1900.

46 *Dawson Daily News*, April 3, 1900. Certainly the government was afraid of losing a territorial election, although it is doubtful that it was concerned about the impact of such a defeat on its chances in the federal election. Aimé Dugas, son of the judge, wrote Israel Tarte, the Minister of Public Works, regarding the government's chances in an election for two councillors: "la grand majorité votera pour deux députés qui seront antagonistes à tout pouvoir actuel. Je ne crois pas que même le vote des hommes de la Police et de la Milice seront suffisants pour pouvoir bouleverser cette majorité" (A. Dugas to Tarte, February 18, 1900, Laurier Papers, vol. 142, p. 42505).

47 *Klondike Nugget*, March 30 and April 6, 1900.

48 *Yukon Sun*, April 11, 1900. "Midnight" was removed from the newspaper's masthead in 1899.

49 *Klondike Nugget*, April 13, 1900.

50 *Ibid.*, April 27, 1900. The *Dawson Daily News* (April 15, 1900) reported that there was little interest in incorporation among leading businessmen because they feared it would bring higher taxes.

51 *Klondike Nugget*, May 3, 1900.

52 Ogilvie to Sifton (telegram), May 2, 1900, file 1–39–1 (Whitehorse), "The Yukon Act," n.p.

53 *Dawson Daily News*, May 7, 1900. Sugrue's motion to appeal to Chamberlain was on the agenda but not discussed in the meeting. The author found no further reference to it.

54 *Klondike Nugget*, May 7, 1900.

55 *Ibid.*, May 14, 1900.

56 See Minto to Laurier, June 17, 1900, Laurier Papers, vol. 159, pp. 46594–96.

57 *Dawson Daily News*, February 8 and 15, 1900; and *Klondike Nugget*, July 19, 1900.

58 Senate, *Debates*, 1900, pp. 213–15.

59 H. of C. *Debates*, 1900, cols. 7773–79 and 7781–84.

60 *Klondike Nugget*, June 2, 1900. W. H. P. Clement, the Legal Adviser, claiming he owed no responsibility to the people of the territory, boycotted Council's public sessions in July and August; because Superintendent Perry had been transferred and Judge Dugas was on leave, Clement prevented Council from attaining its 50-per-cent quorum (*ibid.*, July 10, 1900). Shortly thereafter, Clement, disgruntled as a result of his feuds with Ogilvie over his private law practice and with Girouard and Dugas over government policy towards French Canadians, resigned from the Yukon service and left the territory (*ibid.*, August 24, 1900).

61 P.C. 1724, July 13, 1900.

62 *Klondike Nugget*, June 22, 1900.

CHAPTER FIVE

1 *Klondike Nugget*, July 23 and 28, 1900.

2 Wade to Sifton (telegram), July 20, 1900, and Sifton to Wade (telegram), undated, Sifton Papers, vol. 91, pp. 71059 and 71061.

3 Wade to Sifton, January 5, 1901, *ibid.*, vol. 115, p. 90757.

4 *Ibid.* Wood succeeded Superintendent Perry as Officer in Command of the North-West Mounted Police in the summer of 1900.

5 *Klondike Nugget*, August 15, 1900.

6 Wade to Sifton, January 5, 1901, Sifton Papers, vol. 115, p. 90758.

7 "Petition of the Dawson Board of Trade," Minto Papers, vol. 24, pp. 5–12.

8 Wade to Sifton, January 5, 1901, Sifton Papers, vol. 115, p. 90759.

9 Minto to Laurier, September 5, 1900, Laurier Papers, vol. 169, pp. 48817–21.

10 "Memorandum re Yukon Affairs," Minto Papers, vol. 24, pp. 124–29.

11 Minto's italics.

12 Sam Steele had been well liked by the people of the Klondike, and, when he was transferred to South Africa, many citizens signed a petition protesting the action (*Klondike Nugget*, September 20, 1899). Laurier received a letter from H. J. Woodside, editor of the Liberal *Yukon Sun*, asking the government not to "remove" Steele. "He has been . . . the strongest factor we have here in reconciling the people to conditions, which are unnecessarily hard and unworkable, by his wisdom and fore-thought in handling the force under his command, and in every way assisting the pioneer." The Prime Minister replied that he did not know of Steele's "removal," and suggested that Woodside apply to Sifton for the reason. (Woodside to Laurier, September 12, 1899, and Laurier to Woodside, October 2, 1899, Laurier Papers, vol. 125, pp. 37352 and 37354.)

13 *Klondike Nugget*, July 30, 1900.

14 P. C. 1908, July 31, 1900.

15 *Ordinances*, 1900, c. 33. Although the *Nugget* (August 21, 1900) bitterly complained that a proposed $100 deposit would drive many prospective condidates from the race, the deposit was raised to $200 by the time the ordinance was passed (*Klondike Nugget*, August 30, 1900).

16 *Klondike Nugget*, August 21, 1900.

17 *Ibid.*, August 22, 1900.

18 *Ibid.*, August 27, 1900.

19 *Ibid.*, August 29 and 31, 1900. The preliminary conventions, open to all who wished to attend, resembled the direct primary, an institution that was reaching the peak of its popularity in the United States at that time. In this instance, the delegates were not bound to support a particular aspirant for the nomination, although in preliminaries held before succeeding elections they were.

20 *Ibid.*, September 10, 1900.

21 *Ibid.*, August 29 and 30, 1900.

22 *Dawson Daily News*, April 11, 1905.

23 *Klondike Nugget*, August 31 and September 12, 1900.

24 Yukon Liberals to Laurier (telegram), October 26, 1900, Laurier Papers, vol. 176, p. 50287; and Wade to Sifton, November 17, 1900, Sifton Papers, vol. 91, pp. 71074–75. See also Arthur Wilson to Laurier, December 8, 1900, Laurier Papers, vol. 180, p. 51541.

25 *Klondike Nugget*, September 19, 1900.

26 *Ibid.*, September 20, 1900.

27 *Ibid.*, September 25, 1900.

28 Wilson to Laurier, December 8, 1900, Laurier Papers, vol. 180, p. 51541.

29 *Ordinances*, 1900, c. 32, previously passed in Ottawa as P.C. 1909, July 31, 1900. See also *Klondike Nugget*, August 23, 1900.

30 *Klondike Nugget*, September 6, 1900. Wood wrote Sifton: "In view of the approaching election of two members for the Yukon Council, and the attitude of the Citizens' Committee and other agitators against the Government and officials, I decided to take no action in the matter, and in fact, kept your letter a secret, until after the election, but Ogilvie upset plans by giving the letter to the *News* and *Nugget* verbatim" (Wood to Sifton, September 8, 1900, Sifton Papers, vol. 91, p. 71519).

31 See P.C. 505, July 20, 1900. The hill and bench claims reserved on Bonanza and Eldorado creeks were opened as well (P.C. 2117, September 5, 1900). The promise of a reduced royalty was given by E. C. Senkler, the Gold Commissioner, on September 27 (see *Klondike Nugget*), but Ottawa authorities took no immediate action.

32 *Klondike Nugget*, September 25, 1900.

33 *Dawson Daily News*, October 12, 1900.

34 *Klondike Nugget*, October 13 and 16, 1900.

35 For election results and post-election activities and comment, see *ibid.*, October 17 (extra edition) and 18, and November 30, 1900.

36 Wade to Sifton, October 27, 1900 (telegram), and November 17, 1900, Sifton Papers, vol. 91, pp. 71071 and 71074–77.

37 Yukon Liberals to Laurier (telegram), October 26, 1900, Laurier Papers, vol. 176, p. 50287. A leading Liberal, J. R. Christie, subsequently wrote the Prime Minister, pleading for the appoint-ment of a "popular Liberal Commissioner" (January 8, 1901, *ibid.*, vol. 184, p. 52998).

38 Laurier to T. W. O'Brien (telegram), November 11, 1900, *ibid.*, p. 50293.

39 H. of C. *Debates*, 1901, col. 73.

40 *Klondike Nugget*, February 8, 1901.

41 *Ibid.*, October 25, 1900.

42 See Executive of the Yukon Liberal Association to Laurier (telegram), February 16, 1901, Laurier Papers, vol. 187, p. 53569; and *ibid.*, pp. 53366, 53387, and 53540.

43 Tarte to Laurier, March 17, 1901, *ibid.*, vol. 190, p. 54442; and P.C. 544, March 11, 1901.

44 See William Tramer, "James Hamilton Ross—a Western Public Man," *Manitoba Free Press*, September 6, 1902. See also L. H. Thomas, *The Struggle for Responsible Government in the North-West Territories*, especially pp. 116, 124–26, 135, 144, 146–47, 175, 203, 218–19, 221, 225, 246, 251–54, 259 *n.*; and C. C. Lingard, *Territorial Government in Canada*, pp. 25 *n.*, 36 *n.*, 117 *n.*, 118. It may seem strange that Ross, at the height of his political career in the North-West Territories, accepted the post of Commissioner of the Yukon. The author, unable to locate any sources that enlighted him on Ross's motivation, drew the conclusion that the office was viewed as a stepping-stone to a career in federal politics. Z. M. Hamilton offered another possible explanation when he wrote Ross's obituary: "the emoluments of political life in the Territories in these days were meagre, and Mr. Ross had a fine young family growing up. It was essential that he should make provision for them. Much of his life had been freely given to the service of his country without thought of remuneration. He was offered the position of commissioner of the Yukon [at a salary of $6,000], and he accepted it" (Z. M. Hamilton, "The Late Senator Ross," *Regina Leader-Post*, December 16, 1932).

45 *Klondike Nugget*, December 7, 1900.

46 *Ibid.*, March 29, 1901.

47 Appointed by P.C. 571, March 13, 1901.

48 *Klondike Nugget*, June 7 and November 8, 1901; and *Ordinances*, 1901, c. 30.

49 *Klondike Nugget*, January 21, 1901. The practice of a territorial council's forwarding memorials to Ottawa seeking federal action on certain matters had been common in the North-West Territories (see several references in Thomas, *Struggle*).

50 *Klondike Nugget*, March 22, 1901.

51 P.C. 574, March 13, 1901. The changes were announced publicly on April 1, 1901 (*Klondike Nugget*).

52 *Klondike Nugget*, April 11, 1901.

53 For an account of this transitional period, see *ibid.*, April 7, 10–12, and 16, 1901.

54 London, Ont., Office of the W.C.T.U. to Sifton, June 27, 1900, in file 1443 (Dawson), "Dancehalls and Gambling in the Yukon Territory," Interior Department Records of Field Offices in the Yukon Territory, vol. 5, n.p.

55 Sifton to Ogilvie, July 2, 1900, in *ibid.*

56 Ogilvie to Sifton, July 21, 1900, in *ibid.*

57 Sifton to Ogilvie, August 14, 1900, in *ibid.* See above, p. 36.

58 Ogilvie to Sifton, September 12 1900, in "Dancehalls and Gambling."

59 Ogilvie to Smart, February 27, 1901, in *ibid.* See also *Klondike Nugget*, February 27, 1901.

60 See *Nugget*, February 27 and 28, 1901; and Sifton to Laurier, April 9, 1901, Laurier Papers, vol. 190, pp. 54471–72.

61 *Klondike Nugget*, March 18, 1901. The gambling establishments and dancehalls were closed on March 16. Normally, they would not have operated on the following day, a Sunday.

62 Grant to Sifton, March 19, 1901, Laurier Papers, vol. 190, p. 54470.

63 Smart to Ross, March 30, 1901, in "Dancehalls and Gambling"; and *Klondike Nugget*, November 16, 1901.

64 Based upon *Klondike Nugget*, April 12 and 18, 1901; and an interview with a Dawson City resident who wished to remain anonymous, August 8, 1963.

65 *Ordinances*, 1902, cc. 8 and 24.

66 *Klondike Nugget*, July 11, 1902.

67 *Ibid.*, May 25, 1901.

68 *Ibid.*, October 19, 1900.

69 *Ibid.*, December 21, 1900, and January 8, 1901.

70 *Ibid.*, March 5 and 8, 1901.

71 *Ibid.*, February 28 and March 2, 1901.

72 *Ordinances*, 1901, c. 31. See also *Klondike Nugget*, August 10, 1901.

73 *Klondike Nugget*, July 31, 1901.

74 *Ordinances*, 1901, c. 45.
75 *Klondike Nugget*, November 29 and December 3, 7, and 12, 1901.
76 *Ibid.*, December 20, 1901; and *Ordinances*, 1901, c. 45.
77 See *Klondike Nugget*, issues of December and January, especially January 7, 1902.
78 *Ibid.*, January 10, 1902.
79 *Ibid.*, February 7, 1902.
80 "Report of Commissioner J. H. Ross for 1901–02," *C.S.P.*, 1903, no. 25, *Annual Report of the Department of the Interior for 1901–02*, s. VII, p. 4.
81 *Ibid.*, p. 3; and *Klondike Nugget*, July 31 and November 21, 1901.
82 *Klondike Nugget*, November 9 and December 5, 1901.
83 *Ibid.*, January 30, 1901.
84 The Yukon Representation Act, *Statutes of Canada*, 1902, c. 37, and the Yukon (Amendment) Act, *ibid.*, c. 35. Included among changes in the latter was the following provision: "Every Ordinance made by the Governor in Council and the Commissioner in Council . . . shall remain in force until the day immediately succeeding the day of prorogation of the then next session of Parliament, and no longer, unless during such session of Parliament such Ordinance is approved by resolution of both Houses of Parliament." As far as the author knows, this was Parliament's first attempt to control delegated legislation by means of requiring its submission to a positive resolution. The clause was inserted in the act at the insistence of R. L. Borden, the leader of the opposition (H. of C. *Debates*, 1902, col. 4484).
85 *Dawson Daily News*, June 4, 1902.
86 The change was effected by P.C. 899, May 21, 1902.

CHAPTER SIX

1 P.C. 22, January 12, 1898.
2 H. A. Innis, *Settlement and the Mining Frontier*, pp. 226–27.
3 See excerpts from Treadgold's private memoirs cited in F. Cunynghame, *Lost Trail*, pp. 50–51.
4 Treadgold to Sifton, September 7, 1899, Sifton Papers, vol. 73, p. 54573; and *ibid.*, July 17, 1900, vol. 90, p. 70030.
5 *Ibid.*, July 17, 1900, vol. 90, p. 70029 (my italics).
6 Barwick to Sifton, January 16, 1900, Sifton Papers, vol. 75, pp. 57082–91.
7 P.C. 1293, June 12, 1901.
8 Senkler to P. G. Keyes, Secretary to the Department of the Interior, July 23, 1901, *C.S.P.*, 1903, no. 63, *Correspondence, etc. relating to the Treadgold Hydraulic Mining Syndicate* (hereafter cited as *Treadgold Syndicate*), p. 3.
9 *Klondike Nugget*, July 31, 1901.
10 See *ibid.*, issues of July, August, and September 1901. Issues of the *Dawson Daily News* are missing for these months, but, a year later, when passions ran high over the Treadgold Concession, the *News* (September 2, 1902) took credit for exposing the concession in 1901.
11 Keyes to Senkler (telegram), August 14, 1901, *Treadgold Syndicate*, p. 4.
12 Ross to Sifton, August 16, 1901, Sifton Papers, vol. 110, p. 87015.
13 Except that the syndicate was allowed to record as many claims as it wished without paying entry fees (Sifton to Senkler (telegram), September 6, 1901, *Treadgold Syndicate*, p. 4).
14 The amendment (P.C. 2153, December 7, 1901) was forwarded to Dawson on January 10, 1902 (Keyes to Ross, January 10, 1902, *Treadgold Syndicate*, p. 7), nine days after it took effect. It was yet a month later when Senkler disclosed its terms (*Klondike Nugget*, February 13, 1902).
15 See discussion above, pp. 5–6.
16 *Klondike Nugget*, February 13, 1902; and *Dawson Daily News*, February 13, 1902, cited in *Treadgold Syndicate*, p. 8.
17 *Yukon Sun*, February 14, 1902, cited in *Treadgold Syndicate*, p. 13.
18 *Ibid.*, February 16, 1902, pp. 15–19.
19 Pattullo served as premier of British Columbia from 1933 to 1941.
20 *Klondike Nugget*, February 18, 1902.
21 *Ibid.*, February 19, 1902.
22 *Ibid.*, February 22, 1902.
23 *Ibid.*, February 15, 25, and 26, 1902.

24   *Ibid.*, February 15 and 27, 1902. Apparently Wilson's way was paid by the miners on the creeks and Sugrue's by funds collected at the mass meeting. Congdon, quoted as saying, "It is with the people whether I go or not" (*ibid.*, February 27, 1902), did not go.

25   Sifton to Senkler (telegram), April 17, 1902, *Treadgold Syndicate*, p. 20; and P.C. 662 and P.C. 663, April 21, 1902.

26   *Klondike Nugget*, April 23, 1902.

27   *Dawson Daily News*, April 30, 1902.

28   *Klondike Nugget*, July 25 and 29, 1902.

29   See *Dawson Daily News*, issues of August 1902.

30   *Ibid.*, August 18, 1902.

31   *Ibid.*, August 29, 1902.

32   *Ibid.*, August 25, 1902.

33   For background information on Clarke, see H. J. Morgan, ed., *The Canadian Men and Women of the Time*, 1912, p. 238; H. of C. *Debates*, 1899, col. 5486; *Klondike Miner*, December 14, 1901; and *Dawson Daily News*, August 25, 1902.

34   *Klondike Miner*, December 14, 1901.

35   *Klondike Nugget*, July 7 and 10, 1902.

36   F. T. Congdon, in a letter to Sifton (September 29, 1902, Sifton Papers, vol. 120, p. 95152) said that he and other Liberals worked quietly behind the scenes to secure Clarke's nomination because the Liberals, owing to antipathy towards the government, would have faced certain defeat at the hands of a "respectable" opposition candidate.

37   *Klondike Nugget*, July 19, 1902. See also William Tramer, "James Hamilton Ross—a Western Public Man," *Manitoba Free Press*, September 6, 1902.

38   *Dawson Daily News*, September 8 and 13, 1902.

39   *Klondike Nugget*, September 17 and 19, 1902.

40   *Dawson Daily News*, September 20, 1902.

41   His resignation was accepted by an unnumbered order in council, dated October 16, 1902.

42   *Klondike Nugget*, September 22, 1902.

43   *Dawson Daily News*, September 2 and 5, 1902. See L. H. Thomas, *The Struggle for Responsible Government in the North-West Territories*, pp. 146–47, for an account of the 1887 election contest between Ross and Davin.

44   William Catto, *The Yukon Administration*, pp. 14–15.

45   *Dawson Daily News*, September 4, 1902.

46   Including a settlement of the Alaska Boundary dispute—the only time local politicians referred to it (*ibid.*, September 1 and 19, 1902). Congdon told Sifton (September 29, 1902, Sifton Papers, vol. 120, p. 95151) that the Liberals made pledges on territorial matters only, hoping to win support from Conservative and opposition elements who were disenchanted with Clarke.

47   Unnumbered order in council, November 11, 1902. Dufferin Pattullo had earlier resigned to enter private business. See also Congdon to Sifton (telegram), October 10, 1902, Sifton Papers, vol. 120, p. 95157.

48   *Dawson Daily News*, November 8, 1902.

49   *Ibid.*, November 11 and 12, 1902.

50   *Klondike Nugget*, December 29, 1902.

51   *Ibid.* and *Yukon Sun*, December 3, 1902.

52   *Dawson Daily News*, November 26 and December 3, 1902.

53   *Klondike Nugget*, February 7, 1903. Black, a Yukon councillor from 1905 to 1912, served as Commissioner of the territory (following the Conservative election victory in 1911) from 1912 to 1918, and as the Yukon's Member of Parliament in the years 1921–35 and 1940–49. During the Bennett regime (1930–35), he acted as Speaker of the House of Commons.

54   *Ibid.*, February 14, 1903.

55   M. L. Black, *My Seventy Years*, p. 188. (Mrs. Black sat in the House of Commons for the Yukon from 1935 to 1940.) Too many years have passed to ascertain the truth of these charges of election corruption. Councillor John Pringle, who claimed to be a Liberal, wrote Laurier about the election campaign: "was there ever such a dirty campaign in the interests of a good man [Ross]? . . . Bribes were given, money was paid out of the road fund, [and] . . . lewd women were promised money to dope Clarke men over election day." He also mentioned the alien vote at Miller Creek and Caribou Crossing (Pringle to Laurier, January 3, 1905, cited in H. of C. *Debates*, 1907–8, col. 9591). The reason the allegations of alien voting could not be proved in the courts was that there were no voters' lists.

E*

56 *Klondike Nugget*, February 14, 1903. There is no record of Clarke's going to Ottawa. He had just been through a Yukon Council campaign, and it would seem that he had more than enough excitement to suit him in Dawson.

57 *Ibid.*, December 12, 1902.

58 The Yukon (Amendment) Act, *Statutes of Canada*, 1902, c. 35, s. 1. The constituencies were established by a schedule affixed to *Ordinances*, 1902, c. 29.

59 *Klondike Nugget*, December 4, 1902, and *Dawson Daily News*, December 5, 1902.

60 *Klondike Nugget*, December 5, 1902.

61 *Ibid.*, December 24, 1902.

62 *Ibid.*, December 8, 1902. The *Nugget* reported his withdrawal on December 30.

63 *Ibid.*, January 2, 1903.

64 *Ibid.*, December 26, 29, and 30, 1902, and January 2, 1903; and *Dawson Daily News*, December 17, 1902. James McNamee, a miner, was also nominated for Klondike, but later withdrew (*Klondike Nugget*, December 31, 1902, and January 3, 1903).

65 *Yukon Sun*, January 30, 1903.

66 At a public meeting which Dr. Thompson held for all candidates, William Thornburn delivered a short speech, promising to outline his programme at a mass meeting he intended to hold the next evening (*Klondike Nugget*, January 10, 1903). When he did so, he included every promise made by the other candidates, prompting the *Nugget* (January 12, 1903) to comment that Mr. Thornburn "had evidently benefitted by the speeches of the previous evening."

67 See *ibid.*, January 2–13, 1903.

68 *Ibid.*, January 3, 1903.

69 *Dawson Daily News*, December 17, 1902; and *Klondike Nugget*, December 23, 1902, and January 2, 1903.

70 *Yukon Sun*, January 6, 1903; *Klondike Nugget*, December 30, 1902, and January 10, 1903; and *Dawson Daily News*, December 17, 1902, and January 2, 1903.

71 *Yukon Sun*, January 10, 1903.

72 *Klondike Nugget*, January 12, 1903; and *Dawson Daily News*, December 24, 1902.

73 *Klondike Nugget*, January 12, 1903.

74 See *Yukon Sun* and *Klondike Nugget*, January 14, 1903.

75 *Yukon Sun*, January 17, 1903.

76 Ross to Sifton, December 24, 1902, Sifton Papers, vol. 132, p. 104933; T. W. O'Brien, President of the Yukon Liberal Association, to Laurier (telegram), January 2, 1903, Laurier Papers, vol. 247, pp. 68872–73; and P.C. 306, March 4, 1903. Fred Wade had asked for the appointment (in a telegram to Sifton, September 10, 1902, Sifton Papers, vol. 135, p. 107887), but Ross noted that the former Crown Prosecutor was out of favour with the "French people" (Ross to Sifton (telegram), August 29, 1902, *ibid.*, vol. 132, p. 104901). Wade was later appointed counsel to the Alaska Boundary tribunal.

77 *Klondike Nugget*, February 21, 1903.

78 *Ibid.*, March 6, 1903. The Legal Adviser had informed Wood that it was not within the power of the Acting Commissioner to convene a Council session.

79 Pringle, Landreville, Clarke, and Thompson to Laurier (telegram), March 16, 1903, Laurier Papers, vol. 255, p. 71093; and Laurier to Yukon Councillors (telegram), March 20, 1903, *ibid.*, p. 71095. The latter was reproduced in the *Klondike Nugget* on March 24, 1903.

80 *Klondike Nugget*, March 6 and April 2, 1903; and Charles Reid, Secretary of the Miners' Association, to Laurier (telegram), March 20, 1903, Laurier Papers, vol. 255, p. 71094.

81 *Klondike Nugget*, March 9, 1903.

82 *Ibid.*, March 24, 1903.

83 *Ibid.*, April 13, 1903.

84 *Dawson Daily News*, April 28, 1903.

85 *Ibid.*, April 8, 1903.

86 *Ibid.*, April 9, 1903.

87 *Ibid.*, April 9, 14, and 18, 1903.

88 Council of the Yukon Territory, *Journals* (hereafter cited as *Journals*), 1903, pp. 10 and 12–22; and *Dawson Daily News*, July 3, 1903.

89 *Journals*, 1903, pp. 35–36. H. W. Newlands succeeded Congdon as Legal Adviser and on Council by P.C. 1776, September 14, 1901.

90 *Dawson Daily News*, May 19, 1903.

91   *Journals*, 1903, p. 36. The *News* (March 19, 1903) chastised Lowe severely the next day for siding with the appointed members.

92   *Dawson Daily News*, May 19, 1903. Because of the Legal Adviser's opinion that the right of councillors to advise the Commissioner already existed, the motion was not recorded in the *Journals*. See Thomas, *Struggle*, pp. 154–55, for a discussion of the creation of the Advisory Council in the North-West Territories in 1888.

93   *Dawson Daily News*, May 24, 1903. Congdon said he would not meet any "cabinet" because, to do so would transcend his powers.

94   *Ibid.*, May 21, 1903.

95   *Journals*, 1903, pp. 42–43.

96   *Ibid.*, pp. 44–45; and *Dawson Daily News*, May 7, 1903.

97   *Journals*, 1903, p. 24; and *Dawson Daily News*, May 13, 1903.

98   *Dawson Daily News*, May 13, 1903.

99   *Klondike Nugget*, May 13, 1903.

100 The telegrams were printed in the *Dawson Daily News*, May 21, 1903.

101 *Ibid.*, May 25, 1903; and *Journals*, 1903, p. 44.

102 Dugas to Laurier (telegram), May 17, 1903, Laurier Papers, vol. 265, pp. 73406–8.

103 The petition was dated May 19, 1903. See *Canadian Annual Review*, 1903, p. 235.

104 *Ibid.*, p. 237.

105 *Dawson Daily News*, June 10, 1903.

106 John Carmack, Secretary of the Board of Trade, to Laurier (telegram), July 1, 1903, and Laurier to Carmack, July 3, 1903, Laurier Papers, vol. 271, pp. 74681 and 74780.

107 *C.S.P.*, 1904, no. 142, *Report of the Britton Commission on Hydraulic Mining*, pp. 3–5.

108 *Dawson Daily News*, August 27, 1903.

109 Minto to Laurier, November 10, 1903, Laurier Papers, vol. 289, p. 78725.

110 Willison to Laurier, October 12, 1903, *ibid.*, vol. 285, pp. 77772–77.

111 H. of C. *Debates*, 1903, cols. 11064–87.

112 *Dawson Daily News*, October 1, 1903.

113 *Journals*, 1903, p. 69; *Ordinances*, 1903, c. 14; and *Dawson Daily News*, October 16, 1903.

114 *Dawson Daily News*, December 17, 1903.

115 *Ibid.*, December 18, 1903.

116 *Ibid.*, December 21 and 22, 1903.

117 Congdon to Sifton, November 24, 1903, Sifton Papers, vol. 137, p. 111395.

118 *Dawson Daily News*, January 2, 1904.

119 *Ibid.*, January 4 and 5, 1904. Lithgow was not officially appointed by the cabinet until January 8, 1904 (P.C. 2185).

120 *Dawson Daily News*, January 5, 1904.

121 *Canadian Annual Review*, 1904, p. 353; and P.C. 1179, June 22, 1904.

CHAPTER SEVEN

1   W. S. Wallace, *The Dictionary of Canadian Biography*, p. 129; *Dawson Daily News*, April 22, 1909; PC. 571, March 13, 1901; and P.C. 1776, September 14, 1901.

2   See above, pp. 45–46, 113.

3   H. of C. *Debates*, 1907–8, col. 1126; see also *Canadian Annual Review*, 1904, p. 352.

4   No record was found of the appointments, but frequent references were made to them.

5   See, for example, *Dawson Daily News*, October 15 and May 16, 1903.

6   E. M. Reid, "The Saskatchewan Liberal Machine before 1929," in H. G. Thorburn, ed., *Party Politics in Canada* (1963 ed.), pp. 49–59.

7   T. D. Pattullo, Treasurer of the Yukon Liberal Association to Sifton, March 9, 1904, Sifton Papers, vol. 156, p. 126158.

8   *Dawson Daily News*, March 7, 1904.

9   Pattullo to Sifton, March 9, 1904, Sifton Papers, vol. 156, p. 126158; and W. F. Thompson to Sifton, March 10, 1904, *ibid.*, p. 126156.

10 Congdon to Sifton, March 9, 1904, *ibid.*, p. 126138.

11 *Dawson Daily News*, April 2, 1904.

12 *Ibid.*, April 7, 1904.

13 O'Brien to Laurier (telegram), April 8, 1904, Laurier Papers, vol. 312, p. 84326.

14 *Dawson Daily News*, April 8 and 9, 1904. Congdon's supporters used "Territorial" to differentiate their organization from the Yukon Liberal Association.

15 Bonanza Liberal Club to Laurier, April 9, 1904, Laurier Papers, vol. 312, p. 84334.

16 *Dawson Daily News*, April 14, 1904.

17 J. C. Noel to Laurier, April 9, 1904, Laurier Papers, vol. 312, pp. 84349–53. Noel had replaced F. C. Wade as Crown Prosecutor in 1902.

18 Pattullo to Laurier, April 15, 1904, *ibid.*, vol. 313, pp. 84557–58.

19 Laurier to J. C. Noel, May 3, 1904, *ibid.*, vol. 316, p. 85218; and Laurier to Pattullo, May 6, 1904, *ibid.*, vol. 313, pp. 84560–61.

20 Pattullo to Laurier, June 1, 1904, *ibid.*, vol. 316, pp. 86330–32.

21 Laurier to Pattullo, June 23, 1904, *ibid.*, p. 86334.

22 J. C. Noel to Laurier, June 2, 1904, *ibid.*, p. 86367.

23 Laurier to J. C. Noel, June 21, 1904, *ibid.*, vol. 324, p. 87028.

24 Congdon to Laurier, July 15, 1904, *ibid.*, vol. 328, pp. 88056–57.

25 *Dawson Daily News*, May 7, 1904, was the first to use the nicknames.

26 *Ibid.*

27 *Ibid.*, August 27, 1903.

28 *Ibid.*, December 7, 1903.

29 *Ibid.*, January 16, 1904.

30 *Ibid.*, February 6, 1904; and "The Dawson Conservative Association Constitution," in Sifton Papers, vol. 156, p. 126226.

31 *Dawson Daily News*, January 16, February 12, May 31, July 9 and 25, 1901.

32 *Ibid.*, February 12, 1904.

33 *Ibid.*, April 4 and 5, 1904.

34 *Ibid.*, June 27, 1904; and F. M. Shepard, Secretary of the Yukon Territorial Liberal Association, to Laurier, June 26, 1904, Laurier Papers, vol. 325, pp. 87274–80.

35 *Dawson Daily News*, June 29, 1904. Ross was appointed to the Senate shortly thereafter.

36 *Ibid.*, June 30, 1904.

37 Pattullo to Laurier, July 8, 1904, and Laurier to Pattullo, July 25, 1904, Laurier Papers, vol. 327, pp. 87744 and 87746.

38 The *Sun* became the *News*' morning edition on July 10, 1904 (J. C. Noel to R. Boudreau, Laurier's Private Secretary, July 12, 1904, *ibid.*, vol. 328, p. 88032A). Then only two newspapers were left—the *News* and the *World*. Earlier the *Nugget* had been replaced by the *Dawson Record* (*Nugget*, July 11, 1903), which, in turn, had amalgamated with the *Sun* (*Dawson Record*, October 31, 1903).

39 *Dawson Daily News*, July 15, 1904.

40 *Ibid.*, July 20, 1904; and Pattullo to Laurier, July 20, 1904, Laurier Papers, vol. 328, p. 88151.

41 Woodside to Laurier, July 26, 1904, *ibid.*, vol. 329, pp. 88401–5.

42 Laurier to Woodside, August 16, 1904, *ibid.*, p. 88411.

43 *Dawson Daily News*, July 26, 1904; and *Journals*, 1904, p. 13. Neither Mr. Pringle nor Major Wood attended the session.

44 *Ordinances*, 1904, c. 8.

45 *Dawson Daily News*, July 26, 1904; and *Journals*, 1904, pp. 10–11.

46 *Journals*, 1904, pp. 9 and 11.

47 *Ibid.*, p. 15; and *Dawson Daily News*, July 29, 1904.

48 *Dawson Daily News*, August 5, 1904. When given assent, the bill legalizing dancehalls became *Ordinances*, 1904, c. 4.

49 *Journals*, 1904, p. 25; and *Dawson Daily News*, August 4, 1904.

50 *Dawson Daily News*, June 1, 1904; and *Journals*, 1904, pp. 13–14, 22, and 40.

51 *Journals*, 1904, pp. 22 and 24; and *Dawson Daily News*, August 2, 1904.

52 *Dawson Daily News*, July 30, 1904.

53 *Ibid.*, August 4, 1904.

54 *Canadian Annual Review*, 1904, p. 352.

55 *Dawson Daily News*, July 30, 1904; and *Journals*, 1904, pp. 19 and 26–27.

56 *Dawson Daily News*, August 5, 1904; and *Journals*, 1904, p. 19.

57 *Dawson Daily News*, August 24, 1904.

58 *Journals*, 1904, pp. 12 and 38; and *Ordinances*, 1904, c. 12.

59   Congdon to Sifton, September 26, 1904, Sifton Papers, vol. 156, p. 126290; and *Dawson Daily News*, September 7, 1904.
60   *Dawson Daily News*, September 8 and 9, 1904.
61   *Ibid.*, September 10, 1904.
62   *Ibid.*, September 13, 1904.
63   *Canadian Annual Review*, 1904, pp. 217–18.
64   *Journals*, 1905, p. 11.
65   Congdon to Sifton, September 26, 1904, Sifton Papers, vol. 156, p. 126292.
66   Congdon to Laurier, September 21, 1904, and Laurier to Congdon, October 13, 1904, Laurier Papers, vol. 336, pp. 89893–94.
67   Congdon to Sifton (telegram), October 27, 1904, Sifton Papers, vol. 156, p. 126311.
68   *Dawson Daily News*, October 31, 1904; and Congdon to Laurier, October 29, 1904, Laurier Papers, vol. 341, p. 91219. On Congdon's telegram (see above, *n.* 67), Sifton had scribbled a reply: "I think you should accept."
69   *Dawson Daily News*, October 31, 1904. Actually, Temple remained on the government payroll throughout the campaign (H. of C. *Debates*, 1907–8, col. 1126).
70   *Dawson Daily News*, October 13, 1904.
71   *Ibid.*, October 3, 1904.
72   *Ibid.*, October 15, 1904.
73   McDonald to Laurier, November 4, 1904, Laurier Papers, vol. 342, p. 91456.
74   *Dawson Daily News*, November 4, 1904.
75   Congdon was widely known as the "silver-tongued orator" (see L. B. Berton, *I Married the Klondike*, p. 65).
76   *Dawson Daily News*, November 17, 1904.
77   *Ibid.*, November 17 and 18, 1904.
78   See *ibid.* and *Yukon World*, issues of November and December, 1904; and Z. T. Wood to F. White, December 19, 1904, Sifton Papers, vol. 176, pp. 143096–105.
79   *Dawson Daily News*, December 5 and 7–13, 1904.
80   M. L. Black, *My Seventy Years*, p. 191.
81   *Dawson Daily News*, December 13, 1904.
82   *Ibid.*, December 17, 19 and 24, 1904.
83   *Ibid.*, March 13, 1904.
84   *Ibid.*, November 13, 1905, and May 14, 1906.
85   Yukon Territorial Liberal Association to Laurier (telegram), December 19, 1904, Laurier Papers, vol. 347, p. 92848. Several Dawsonites telegraphed the Prime Minister on December 23 asking him not to reappoint Congdon (*ibid.*, p. 92931).
86   Congdon to Sifton (telegram), December 20, 1904, Sifton Papers, vol. 156, p. 126338; and *Dawson Daily News*, December 26, 1904.
87   P.C. 2284, December 20, 1904.
88   Wood to Wade, November 28, 1904, Sifton Papers, vol. 175, p. 142477.
89   Wood to White, December 19 and 22, 1904, *ibid.*, vol. 176, pp. 143096–105 and 143107.
90   O'Brien to Laurier (telegram), December 20, 1904, Laurier Papers, vol. 347, p. 92828; Woodside to Laurier, December 21, 1904, *ibid.*, vol. 348, p. 92885; and Woodside to Laurier, July 26, 1904, *ibid.*, vol. 324, p. 88405.
91   McDonald to Laurier (telegram), December 21, 1904, *ibid.*, vol. 348, p. 92891.
92   Girouard to Laurier, November 7, 1904, *ibid.*, vol. 343, p. 91859.
93   H. B. Gilmour to Laurier (telegram), November 10, 1904, *ibid.*, vol. 344, p. 92065; and Ross to Sifton, December 3, 1904 (telegram), Sifton Papers, vol. 171, p. 138455. See also C. J. V. Spratt to Laurier (telegram), December 28, 1904, Laurier Papers, vol. 348, pp. 93030–31.
94   *Ordinances*, 1904, c. 18.
95   *Dawson Daily News*, January 7, 1905.
96   *Ibid.*, December 29, 1904.
97   *Ibid.*, January 9, 16, 25, and 27, and February 9, 1905.
98   *Ibid.*, February 6 and 8, 1905.
99   *Ibid.*, March 2, 1905; and Sifton to A. Thompson (telegram), December 27, 1904, in *ibid.*, December 29, 1904.
100 J. W. Dafoe, *Clifford Sifton in Relation to His Times*, p. 288.
101 *Dawson Daily News*, March 7, 1905.

102   See *ibid.*, issues of March 1905.

103   Even though only one "Tab" was nominated, the *News* (March 30, 1905) was afraid that Macaulay, placed in the election as a "feeler," would reinstate the whole Congdon mob if elected.

104   *Ibid.*, March 29, 1905. Just before nominations closed, a deputy returning officer in the recent federal election announced that he would run in Klondike to split the English-speaking vote with Black, thereby allowing Maxime Landreville, with French-Canadian support, to win (*ibid.*, March 23, 1905). However, both of Black's prospective opponents filed their nomination papers too late to become candidates (*ibid.*, March 29, 1905).

105   *Ibid.*, April 10 and 11, 1905.

106   *Ibid.*, April 10, 1905.

107   See *ibid.*, issues of April 1905, especially April 10 and 11.

108   *Ibid.*, April 11, 1905. The reference to the brewing industry was personal because O'Brien had owned the only local brewery.

109   "Report of Assistant Commissioner Wood for 1905," *C.S.P.*, 1906, no. 28, *Annual Report of the Commissioner of the North-West Mounted Police Force for 1905*, s. III, p. 17.

110   Because there were still official voters' lists, it is difficult to estimate the percentage accurately. The final results were listed in *Dawson Daily News*, April 13 and May 12, 1905.

111   Although Gillespie was not the regular party candidate, he agreed to work towards Y.I.P. goals (*ibid.*, April 13, 1905).

112   *Ibid.*, April 13, 1905.

113   Clarke to Laurier (telegram), April 17, 1905, Laurier Papers, vol. 362, p. 96651.

114   Laurier to Clarke, April 20, 1905, *ibid.*, p. 96652; and Clarke to Laurier, May 9, 1905, *ibid.*, vol. 365, pp. 97337–39.

115   *Dawson Daily News*, May 5, 1905.

116   J. C. Noel to Laurier, April 18, 1905, Laurier Papers, vol. 362, pp. 96665–66; and D. MacRae to Laurier, May 2, 1905, *ibid.*, p. 97104.

117   Laurier to J. C. Noel, May 8, 1905, *ibid.*, p. 96669; and Laurier to A. Noel, April 27, 1905, *ibid.*, p. 96924.

118   Laurier to A. Noel, June 2, 1905, *ibid.*, p. 97088; and June 8, 1905, *ibid.*, vol. 366, p. 97627.

119   P.C. 968, May 27, 1905.

120   By naming the *World* as Official Gazette and by refusing to appoint a three-man commission to govern Dawson.

121   By seizing the civic administration prior to the plebiscite on the Dawson city charter.

122   Judge Craig had no power to prevent Congdon from carrying out the plebiscite, but, in his official capacity, the judge condemned the Commissioner and the mayor of Dawson for their behaviour.

CHAPTER EIGHT

1   Particularly when a consolidated mining code for the Yukon came before the Senate in 1906 (Canada, Senate, *Debates*, 1906, pp. 853–69).

2   Compare reports of the two receptions in *Dawson Daily News*, July 1 and 4, 1905.

3   *Ibid.*, July 8, 1905.

4   McInnes to Laurier, July 24, 1905, Laurier Papers, vol. 375, pp. 99964–65.

5   J. C. Noel to Laurier, September 5, 1905, *ibid.*, vol. 380, p. 101011; Laurier to Congdon, July 28, 1905, *ibid.*, vol. 374, p. 99692; and Congdon to Laurier, *ibid.*, vol. 381, p. 101360.

6   Thompson to Laurier, November 5, 1905, and Laurier to Thompson, December 7, 1905, *ibid.*, vol. 386, pp. 102914–15 and 102817.

7   *Dawson Daily News*, April 1, 1906.

8   H. of C. *Debates*, 1905, cols. 7021–59.

9   *Ibid.*, cols. 7074–79.

10   *Ibid.*, col. 7085.

11   *Dawson Daily News*, August 28, 1905. In his journey north in 1897, Sifton got only as far as the Alaska panhandle.

12   See *ibid.*, August 30 and 31 and September 1, 1905, for accounts of Oliver's visit.

13   The Y.I.P. representatives sought unsuccessfully to secure the appointment of a committee to

investigate Congdon's role in the Dawson City plebiscite (*Journals*, 1905, p. 11). They were also defeated in attempts to abolish the office of King's Printer and to open government printing to public tender (*ibid.*, p. 12).

14 *Dawson Daily News*, August 23, 1905.
15 *Journals*, 1905, p. 14; and *Dawson Daily News*, August 25, 1905.
16 *Journals*, 1905, pp. 16–17; and *Dawson Daily News*, September 6, 1905.
17 *Dawson Daily News*, September 6, 1905.
18 *Ibid.*, September 11, 1905.
19 *Journals*, 1905, p. 24.
20 *Ibid.*, pp. 33–34.
21 *Ibid.*, pp. 10 and 26.
22 *Ibid.*, p. 18.
23 *Dawson Daily News*, August 26, 1905.
24 *Ibid.*, January 6, 1906.
25 *Ibid.*, February 1, 1906.
26 *Ibid.*, November 21 and December 22, 1905.
27 *Ibid.*, November 23, 1905, and succeeding issues.
28 *Ibid.*, January 18, 1906.
29 *Ibid.*, February 10, 1906. The petitions of the two groups may be found in Laurier Papers, vol. 402, pp. 107158 and 107161.
30 *Dawson Daily News*, May 5, 1906.
31 *Ibid.*, January 9, 1908.
32 P.C. 1016, May 26, 1906 (later upheld in the Territorial Court—*Dawson Daily News*, October 29, 1906); and the Yukon Placer Mining Act, *Statutes of Canada*, 1906, c. 39.
33 *Dawson Daily News*, February 14 and March 19, 1906.
34 *Ibid.*, August 20, 1906.
35 *Ibid.*, March 29, 1906.
36 H. of C. *Debates*, 1906, cols. 2886–89.
37 *Dawson Daily News*, May 12, 1906.
38 *Ibid.*, May 16, 1906.
39 *Ibid.*, May 22, 1906.
40 H. of C. *Debates*, 1906, cols. 5104 and 5114.
41 *Ibid.*, cols. 6553–54.
42 *Journals*, 1906, pp. 19 and 23.
43 *Dawson Daily News*, July 13, 1906.
44 *Journals*, 1906, p. 37.
45 *Ordinances*, 1906, cc. 5 and 9.
46 See *Canadian Annual Review*, 1906, p. 511; *Dawson Daily News*, March 1 and June 18, 1906; and *Journals*, 1906, p. 11.
47 H. of C. *Debates*, 1906–7, col. 4537.
48 McInnes to Laurier, June 19, 1906, Laurier Papers, vol. 417, pp. 111395–96.
49 Wells to Laurier, August 13, 1906, *ibid.*, vol. 423, pp. 112880–87 and 112891.
50 Laurier to McInnes, September 14, 1906, *ibid.*, vol. 427, p. 113483; and McInnes to Laurier, October 10, 1906, *ibid.*, vol. 423, pp. 112897–98.
51 MacRae to Laurier, November 1, 1906, *ibid.*, p. 112901.
52 Thompson to Laurier, October 28, 1906, *ibid.*, vol. 429, p. 114583; Pattullo to Laurier, November 12, 1906, *ibid.*, vol. 432, p. 115520; and Resolution of Yukon Liberal Association, November 10, 1906, *ibid.*, p. 115521,
53 Wells to Laurier, November 28, 1906, *ibid.*, vol. 423, pp. 112907–8.
54 White to Laurier, August 23, 1906, *ibid.*, pp. 113081–82.
55 *Dawson Daily News*, November 8, 1906; and *Canadian Annual Review*, 1906, p. 597.
56 *Dawson Daily News*, January 7, 1906.
57 Laurier to McInnes, September 14, 1906, Laurier Papers, vol. 427, p. 113483. On February 14, 1907, Laurier was asked if formal charges of misconduct had been laid against McInnes. The Prime Minister told the House of Wells' letter, but noted that the complaints in it had been completely repudiated (H. of C. *Debates*, 1906–7, col. 2978).
58 P.C. 756, April 9, 1907.

CHAPTER NINE

1 L. B. Berton, *I Married the Klondike*, p. 14 (Mrs. Berton's italics).

2 *Dawson Daily News*, January 5, 1907.

3 The proceedings of the meeting were not mentioned in the *Dawson Daily News*. Sam Hughes, a Conservative member of Parliament, read the minutes and resolutions in the House of Commons (H. of C. *Debates*, 1906–7, cols. 5677–79).

4 Resolution of the Yukon Territorial Liberal Association, January 12, 1907, Laurier Papers, vol. 442, p. 118111A.

5 H. of C. *Debates*, 1906–7, col. 5678; and Pringle to Oliver, January 19, 1907, *ibid.*, 1907–8, col. 9623 (my italics).

6 *Toronto News*, March 11, 1907, *ibid.*, 1906–7, cols. 4542–43.

7 Pringle to Laurier, May 27, 1902, *ibid.*, 1907–8, cols. 9583–88.

8 *Ibid.*, January 3, 1905, cols. 9589–94.

9 Laurier to Pringle, February 6, 1905, *ibid.*, col. 9594.

10 Memorandum of F. T. Congdon re charges laid by the Rev. John Pringle, *ibid.*, cols. 9595–98.

11 *Journals*, 1904, p. 13; and *Dawson Daily News*, July 14, 1903.

12 According to a letter from Pringle to Laurier, November 30, 1906, H. of C. *Debates*, 1907–8, col. 9599.

13 Pringle to Laurier, July 31, 1907, *ibid.*, col. 9600.

14 As far as Lithgow was concerned, Pringle did not state much more publicly than he did privately to Oliver in his letter of January 19 cited above. With respect to Girouard, Pringle produced several affidavits alleging that the Registrar was frequenting the home of a prostitute when he was supposed to be attending to office duties on the day of the Thompson–Congdon election. Apparently several men from the Thompson campaign sought out Girouard, and chased him, half-naked, after he had escaped through the back door of the house (see *ibid.*, cols. 9658–59).

15 *Dawson Daily News*, July 1, 1907; and unnumbered order in council of June 17, 1907.

16 *Dawson Daily News*, July 15, 1907.

17 Henderson to Oliver, December 7, 1907, H. of C. *Debates*, 1907–8, col. 9605; and *Toronto News*, March 11, 1907, *ibid.*, 1906–7, col. 4542.

18 *Dawson Daily News*, March 9 and April 2, 1907.

19 *Ibid.*, April 3, 1907.

20 *Ibid.*, April 12, 1907.

21 *Ibid.*, April 5, 1907. The *Yukon World* was being published as the morning edition of the *News*.

22 Out of 2,660 eligible voters 1,517 exercised their franchise (see *ibid.*, April 30 and May 1, 1907).

23 *Ibid.*, April 17, 1907.

24 See V. O. Key, Jr., *Southern Politics*, pp. 37–39.

25 Henderson to Oliver, December 7, 1907, H. of C. *Debates*, 1907–8, col. 9606; and *Ordinances*, 1907, c. 9.

26 *Dawson Daily News*, August 14, 15, and 29, 1907; and *Journals*, 1907, p. 46.

27 Henderson to Oliver, December 7, 1907, H. of C. *Debates*, 1907–8, col. 9606.

28 Oliver to Pringle, August 28, 1907; Henderson to Oliver, November 8, 1907; and Oliver to Pringle, November 14, 1907, *ibid.*, cols. 9601 and 9603.

29 Henderson to Oliver, November 8, 1907, and Oliver to Pringle, November 14, 1907, *ibid.*, col. 9603.

30 Henderson to Oliver (telegram), December 17, 1907, *ibid.*, col. 9604.

31 *Toronto News*, January 28, 1908, *ibid.*, col. 9612.

32 *Dawson Daily News*, January 15 and 17, 1908.

33 *Ibid.*, February 18 and 25, 1908.

34 *Ibid.*, March 28, 1908.

35 The debate on the Pringle affair is in H. of C. *Debates*, 1907–8, cols. 9580–9693.

36 *Dawson Daily News*, March 20, 1908.

37 *Ibid.*, July 23 and 25, and April 1, 1908; and *Journals*, 1908, pp. 11 and 18.

38 *Canadian Annual Review*, 1908, p. 544.

39 L. Berton, *I Married*, p. 36.

40 *Canadian Annual Review*, 1908, p. 542.

41 Francis Cunynghame, *Lost Trail*, pp. 59–60.

42 *Dawson Daily News*, October 16 and 17, 1906.

43   H. A. Innis, *Settlement and the Mining Frontier*, pp. 244–45.

44   *Ibid.*, p. 262; and *Dawson Daily News*, March 30, 1907.

45   *Dawson Daily News*, August 18, September 8 and 11, and issues of October and November 1908. The last reference to the work of the association was in *ibid.*, November 23, 1908.

46   H. of C. *Debates*, 1906–7, cols. 4521–23. During the 1907 session of the Yukon Council, George Black proposed another motion requesting the establishment of an advisory committee on finance. He received support only from Dr. LaChapelle. (*Journals*, 1907, p. 26; and *Dawson Daily News*, August 9, 1907.)

47   A. Thompson, "Government of Yukon," *Alaska-Yukon Magazine*, V (1908), p. 414.

48   See the Yukon (Amendment) Act, *Statutes of Canda*, 1908, c. 76.

49   See, for example, R. G. Robertson, "The Evolution of Territorial Government in Canada," in J. H. Aitchison, ed., *The Political Process in Canada*, pp. 141–42 and 151–52; and L. Wilson, "How Canada Plans to Give Self-Government to Our Northland," *Financial Post*, January 23, 1960.

50   See L. H. Thomas, *The Struggle for Responsible Government in the North-West Territories*, pp. 152–55. In 1888 the Legislative Assembly of the North-West Territories was not made fully elective because three of the twenty-five prospective members were to be judges appointed by the federal government to sit as non-voting members responsible for drafting legislation and giving legal advice. However, because the Lieutenant Governor was to be barred from deliberating with the Assembly and the three judges were not to be regarded as representatives of the executive, a situation almost identical to the one envisioned by the 1908 amendment would have occurred had not Nicholas Flood Davin, the Member of Parliament for Assiniboia, insisted upon the establishment of an executive council. Sir John A. compromised and inserted a clause constituting the Advisory Council on Finance. Actually, Macdonald deviated even further than Laurier from accepted practices by not conferring upon the Lieutenant Governor the power to dissolve the Assembly before the completion of its three-year term.

51   H. of C. *Debates*, 1907–8, cols. 10529–30.

52   Canada, Senate, *Debates*, 1907–8, pp. 1233–34.

53   *Ibid.*, p. 1234.

54   H. of C. *Debates*, 1907–8, col. 10530.

55   See *C.S.P.*, 1899–1909, no. 1, *Annual Report of the Auditor General*.

56   See P.C. 439, April 20, 1905; P.C. 64, May 31, 1906; H. of C. *Debates*, 1906–7, col. 6252; and *ibid.*, 1907–8, col. 10108.

57   *Dawson Daily News*, December 23, 1908.

58   *Ibid.*, March 21, 1908.

59   *Ibid.*, October 23, 24, and 29, 1908.

60   *Ibid.*, issues of October, November, and December 1908, and January 1909. Joe Clarke's antics, as usual, provided newspaper reporters with the opportunity of adding colour to their stories on the election campaign. The following is a description of Clarke's behaviour at a mass meeting: "[The meeting's] . . . grand finale came about midnight, when Joe Clarke with dishevelled locks, flushed countenance and his voice quivering with the righteous indignation he felt, in replying to the previous speakers came near having a hemorrhage and going straight up through the ceiling. . . . Joe clawed the air . . . paced up and down before the footlights and yelled above the din and confusion that he was the most abused and persecuted man on earth and he did not propose to stand for it." (*Ibid.*, November 28, 1908.)

61   *Ibid.*, January 20, 1909. The final results were Congdon, 992; Black, 726; Lowe, 482; and Clarke, 265 (*ibid.*, February 16, 1909).

62   *Ibid.* As a final melodramatic gesture, Clarke wrote an open letter to "the people of the Yukon." Entitling it "Farewell and Not au Revoir," he said, in part: "I quit. I will . . . leave the Yukon for keeps. Broke, down and out, with health galore and a clear conscience as my only assets. . . . Being not even the senior minority representative, I owe the Yukon no service; that they did not want any from me, they have amply proved. Hearts do not break very easy, and the separation of two thousand miles may even take the sting out of such venom as my untruthful opponents . . . are still indulging in, even after such a defeat. Of course, I am sore, disappointed and cast down, but few will ever realize it after I once take the stage for the outside. An eye for an eye and a tooth for a tooth. Others have been driven out of the Yukon for their own good. As each individual has been to me, I am to them." (*Ibid.*, January 23, 1909.)

Clarke moved to Edmonton, and just three years after his departure from the Yukon, he was married, out of debt, and an alderman on the city council (*ibid.*, February 2, 1912). Elected mayor of

Edmonton in 1918 (*ibid.*, January 2, 1919) and again in later years, he died with a durable memorial to his name—Clarke Stadium, home of the Edmonton Eskimos.

CHAPTER TEN

1   See H. A. Innis, *Settlement and the Mining Frontier*, p. 265.
2   Appendix B, "Gold Production in the Yukon, 1885–1918"; and *Dawson Daily News*, November 7, 1908.
3   See M. L. Black, *My Seventy Years*, p. 231 ff., for a discussion of the activities of Yukon soldiers in World War I.
4   The figure of 1,475 Indians includes 80 migratory Eskimos who happened to be in the territory when the census was taken (Canada, Dominion Bureau of Statistics, *Census of Canada*, 1921, vol. I, pp. 356–57). The population in 1911 had been 8,512 (Canada, Census and Statistics Office, *Census of Canada*, 1911, vol. I, p. 169).
5   This conclusion is drawn from a perusal of reports in the *Dawson Daily News*, but see also L. B. Berton, *I Married the Klondike*, pp. 44–45.
6   *Dawson Daily News*, March 5, 1920. See February and March issues of that newspaper for an account of the activities of the People's Prohibition Movement, whose leaders were mostly drawn from the ranks of Dawson's women. Prohibition was made law by *Ordinances*, 1920, cc. 9 and 10.
7   *Dawson Daily News*, June 1, 1909, and January 22, 1910. The latter contains a detailed article on the activities of the "citizens' committee."
8   *Ibid.*, March 15, 1911.
9   L. B. Berton, *I Married*, pp. 119–20.
10   *Dawson Daily News*, July 10, 1911. Henderson's resignation was confirmed in P.C. 26–2721, November 30, 1911, and Wilson was appointed Administrator with full powers to act in the Commissioner's absence by P.C. 2059, October 9, 1909.
11   P.C. 225, January, 1912.
12   *Dawson Daily News*, August 15 and September 25, 1911. Thompson was chosen by a Conservative convention three days after the general election results were announced.
13   See *ibid.*, September 12 to October 23, 1911.
14   Incomplete returns gave Thompson 1,150 votes and Congdon 750 (*ibid.*, October 24, 1911). No reference was found to the final results.
15   *Ibid.*, January 1, 1918. Congdon's intentions to run as a Laurier Liberal are apparent from the fact that he did not repudiate certain letters and speeches that were quoted by Dr. Thompson during the course of the campaign (see *ibid.*, issues of January 1918, especially January 17).
16   *Ibid.*, November 13, 1917, and January 9, 1918.
17   *Ibid.*, issues of January 1918, especially January 16 and 17.
18   *Ibid.*, January 29, 1918. Final results, published in *ibid.*, February 18, 1918, gave Congdon 776 out of a total of 1,442 votes.
19   A *News* correspondent (*ibid.*, February 28, 1918) reported in February, three months before the dispute was settled, that these figures would result from the allotment of Unionist votes to Thompson and Laurier Liberal ones to Congdon. Apparently Yukon soldiers voted before the general election, long before it was apparent that there would be two Unionist candidates in their constituency. For a brief account of the controversy, see *ibid.*, May 22 and 23, 1918; for details of the role the House of Commons played in settling it, see H. of C. *Debates*, 1918, pp. 735, 1835, 2067, 2097–2100, 2194, 2209, 2215–41, 2382, 2504–6.
20   *Dawson Daily News*, issues of June 1909 (especially June 10), February and March 1915, February and March 1917, and April 1912.
21   See *Journals*, 1909 and 1910; and *Dawson Daily News*, issues of July and August 1909, and May and June 1910. At the end of the 1910 session, Commissioner Henderson reserved four bills (*Journals*, 1910, pp. 76–77), which became null and void when the federal Minister of Justice decided in February 1911 to take no action to implement them. (*Sessional Papers of the Council of the Yukon Territory*, 1911, p. 31. The sessional papers may be found in an appendix to *Journals*, 1911.)
22   See *Journals*, 1909–18.
23   *Ibid.*, 1912–15.
24   Council was reduced to three members in 1919 (The Yukon [Amendment] Act, *Statutes of*

Canada, 1919, c. 9), and then increased in size to five in 1951 (*ibid.*, 1951, c. 23) and seven in 1960 (*ibid.*, 1960, c. 24). In this last case, the act amended was a new one—The Yukon Territory Act, *Statutes of Canada*, 1953, c. 53.

25   See F. B. Fingland, "Recent Constitutional Developments in the Yukon and the Northwest Territories," *University of Toronto Law Journal*, XV, 2 (1964), pp. 306–10; and R. G. Robertson, "The Evolution of Territorial Government in Canada," in J. H. Aitchison, ed., *The Political Process in Canada*, pp. 151–52.

26   Early in 1967, a newspaper columnist reported that two Yukon councillors—Don Taylor and John Watt—were seeking to secure provincial status for the Yukon as a Canadian centennial project. Erik Nielsen, Progressive Conservative member of Parliament for the territory, promised to lend his support to the campaign. Both in content and style, the comments of these three men were similar to those of territorial politicians early in the century. For example, Mr. Watt stated: "We've had nothing but a continuous brainwashing on this Council by Ottawa. Ottawa's been telling us we aren't ready for self-government. We'll have the last word on that." Even more strongly in the tradition of Joe Clarke, Mr. Nielsen said: "The population in Manitoba [when it became a province] was . . . about the same as it is now in the Yukon and the two situations are remarkably similar. [A] rebellion sparked province-hood for Manitoba and could as well do it for the Yukon." (See Bruce West, "11th Province," *Globe and Mail* [Toronto], January 20, 1967.) Later in that year, most of the candidates in a Council election ran on a platform of greater territorial autonomy. Mr. Watt was defeated in Whitehorse West, but his victorious opponent was also a strong supporter of increased popular control and responsibility (see Canadian Press release in *Peterborough Examiner*, September 12, 1967).

27   Black, *Seventy Years*, p. 226.
28   *Dawson Daily News*, April 5, 1918.
29   *Ibid.*, April 8 and 12, 1918.
30   The Yukon (Amendment) Act, *Statutes of Canada*, 1918, c. 50.
31   *Dawson Daily News*, April 12, 1918.
32   *Ibid.*, April 13 and 14, 1918.
33   *Ibid.*, April 17 and 25, 1918.
34   *Ibid.*, April 14 and May 1, 1918.
35   *Ibid.*, May 6, 1918.
36   *Ibid.*
37   Royal assent was given on May 24. Only a few questions were asked and comments made during the stages of second reading and committee consideration (see H. of C. *Debates*, 1918, pp. 982–83; and Canada, Senate, *Debates*, 1918, pp. 334–35).
38   *Dawson Daily News*, January 31, 1919. The enabling legislation was passed by Parliament later in the year (see The Yukon [Amendment] Act, *Statutes of Canada*, 1919, c. 9). The office of Commissioner was reinstated in the 1940's (C. C. Lingard, "Administration of the Canadian Northland," *Canadian Journal of Economics and Political Science*, XII (February 1946), p. 53).
39   L. B. Berton, *I Married*, p. 162.

BIBLIOGRAPHY

PRIVATE PAPERS[1]

Papers of Charles Constantine.
Papers of Clifford Sifton.
Papers of the Fourth Earl of Minto, vol. 24.
Papers of Sir Wilfrid Laurier.

NEWSPAPERS

Dawson Daily News, 1900–20, microfilm, National Library of Canada, Ottawa.
Dawson Record, 1903, microfilm, National Library of Canada, Ottawa.
Dawson Sunday Gleaner, 1899, Public Archives of British Columbia, Victoria.
Klondike Miner, 1899, Public Archives of British Columbia, Victoria; 1901–2, private collection of (Mrs.) Athol Retallack, Dawson City.
Klondike Nugget, 1898–1903, microfilm, University of Washington Library, Seattle.
Yukon Sun, 1898–1904, microfilm, National Library of Canada, Ottawa.

GOVERNMENT PUBLICATIONS AND DOCUMENTS

A. GOVERNMENT OF CANADA

AGRICULTURE, DEPARTMENT OF, *The Statistical Year-Book of Canada*, 1899–1904.
CENSUS AND STATISTICS OFFICE, *Census of Canada*, 1901 and 1911.
—— *Special Report on the Foreign-born Population*, 1915.
COLLINS, F. H., *The Yukon Territory*, Queen's Printer, 1955 (a brief presented to the Royal Commission on Canada's Economic Prospects).
GOVERNOR IN COUNCIL, Orders in Council relating to the Yukon, 1894–1920 (five volumes in the Mining Recorder's Office, Dawson City).
HOUSE OF COMMONS, *Debates*, 1898–1920.
INTERIOR, DEPARTMENT OF, *The Administration of the Yukon*, undated (probably 1928), mimeo.
—— Files relating to the administration of the Yukon, 1897–1909 (in government offices, Whitehorse and Dawson City[2]).
—— Interior Department Records of Field Offices in the Yukon Territory, 1898–1909 (in Public Archives of Canada, Ottawa[3]).
—— *The Yukon Territory*, 1926.
—— *The Yukon Territory: Its History and Resources*, 1907, 1909, and 1916.
—— *Yukon: Land of the Klondike*, prepared by F. H. Kitto, 1930.
MINES AND RESOURCES, DEPARTMENT OF, *The Yukon Territory: Administration, Resources and Development*, 1943 and 1944.

---

[1] In the Public Archives of Canada, Ottawa.
[2] The location of material cited from these files has been indicated in parentheses.
[3] In all references to files of the Department of the Interior in the Public Archives of Canada, "Dawson" has been placed in parentheses to indicate that the files were numbered in accordance with the system used for the files found in Dawson City.

MINES AND RESOURCES, DEPARTMENT OF, *Yukon Territory: History, Administration, Resources and Development*, prepared by W. F. Lothian, 1947.

NATIONAL DEFENCE, DEPARTMENT OF, *Note on the Yukon Field Force*, 1950, mimeo.

NORTHERN AFFAIRS AND NATIONAL RESOURCES, DEPARTMENT OF, *The Yukon: Its Riches and Resources*, 1957 and 1962.

RESOURCES AND DEVELOPMENT, DEPARTMENT OF, *Yukon Territory: A Brief Description of Its History, Administration, Resources and Development*, 1950.

SENATE, *Debates*, 1899–1920.

SENATE, *Journals*, 1898.

Sessional Papers

Annual Report of the Auditor General, 1898–1909, no. 1.

Annual Report of the Commissioner of the North-West Mounted Police Force, 1894–96, no. 15; 1897–99, no. 13; and 1900–5, no. 28.

Annual Report of the Commissioner of the Royal North-West Mounted Police Force, 1906–7 to 1909, no. 28.

Annual Report of the Department of the Interior, 1895–96, no. 13; 1897–99, no. 15; and 1900–20, no. 25.

Correspondence between Ottawa and Regina respecting Liquor Permits, 1898, no. 51a.

Correspondence etc. relating to the Treadgold Hydraulic Mining Syndicate, 1903, no. 63.

Evidence Taken before the Commission Appointed to Investigate Charges of Alleged Malfeasance of Officials of the Yukon Territory, 1899, no. 87a.

Gold Production in the Yukon, 1885–97, 1898, no. 30a.

Letters and Reports from Major Walsh, 1898, no. 38b.

Report of the Britton Commission on Hydraulic Mining, 1904, no. 142.

Report of Commissioner Ogilvie for 1898–99, 1900, no. 33u.

Report of Inspector Constantine for 1895, 1896, no. 15a.

Report of the Ogilvie Commission of Inquiry, 1899, no. 87.

Special Report of Commissioner Henderson for 1907–08, 1907–8, no. 25c.

SMITH, GORDON W., *Territorial Sovereignty in the Canadian North: A Historical Outline of the Problem*, Northern Co-ordination and Research Centre, 1963.

Statutes of Canada, 1898–1960.

B. GOVERNMENT OF THE YUKON TERRITORY

Council, *Journals*, 1903–20.

Ordinances of the Yukon Territory, 1898–1920.[4]

BOOKS AND ARTICLES

ADNEY, TAPPAN, *The Klondike Stampede*, New York, Harper and Brothers, 1900.

BANKSON, R. A., *The Klondike Nugget*, Caldwell, Idaho, Caxton Printers, 1935.

BERTON, LAURA B., *I Married the Klondike*, Boston, Little Brown, 1952.

BERTON, PIERRE, *The Klondike Fever*, New York, Alfred A. Knopf, 1958.

BLACK, MARTHA L., *My Seventy Years*, London, Thomas Nelson and Sons, 1938.

BORDON, HENRY, ed., *Robert Laird Borden: His Memoirs*, Toronto, Macmillan, 1938.

BROWN, J. N. E., "The Evolution of Law and Government in the Yukon Territory," in S. MORLEY WICKETT, ed., *The Municipal Government of Toronto*, Toronto, University of Toronto Press, 1907, pp. 197–212.

Canadian Parliamentary Guide, 1901–20.

CATTO, WILLIAM, *The Yukon Administration*, Dawson, King St. Job Office, 1902.

CUNYNGHAME, FRANCIS, *Lost Trail*, London, Faber and Faber, 1953.

---

[4] Only the ordinances passed and given assent between 1903 and 1920 were published. The author found the rest in a bound volume in the Mining Recorder's Office, Dawson City.

DAFOE, J. W., *Clifford Sifton in Relation to His Times*, Toronto, Macmillan, 1931.
DAWSON, W. F., *Procedure in the Canadian House of Commons*, Toronto, University of Toronto Press, 1962.
FETHERSTONHAUGH, R., *The Royal Canadian Mounted Police*, New York, Carrick and Evans, 1938.
FINGLAND, F. B., "Recent Constitutional Developments in the Yukon and the Northwest Territories," *University of Toronto Law Journal*, XV, 2 (1964), pp. 299–316.
FLEMING, G. S., "The Yukon Telegraph Service," *Dawson Daily News*, August 17, 1917.
HAMILTON, Z. M., "The Late Senator Ross," *Regina Leader-Post*, December 16, 1932.
HASKELL, W. B., *Two Years in the Klondike and Alaskan Gold-Fields*, Hartford, Hartford Publishing Company, 1898.
HAYDON, A. L., *Riders of the Plains*, Toronto, Copp Clark, 1910.
HOPKINS, J. CASTELL, ed., *Canadian Annual Review*, 1902–9.
INNIS, H. A., *Settlement and the Mining Frontier*, vol. IX, in W. A. MACKINTOSH and W. L. G. JOERG, eds., *Canadian Frontiers of Settlement*, Toronto, Macmillan, 1939, pp. 171–413.
KEY, V. O., JR., *Southern Politics*, New York, Vintage Books (Random House), 1949.
LEECHMAN, DOUGLAS, "Yukon Territory," *Canadian Geographical Journal*, XL (June 1950), pp. 240–67.
LINGARD, C. C., "Administration of the Canadian Northland," *Canadian Journal of Economics and Political Science*, XII (February 1946), pp. 45–74.
——— *Territorial Government in Canada: The Autonomy Question in the Old North-West Territories*, Toronto, University of Toronto Press, 1946.
LONGSTRETH, T. MORRIS, *The Silent Force*, London, Philip Allan, 1938.
MACBETH, M. A., *Policing the Arctic*, London, Hodder and Stoughton, 1932.
MORGAN, H. J., ed., *The Canadian Men and Women of Our Time*, Toronto, William Briggs, 1912.
OGILVIE, WILLIAM, *Early Days on the Yukon*, London, John Lane, 1913.
PHILLIPS, R. A. J., "The Klondike Legend," *Canadian Geographical Journal*, LXIV (March 1962), pp. 76–85.
REID, ESCOTT M., "The Saskatchewan Liberal Machine Before 1929," in HUGH G. THORBURN, ed., *Party Politics in Canada*, Toronto, Prentice-Hall, 1963, pp. 49–59.
ROBERTSON, R. G., "The Evolution of Territorial Government in Canada," in J. H. AITCHISON, ed., *The Political Process in Canada*, Toronto, University of Toronto Press, 1964, pp. 136–52.
STEELE, HARWOOD, *Policing the Arctic*, Toronto, Ryerson Press, 1925.
THOMAS, L. H., *The Struggle for Responsible Government in the North-West Territories*, Toronto, University of Toronto Press, 1956.
THOMPSON, ALFRED, "Government of Yukon," *Alaska-Yukon Magazine*, V (1908), pp. 413–14.
TOMKINS, STUART R., "The Klondike Gold-Rush: A Great International Adventure," *British Columbia Historical Quarterly*, XVII, 3 (1953), pp. 223–29.
——— *Alaska: Promyshlennik and Sourdough*, Norman, University of Oklahoma Press, 1945.
TRAMER, WILLIAM, "James Hamilton Ross—a Western Public Man," *Manitoba Free Press*, September 16, 1902.
TYRRELL, J. B., "The Yukon Territory," in A. SHORTT and A. C. DOUGHTY, eds., *Canada and Its Provinces*, Toronto, Glasgow, Brook & Company, vol. XXII, 1914, pp. 585–636.
WADE, F. C., "A Business Talk on the Yukon," *The Canadian Magazine*, XIX (May 1902), pp. 25–31.
WALLACE, W. S., *The Dictionary of Canadian Biography*, Toronto, Macmillan, 1945.
WEST, BRUCE, "11th Province," *Globe and Mail* (Toronto), January 20, 1967.
WILSON, LESLIE, "How Canada Plans to Give Self-Government to Our Northland," *Financial Post*, LIV, January 23, 1960.
WINSLOW, KATHRYN, *Big Pan-Out*, New York, W. W. Norton, 1951.
WOODSIDE, H. J., "Dawson As It Is," *The Canadian Magazine*, XVII (September 1901), pp. 403–13.
WOODWORTH, C. M., "How to Save the Yukon," *The Canadian Magazine*, XXIV (June 1905), pp. 317–20.

THESES

JUDY, R. D., "Territorial Government: the Canadian Northwest Territories and the Yukon," Ph.D. dissertation, University of California, 1959.

LLOYD, TREVOR, "The Geography and Administration of Northern Canada," Ph.D. dissertation, Bristol University, 1947.
MORRISON, D. R., "The Politics of the Yukon Territory, 1898–1908," M.A. thesis, University of Saskatchewan, 1964.

INTERVIEWS

FAULKNER, MISS VICTORIA, for years secretary to the Commissioner of the Yukon Territory, Whitehorse, August 13, 1963.
FINGLAND, F. B., Administrative Assistant to the Commissioner of the Yukon, Whitehorse, August 1, 1963.
HEBERT, TOM, a dog-driver for Major J. M. Walsh in 1878–93, Dawson City, August 8, 1963.
TROBERG, R. E., Historian of the Dawson Order of Pioneers, Bonanza Creek, August 8, 1963.
A resident of Dawson City from 1899 to the present who wished to remain anonymous, Dawson City, August 8, 1963.

INDEX